# THE CATHOLIC EMANCIPATION CRISIS IN IRELAND, 1823-1829

BY JAMES A. REYNOLDS

GREENWOOD PRESS, PUBLISHERS
WESTPORT, CONNECTICUT

*Copyright 1954 by Yale University Press*

Reprinted with the permission
of Yale University Press

First Greenwood Reprinting 1970

Library of Congress Catalogue Card Number 74-95134

SBN 8371-3141-3

Printed in the United States of America

DOMINO EMINENTI

PATRONOQUE BENIGNO

FRANCISCO CARDINALI SPELLMAN

D. D. D.

AUCTOR

# *Preface*

Few political movements have exercised such profound influence on the history of modern Ireland or, indeed, on the constitutional and political development of 19th-century England as the Irish struggle for Catholic Emancipation in the years 1823–29. This judgment, first a surmise engendered by my reading of late British history, assumed increased validity in the course of researches in Ireland and in England into the activities of Daniel O'Connell and the Catholic Association. I think it warrants exposition. The study in hand, therefore, is an attempt to show how a pressure group, of surprising proportions and clamor, not only forced from a reluctant British government a major constitutional reform but also, and perhaps more significantly, became the prototype for subsequent agitations in Ireland.

My gratitude in the first instance, for his understanding and generosity in affording me leisure to pursue this investigation, is due my ordinary, Francis Cardinal Spellman, archbishop of New York. More proximate to the historical problem is Professor Lewis Curtis of Yale. He first suggested the research, was its inspiration in labor, sponsored its baptism as a doctoral dissertation, and has seen its confirmation as a book. Others who have made constructive criticism of the manuscript are Professors William Dunham, Archibald Foord, and Basil Henning, all of Yale, and John Kelleher of Harvard.

Farther afield my thanks go to the archbishop of Dublin, the Most Reverend John McQuaid, for permission to search among the collections of "Catholic Proceedings" in the Dublin archdiocesan archives, to Professor John Wardell, late of Trinity College, Dublin, for use of the journal of G. E. Ross-Lewin, to Professor R. B. McDowell, also of Trinity, and to Mr. Maurice O'Connell.

The staffs of the following institutions have also given gracious assistance: the Sterling Memorial Library at Yale, the Irish State Paper Office, the National Library of Ireland, the Royal Irish

Academy, the library of University College, Dublin, the British Museum, the Public Record Office, London, and the archives of the Congregation of the Propagation of the Faith, Rome.

For permission to reprint material from their copyright books I am indebted to E. P. Dutton and Co., publishers of Sir Herbert Maxwell, ed., *The Creevey Papers*, and to Methuen and Co., Ltd., publishers of Edmund Curtis and R. B. McDowell, eds., *Irish Historical Documents, 1172–1922*.

Finally I am grateful to the editorial board of the Yale Historical Publications, to members of the Yale University Press, and in particular to Miss Ella Holliday for her painstaking work in styling the manuscript.

J. A. R.

# Contents

# *Abbreviations*

| | |
|---|---|
| AHD, CP | Archbishop's House, Dublin, Catholic Proceedings |
| BM, PP | British Museum, Peel Papers |
| BM, WP | British Museum, Wellesley Papers |
| DEM | Dublin *Evening Mail* |
| DEP | Dublin *Evening Post* |
| ISPO, CAP | Irish State Paper Office, Catholic Association Papers |
| ISPO, CSORP | Irish State Paper Office, Chief Secretary's Office Registered Papers |
| ISPO, OP II | Irish State Paper Office, Official Papers, Second Series |
| ISPO, SCP | Irish State Paper Office, State of the Country Papers |
| NL, CA MSS | National Library of Ireland, Catholic Association Manuscripts |
| NL, O'C MSS | National Library of Ireland, O'Connell Manuscripts |
| NL, WP | National Library of Ireland, Wellesley Papers |
| PRO, FO | Public Record Office, London, Foreign Office |
| PRO, HO | Public Record Office, London, Home Office |
| RIA | Royal Irish Academy |
| UCD, O'C P | University College, Dublin, O'Connell Papers |

# 1. *Political Pressure Groups in Britain before 1823*

PRESSURE groups perform an important function in modern democratic government. They call attention to the grievances of particular classes and segments of society whose interests established political parties cannot, or perhaps will not, sufficiently represent. Thus, despite frequent accusation of sinister dealings, especially in the matter of lobbying, such organizations have come to be accepted as a necessary part of our political system.[1] Their place and function are more readily appreciated than is the history of their gradual development.

Pressure groups engineered violent revolutions in 18th-century America and France. In the British Isles they fomented revolutions no less radical because they were bloodless. As a result, the first half of the 19th century saw three great constitutional reforms which, along with the leaven of Methodism and the evangelical revival, abolition of the slave trade and slavery, humane factory legislation, and the rise of trade unionism, renovated the United Kingdom. Each of the three, Catholic Emancipation, parliamentary reform, and repeal of the Corn Laws, was won by means of pressure brought to bear on government by powerful extraconstitutional organizations.

In mid-18th-century England Methodism presented a remarkable example of enthusiasm and organization aimed at moral reform. Through a gradually developing, hierarchical structure of associations, John Wesley was able to give social reinforcement to the new evangelism he was preaching within the Anglican Church. At the base of the pyramid were small groups of from five to twelve converts banded together in classes, several of which formed a society. The societies, in turn, were grouped by districts, the districts by provinces or nations, all constituting "the People

1. For a detailed study of the role of pressure groups in government see V. O. Key, Jr., *Politics, Parties, and Pressure Groups* (3d ed. New York, 1952).

Called Methodists, or the United Societies," in reality a vast mass movement cemented not only by common religious inspiration but, very practically, by the efforts of circuit overseers and itinerant preachers, by zealous use of the newspaper and pamphlet press, and by an ingenious system of penny-a-week dues paid by each member through his class leader to the stewards of the societies. The word society, as Wesley noted in 1748, was "a very innocent name, and very common in London, for any number of people associating themselves together." [2] Association, already in the air, soon became a term almost synonymous with Methodism.

In the realm of political agitation the advantages of common action, so strikingly depicted in the huge open-air meetings of Wesley and Whitefield and in the fervor of thousands of converts, class leaders, stewards, and traveling preachers, were not so early realized. Despite occasional flurries of excitement, such as the remonstrance of 1733 against Walpole's excise scheme and that of 1763 in the southwestern counties against the cider tax, it was only after John Wilkes was twice elected by the Middlesex freeholders and thrice expelled from the House of Commons that practically the first attempt was made at organization for political purposes. The Society of the Supporters of the Bill of Rights, founded in 1769 by the friends of Wilkes, summoned numerous meetings of protest against the invalidation of his re-election. The society soon fell to pieces owing to personal quarrels. Yet it was the beginning of a long succession of associations that were to carry on intermittently until 1832 the predominant agitation, that for parliamentary reform.[3]

The first period of intense activity after the Wilkes episode came in 1780–84 with the formation of societies for constitutional information and of county associations for economical and parliamentary reform based on the model of Christopher Wyvill's Yorkshire Association. Although in 1780 delegates from all over the

2. John Wesley, "A Plain Account of the People Called Methodists" (1748), p. 250, in Thomas Jackson, ed., *The Works of the Rev. John Wesley* (London, 1872), *8*, 248–268.

3. The Catholic Relief Act of 1778 precipitated a rash of Protestant associations in England and Scotland under the leadership of Lord George Gordon, whose demand for repeal of the act ended in the notorious Gordon riots of 1780. More lasting than Gordon's campaign and contemporaneous with the movement for parliamentary reform was that for abolition of the slave trade. An association founded in 1787 to raise funds and to circulate information about the horrors of the traffic became a central body with societies in the chief towns. Public meetings and petitions brought about a notable triumph of public opinion in the abolition of the slave trade in 1807.

country did assemble in convention in London, Wyvill's plan for a national association linking in common action standing committees appointed by the reformers of each county was never fully realized. County, city, and town meetings and committees, as well as the tactic of bombarding Parliament with monster petitions, proved, as did the reformist literature of the constitutional information societies, ineffectual in converting an aristocratic legislature to reform. The network of county associations, which at the height of the movement had numbered about twenty-six in England and Wales, disappeared after 1784.

Not until six years later, amid the contagion of the French Revolution, was there a revival. In 1792 appeared the Society of the Friends of the People, and in the same year Thomas Hardy founded the London Corresponding Society, which soon became a central committee with thirty branches. Within two years most of the societies disintegrated with the treason trials of their leaders and the promulgation of the two acts of 1795 against corresponding societies and seditious meetings.[4] For approximately fifteen years thereafter little was heard of reform, until Francis Place carried through the election of Sir Francis Burdett for Westminster on the crest of public enthusiasm, and the cry was taken up anew in reform unions and Hampden clubs. But again the government stepped in, this time with the four acts of 1817 and the six acts of 1819. For the whole of the 1820's, although one notes occasional speeches of such reformers as Burdett, Cobbett, Hunt, Brougham, Lords Grey and Russell, popular political agitation, under the shadow of the repressive acts and lulled by economic recovery from postwar depression, failed to disturb the United Kingdom—with one important exception, Ireland.

John Bull's other island had always been turbulent. But the organization of its discontented population, Protestant as well as Catholic, for peaceful political agitation, as opposed to the more traditional Irish resort to rebellion, began during the reign of George III. It had three main objectives: independence for the Irish Parliament, parliamentary reform, and repeal of the penal laws against Catholics.

For nearly three centuries Poynings' Law of 1494 had shackled the Irish Parliament.[5] It was denied control over finances, the

4. The London Corresponding Society revised its constitution to avoid the operation of the acts, but it was formally suppressed in 1799.

5. For the latest reassessment of Poynings' Law see H. G. Richardson and G. O. Sayles, *The Irish Parliament in the Middle Ages* (Philadelphia, 1952), pp. 269–281.

army, and the ministers of state, who were named by and were responsible to the English Government alone. After 1692 a procedure called "Heads of Bills" enabled either house to propose a bill which, if approved by the Irish Council, was then passed by the Irish Parliament and submitted to the King's privy council, who could approve, change, or reject it. If the bill returned from England, the Irish Parliament had to accept or reject it in full. Thus no legislation could be passed which was unacceptable to the British Government. Moreover, while the English Parliament could make its laws applicable in Ireland and had been able thus to exclude the sister island from the benefits of colonial trade, to limit her exports, and to suppress industries which, like the wool trade, threatened those in England, the companion body in Dublin was not permitted to pass important laws already in force in England.

The consequent subjection of Ireland to purely English interests had formed the theme, early in the century, of the bitter protests of Dean Swift and Bishop Berkeley. Irishmen treasured their words, and the spirit of incipient nationalism which they had voiced was reinvigorated in 1779 by three other Anglo-Irish patriots, Grattan, Flood, and Charlemont, in the formation of the Irish Volunteers. Ostensibly a military organization, mobilized for the defense of the island at an hour when Britain, hard pressed by rebellious American colonies, was threatened with invasion by France, the Volunteers soon showed that their primary aims were political and commercial. An almost completely Protestant body, they proclaimed, in the eighty thousand men whom they eventually mustered to arms and pledged, as Swift had once advised, to wear only cloth of Irish manufacture, the birth of a new Irish patriotism.[6] England's distress, her panic at the weakness of Ireland's defenses and the uncertain loyalty of her inhabitants, proved then to be Ireland's opportunity. Northern Presbyterians and southern Protestants in their Volunteer conventions, inspired by Flood's insistence that the Volunteers would remain on foot until they had exacted Ireland's rights, as well as by Grattan's hope of eventual alliance with the great body of their Catholic fellow countrymen, won in 1779 removal of most of the trading restrictions and, three years later, repeal of Poynings' Law. Here Grattan was content

6. In 1780 when the delegates of the English county associations met in a national convention in London, they were viewed with suspicion. Associations and conventions of so threatening a nature had appeared lately in America and in Ireland that the very terms were ominous.

to trust England's word. Flood, on the other hand, colder and more suspicious, insisted that the British Parliament positively renounce its pretension to bind Ireland by its acts. Even this "the weary Titan" decided to accept, and in 1783 the Renunciation Act guaranteed Irish legislative independence.

The Irish Parliament remained, nevertheless, a source of contention. It was less representative and more corrupt than its English prototype, and although restored to a species of autonomy, it was still subject to the interference of the English Government. In the lower house more than two-thirds of the three hundred members owed their seats to wealthy patrons, while from one-third to one-half were placemen or pensioners of the Crown, amenable to the dictation of a few influential borough holders bribed to care for British interests. In the Lords the bishops and peers proved dependable agents of the power across the sea to whose favor and protection they owed their sees and their estates.

While Grattan proposed to purify this legislature from within by reducing the pensions list and the number of bought placemen, Flood wanted to increase the Protestant electorate and make Parliament more representative. Grattan, loyalist and imperialist, was ready to show his confidence in England by disbanding the Volunteers. Flood, whose importance as a realist and prophet has been obscured by Grattan's greater popularity, insisted that the Volunteers be maintained as a wedge for reform. For a time Flood's policy prevailed. But when Parliament rejected his reform bill of 1784, the Volunteers, many of whose leaders, like Grattan, thought they had gone too far in attempting by a show of force to intimidate the government, went into decline. They gave way to another group of Protestant patriots, republicans like Wolfe Tone and Napper Tandy, who, hoping to join the Catholics with the democratic Presbyterians of Ulster, founded in 1791 the Society of United Irishmen. Like the Volunteers, the United Irishmen demanded reform, and like them they were rebuffed. Their leaders, exasperated by the failure and by the Convention Act of 1793 outlawing organizations calling themselves representatives of the people, turned the society from an open movement for parliamentary reform into a military conspiracy. The climax came in the Rebellion of 1798. Two years later the Act of Union put an end to the Irish Parliament.

Irish agitation, failing to reform the legislature which it had made independent, was concerned with yet a third objective, one which, while benefiting a minority of Englishmen, was from the beginning primarily an Irish question. Popularly known as Catholic Emancipation, it involved the repeal of the rigorous code of penal laws that had, since the defeat of James II at the Boyne, proscribed the religion of the majority of Irishmen.

During the 18th century race and religion split Irish society into three sharply defined and hostile factions: the Anglo-Irish of the Established Church, the Ulster Presbyterians of Scottish origin, and the native Irish. At the last of these, who were almost all Roman Catholics, were aimed the penal laws, enacted between 1695 and 1746 for the purpose of preserving a small minority, the Protestant ascendancy, in possession of all political power and of great tracts of land confiscated from Catholic proprietors. The laws constituted, in the opinion of Edmund Burke, "a machine of wise and elaborate contrivance, and as well fitted for the oppression, impoverishment, and degradation of a people, and the debasement, in them, of human nature itself, as ever proceeded from the perverted ingenuity of man." [7]

The penal code banished from the island all Catholic prelates and religious orders and permitted only one priest, registered with the authorities, to minister to each parish. A Catholic landholder who had somehow managed to survive the spoliations and plantations under James I, Cromwell, and William III might not take a lease of more than thirty-one years, obtain the land of a Protestant by gift, sale, or inheritance, or even own a horse valued at more than £5, and on his death his estate was divided, by what was known as the Gavelkind Act, among all his sons, unless the eldest conformed in religion and thus, according to the usual English law of primogeniture, made himself sole heir. Although they paid additional taxes, Catholics could not vote, sit in Parliament, or hold any municipal office, enter the legal profession, the army and navy, or trades allied with publishing and the making and sale of arms, serve as apprentices in the shop of a Protestant, or, if tradesmen themselves, employ more than two apprentices. They might not have their own schools, be teachers, or send their children abroad to be educated. If a child wished to conform to the Established Church he could be taken from his parents to be reared, as were all orphans, by Protestant guardians.[8]

7. Letter to Sir Hercules Langrishe, Jan. 3, 1792, in *The Writings and Speeches of the Right Honourable Edmund Burke* (Beaconsfield ed. Boston, Little, Brown & Co., 1901), *4*, 305.

8. For a detailed account of the penal laws see W. E. H. Lecky, *A History of Ireland in the Eighteenth Century* (new ed. London, 1892), *1*, 136–171.

The penal code failed to extirpate the Catholic religion. Indeed, it was not systematically enforced, and once the intransigent Romanism of the native Irish proved itself, the Church of Ireland, largely an instrument of the political-economic monopoly, seldom showed enthusiasm for large-scale conversions. But the laws, especially those affecting property holding, did succeed in making Ireland an island of sharp contrasts: of mud huts and stately manors, of graceful Georgian Dublin and of country towns wretched as African kraals, of hedge schools and Trinity College, of the squalor of the Coombe and the elegance of Merrion Square. And the code drove to the Continent the Catholic gentry, natural leaders of the peasantry, the "wild geese" whose flight beyond the sea was recalled in the songs of the common people who remained behind, "little better than hewers of wood, and drawers of water, . . . out of all capacity of doing any mischief, if they were ever so well inclined." [9] Finally, the penal laws succeeded in erecting a barrier of suspicion and hostility between Catholic and Protestant that remains to the present day.

For a time, in the latter half of the 18th century, it seemed that the barrier might be broken down. In 1750 Catholics were admitted to the lesser grades of the army, and in 1771 the Bogland Act enabled them to take leases for sixty-one years of not more than fifty acres of unprofitable land, to be free of taxes for seven years. Not only were the anti-Catholic statutes no longer enforced with the savagery of the reigns of Anne and George I; a sense of political grievance common to all three sections of Irish society tended to weaken their distrust of one another. Both the Volunteers and the United Irishmen made some degree of emancipation part of their program. But the main impetus toward relaxation of the penal code came from the Catholics themselves. In 1759 they set up the first of a series of committees, boards, and associations to demand civil equality. Within four years this initial committee disintegrated through internal dissension: the Catholic aristocracy resented the challenge made to their leadership of the movement by an upstart, middle-class group of merchants. In 1773 the committee was revived and through its pressure was partly responsible for the relief acts of 1778 and 1782. The former permitted Catholics who took an oath of allegiance to take leases of land of indefinite tenure, although not freeholds; they might inherit land on the same terms as Protestants; and the Gavelkind Act was repealed.

9. Dean Swift, "A Letter Concerning the Sacramental Test" (1708), in Sir Walter Scott, ed., *The Works of Jonathan Swift* (2d ed. Boston, 1883–84), *8*, 354.

The Act of 1782, while sweeping away laws against education, residence of the regular clergy and of unregistered parish priests, and the bearing of arms, enabled Catholics to purchase, hold, and bequeath freehold land and leases.

Gradually the middle-class Catholics, emboldened by their gains, wrested control of the movement from the more timid aristocracy. The Catholic Committee of 1792, following the example of the Volunteers and the United Irishmen, met in a national convention significantly reminiscent of the French Directory. Delegates attended from every county in Ireland. The Protestant Wolfe Tone acted as their secretary, a disturbing portent of possible coalition of the Catholic masses with the democrats of Ulster, perhaps in the Society of United Irishmen where Belfast Presbyterians were showing marked pro-Catholic sympathies. The Relief Act of 1793 was the result. Besides admitting Catholics to the same parliamentary and municipal franchise enjoyed by Protestants, it repealed all their remaining disqualifications with the exception of the oath of supremacy, the declaration against transsubstantiation, and the assertion that the invocation of saints and the sacrifice of the Mass were superstitious and idolatrous. While Irish Catholics were thus still debarred from both houses of Parliament, from higher offices in the civil administration, from the posts of sheriff and subsheriff of counties, from the inner bar and the judicial bench, and from promotion in the military establishment beyond the rank of colonel, they were no longer excluded from university degrees, from commissions in the army and navy, from magistracies, and from grand juries. It seemed probable that even the galling oaths, the last obstacle to equality before the law, might soon be removed. But the hope, the high hope of the delegates of 1792, was blighted by the Rebellion of 1798 and the Union.

After 1800 Protestants of North and South drew closer to each other in their mutual distrust of the native Irish and in their anxiety to preserve the legislative union, originally opposed by many of them but which they soon came to recognize as the bulwark of their ascendancy.[10] They produced, indeed, such "Catholics" as the revered Grattan and his successor as foremost Irish champion of emancipation, William Plunket, the Duke of Leinster, and other

10. A number of Presbyterian ministers had been rebels in 1798. Yet the failure of the rebellion and the religious note that had been given to it left the Presbyterians disillusioned over the union of all Irishmen regardless of creed. In 1802 the government, in a successful attempt to wean them from disloyalty, increased the *Regium Donum* to Presbyterian ministers to scales ranging from £50 to £100, paid by the state to loyal ministers.

members of Parliament of the stature of Vesey Fitzgerald of Clare, Thomas Spring-Rice of Limerick, and Maurice Fitzgerald of Kerry. Yet the rank and file of the ascendancy party, squireens and middlemen, thinly scattered among a hostile population, with their fortunes based on confiscation, regarded the Protestant constitution as the fundamental principle in politics. Dominated by great families like the Beresfords, who were said to fill one-fourth of all the places in Ireland with their dependents and connections,[11] and with the aid of an oligarchy of government officials led by Henry Goulburn, Thomas Manners, and William Gregory,[12] noblemen such as the Marquis of Waterford, the Earls of Clancarty, Mayo, and Longford, Bishops represented by William Magee of Dublin and John Jebb of Limerick, and hundreds of parsons, judges, and lawyers, the Irish Protestant gentry constituted in practice, if no longer in law, the Irish state and society. Inferior on the whole to the corresponding class in England, inheriting traditions of violence, extravagance, and intolerance, as well as a general tone of dissipation and political profligacy, all vices arising from irresponsible, often tyrannical relations to their tenants, the Irish squirearchy depressed the level of public spirit far below that of the other island. Landowners in 1800 sold their pocket boroughs for peerages, and all classes regularly bartered their services for places in the revenue, the law, and the church.[13] Ruling through Dublin Castle, they still looked upon themselves as England's garrison, withstanding the pretensions of the "mere Irish," potential rebels, who protested through a handful of noisy agitators.

The hope of the Catholics lay now across the Irish Sea, in Westminster rather than in College Green, and for the first twenty-eight years of the new century their bitterest complaint centered on the failure of the united Parliament to grant the full emancipation refused by their own legislature and on the expectation of which, a prospect carefully fostered by the government of Pitt, they had been induced in 1800 not to oppose the Union and to trust in the beneficence of the imperial Parliament. In 1799 the govern-

11. Edward Wakefield, *An Account of Ireland, Statistical and Political* (London, 1812), *2*, 384.

12. Goulburn was chief secretary of Ireland, 1821–27; Manners, lord chancellor, 1807–27; and Gregory, undersecretary, 1812–31.

13. "I found in Ireland," wrote Robert Peel of his own term as Irish chief secretary, "that every official man . . . thought he had a right to quarter his family on the patronage of Government." Peel to Henry Goulburn, Jan. 6, 1826, in Charles S. Parker, ed., *Sir Robert Peel from His Private Papers* (London, J. Murray, 1891–99), *1*, 60. For more letters of Peel on the corruption of the Irish Government see *ibid.*, 271–286.

ment had discreetly sounded the Catholics through their aristocratic leaders and their bishops on the question of the proposed Union. The peers, headed by Lords Kenmare and Fingall, readily consented. The hierarchy passed resolutions accepting an informal offer of state payment of the clergy and admitting the right of the government in return to confirm the appointment of Irish bishops and parish priests, the so-called veto power. Only the lower orders of the Catholics, emboldened by the maiden speech of a rising young barrister, Daniel O'Connell, subscribed to his passionate declaration that he would sooner have the penal code back than lose the national Parliament. To no avail. The Union was managed adroitly. Thereafter the House of Lords in England proved adamant in rejecting the petitions of a Catholic Committee of 1809 and a Catholic Board of 1813. The former was suppressed under the terms of the Convention Act; [14] the latter broke up on the veto question. But both had brought into national prominence the figure of Daniel O'Connell. His was to be the dominant spirit henceforth in Catholic agitations. By 1808 he had nerved the bishops, by means of his first great success in demonstrating that the rural Catholics did not want government-approved bishops or the parish priests such bishops might appoint, to reject any veto clause in emancipation. With the Catholic peers he was less successful, and hence the demise of the Catholic Board of 1813.

The veto continued to be the impasse. Catholic relief bills of 1813 and 1821 foundered on it. In 1814, when Monsignor Quarantotti, vice-prefect of the Congregation *De Propaganda Fide* in Rome, at the behest of English Catholics, issued a rescript in favor of accepting the veto, O'Connell denounced him as a meddling Italian ecclesiastic. Assemblies of indignant clergy and bishops declared that the rescript was nonobligatory. But the peers and some of the middle-class Catholics, led by the barrister Richard Sheil, were in sympathy with their English coreligionists. Thus the Catholics in Ireland were distracted by the intrigues of opposing factions: O'Connell, the clergy, and most of the laity antivetoists; Sheil and the Lord Fingall type of Catholic vetoists.

Some progress had been made, indeed, since 1759: not a few of the middle-class merchants and many of the upper clergy showed themselves more radical. But still a fundamental cleavage existed within the Catholic body, between the great mass of the peasantry

14. The Convention Act effectively precluded what had been the main resource of the Catholics in the 18th century, the delegation which made of their various committees and boards representative assemblies.

on the one side and the small, relatively prosperous middle class and the remnant of an aristocracy on the other. The split, dating back over a hundred years, has considerable bearing on the organization and conduct of the 18th-century Catholic Church in Ireland, with its largely peasant-born lower clergy and its respectably born upper clergy and hierarchy. It explains much of the weakness of the Catholics as a body at the end of the 18th century and the beginning of the 19th, for example, the general failure and the local victories of the 1798 rebels, and the slowness of various Catholic boards and committees in following up and consolidating the concessions they won. For a major effect of the penal code was that a Catholic who did make money—and a surprising number did—was forced into a role similar to that of the English Quaker. He could not invest in land, or live ostentatiously, or be a gambling buck, or keep horses and hounds, or engage in any of the gentlemanly pursuits by which the bulk of the Anglo-Irish gentry so regularly ruined themselves. As a result, the well-to-do Catholics were reserved, cautious, respectable people with an eager eye for good investments. And they were mainly urban. They spoke English, took to English, or Anglo-Irish, ways, and often looked for their model to the English Catholics, so loyal, so genteel, and so gently conservative. A less revolutionary group can scarcely be imagined.

When such leaders are contrasted with the Irish-speaking, poverty-stricken, politically nonexistent peasantry, it is not difficult to see why the vague maneuvers and timid aspirations of various Catholic committees and boards raised so few ripples outside Dublin; why hearty souls, like Wolfe Tone, despised the urban Catholics as so many sheep. Only in the brief association of the advanced Catholics, like John Keogh, with the United Irishmen, and the United Irishmen's mismanaged association with agrarian secret societies of the peasantry, was some sort of connection established. The connection was too faulty in 1798, and after that there was none for years.

On the eve of 1823, then, the cause of emancipation seemed utterly becalmed and the Catholics themselves disheartened under grievances from which their recent passivity had gained them, from an unrelenting Protestant ascendancy at home and a heedless Parliament across the water, no more respite than had their former clamor. There were no public meetings, no petitions, no organization such as had won relief in the past century and carried on, however feebly, the tradition of protest for the two decades since the Union. George IV, indeed, visited his second kingdom in 1821 and thus presented the Irish with their first sight of a sovereign since the Boyne. On leaving Ireland he had directed Lord Sidmouth to address to his loyal subjects a letter counseling them to avoid every cause of irritation and to continue the mutual forbearance which his appearance among them had induced.[15] The Catholics, remembering perhaps that the author of the letter, as prince of Wales, had promised in 1807 never to forsake their interests, interpreted the gesture as a possible return to first fervor, and their optimism seemed confirmed shortly afterward when George consented to the appointment as viceroy of the Marquis Wellesley, a pro-Catholic, in succession to the narrow-minded ultra-Tory Earl Talbot. But with the exception of Wellesley and his attorney general, William Plunket, the Irish Government was as firmly Protestant and, to the native Irish, as foreign as ever. And even the King's sentimental outburst on quitting Ireland was belied by his implacable hostility to emancipation, a step which he asserted, with no less vehemence than had his father, would be tantamount to a violation of his coronation oath. The House of Lords and the high Tories shared their sovereign's animosity. Liberal Tories, Whigs, and Radicals were friendly; in the Commons they had twice passed Catholic relief bills; and their numbers and talents had compelled Lord Liverpool since 1812 to leave emancipation an open question in his cabinet. But the prospect of the Whigs overthrowing Liverpool and forming a government of their own strong enough to carry their favorite measure was slight.

Removal of the last remaining legal disqualifications appeared remote, all the more hopeless in that the future lay not with oligarchic boards and committees who sought to persuade Parliament only by means of humble petitions. It lay with the people. And the people? Cultivating their patches of rack-rented land or working as day laborers in the towns, living in constant fear of the land-

15. During the visit the Catholics, led by O'Connell and the Earl of Fingall, showed marked devotion to the King. Their conduct provoked from Byron his scornful "Irish Avatar":

> Wear Fingall thy trappings! O'Connell proclaim
>   His accomplishments—His!!!—and thy country convince
> Half an age's contempt was an error of fame,
>   And that Hal is the rascallest, sweetest young prince. . . .
>
> Till now I had envied thy sons and their shore.
>   Though their virtues were hunted, their liberties fled,
> There was something so warm and sublime in the core
>   Of an Irishman's heart, that—I envy *thy dead.*

lord, the tithe proctor, and the magistrate, they could scarcely be expected to rally to a cause which seemed far above the interests of the common man. They were weary of speeches about Catholic Emancipation, of futile debates in the House of Commons, of petitions ignored, of relief bills which would make their clergy salaried agents of the state. Of what practical benefit would emancipation be to them? That Catholic gentlemen should have their seats in Parliament and hold public office was an aim worthy of sacrifice —for Catholic gentlemen.

Yet the masses were soon to embrace enthusiastically the cause of the gentlemen. Within six years from 1823 the Irish people, mobilized by the Catholic Association, presented the first successful combination for political purposes of the peasantry and the middle class. It is an exciting story and one whose importance in the constitutional, political, and social history of both England and Ireland has not been sufficiently emphasized. Few men would have thought, in 1823, that the Catholic Association of Ireland would grow from a small clique of agitators into an island-wide network of meetings and committees, that the Catholic clergy would join the demagogues and help to provide them with a party chest, and that the association, by conducting a propaganda campaign designed to draw attention to the troubled state of Ireland, by threatening Parliament with alarming constitutional crises, especially in the field of parliamentary elections, by harassing both the Irish and the English executive governments, and by exploiting the threat of physical force, would make the Catholic question the most pressing issue in British politics. The Catholic Association became a colossus of democratic power unprecedented in the annals of political organization in the British Isles and, indeed, "one of the most powerful political bodies known in history." [16] In 1825 its leaders boasted: "If there were no record of the means by which this singular union was effected, the future historian would pause when it became his duty to narrate the fact. Fellow countrymen, you know with what facility this great object was achieved." [17] The boast was no idle one. The records do remain, and historians have narrated the fact. But they have not paused long enough to do justice to the records.

16. W. E. H. Lecky, *Leaders of Public Opinion in Ireland* (New York, 1903), *2*, 59.

17. "Farewell Address of the Catholic Association to the Catholics of Ireland," March 18, 1825, *DEP*, March 19, 1825.

# 2. The Popish Parliament, 1823-1829

ONE evening in the spring of 1823 Daniel O'Connell and Richard Sheil dined together at the home of a mutual friend in the Wicklow Mountains. The meeting was a sort of reconciliation for the two barristers who had been leaders of opposite factions in the long veto squabble. Now as they sat at table they forgot their differences in lamenting the deplorable apathy of the Catholics, a topic almost as depressing as the sight of heavy, gray clouds lowering over the turf-sodden Wicklow moors. Yet out of the conversation emerged a plan, the idea of a new association. Sheil doubted that the time was suitable, that the plan would work. O'Connell, with characteristic energy, promised he would make it work.

O'Connell and Sheil sent an announcement of their intention to the principal Catholics and succeeded in bringing together about sixty of them for a preliminary meeting at Dempsey's Tavern in Dublin on April 25.[1] While it was probably as much Dempsey's reputation for dressing beefsteaks as any enthusiasm for another agitation that attracted the original group, they agreed to sign a requisition for an aggregate meeting [2] to consider and to vote upon the project of founding an association. The aggregate meeting filled Townsend Street Chapel [3] and the ways leading to it. It unanimously approved O'Connell's outline of his plan. Three days later, with seventy members enrolled, the new organization drew

1. There are varying accounts of the number who attended the first meeting. Thomas Wyse, *Historical Sketch of the Late Catholic Association of Ireland* (London, 1829), *1*, 199, says it was not more than twenty, but the *DEP*, April 26, 1823, reported that about sixty signed an address "in the course of a few minutes within the room."

2. Aggregate meetings, an old feature of Catholic agitations, were large public assemblies at which resolutions prepared by smaller meetings were submitted for general approval. Held in the principal towns throughout the country, they were the mainstay of the Irish leaders after the Convention Act forbade conventions of delegates.

3. Since penal times Catholic places of worship were known as chapels as distinct from Protestant churches.

up a constitution proclaiming that its purpose was "to adopt all such legal and constitutional measures as may be most useful to obtain Catholic Emancipation," disclaiming any representative authority for the members, making provision, in order to guard against even the suspicion of secrecy, for admission of newspaper reporters to all meetings and for public display of the minute books and roster of members, setting the annual subscription for membership at one guinea, and naming Saturday at three o'clock as the weekly hour of meeting, when ten members must be present to form a quorum.[4]

The quorum rule proved irksome. Whatever the initial enticement, Dempsey's steaks or the prospect of some rousing Irish oratory, the meeting rooms, established over Coyne's Book Shop in Capel Street, soon presented a rather forlorn appearance, scarcely like that of an arrogant "Roman Catholic Parliament of Ireland," as the Dublin *Evening Mail*, an ascendancy paper, contemptuously described the new association.[5] An oblong table extended through the center of two large rooms with the chairman's seat at the head and places for secretaries, reporters, and clerks on both sides. There were no ministerial or opposition benches, no elbow cushions for even the most respected auditor, and the members who attended were obliged to stand throughout the proceedings. Few of the more than one hundred who had subscribed bothered to make the effort. On six occasions during the first year, when not even ten members appeared, it was necessary to adjourn scheduled meetings, while on some Saturdays only the last-minute arrival of the tenth saved the day.[6] If one were to judge from the attendance he might readily have agreed with the chief secretary of Ireland, Henry Goulburn, that the whole business was rather dull than

4. "Rules and Regulations of the Catholic Association of Ireland," Wyse, *Historical Sketch, 2,* Appendix xiv, xxxvii–viii.

5. *DEM,* May 26, 1823. The phrase immediately became popular among ultra Protestants, who wrote frequently to Peel at the Home Office to complain of the violent proceedings of "this popish Parliament" and to condemn it, prematurely indeed, as an "imperium in imperio." BM, PP, Add. MSS 40304, 40334, 40370, 40397. Peel himself noted that the association was adopting "the forms of Parliament." Peel to Marquis Wellesley, June 20, 1823, *ibid.,* 40324, fol. 167. One year later, when they had more reasonable cause for alarm, the Dublin Protestants petitioned the House of Commons to suppress this impertinent assembly which was daily mocking Parliament by constituting itself a rival legislature. Petition presented in the House of Commons by Charles Brownlow, May 31, 1824, T. C. Hansard, ed., *The Parliamentary Debates,* 2d Ser., *11,* 943–948.

6. On one occasion O'Connell coerced two young priests whom he found browsing in the bookshop beneath the meeting rooms into attending in order to form a quorum of ten members.

mischievous, and that it looked as if the association would die a natural death.[7]

Such a judgment overlooked at least one important element in the situation. The proceedings of the new body, although the work of a handful of men, were setting a pattern for the future by pushing on, over the objections of more timid members, to a bold policy of protesting and petitioning against a whole litany of grievances, instead of limiting discussion to the general question of Catholic Emancipation. The topics of debate ranged from the concrete and limited annoyance of exclusion of Catholic commercial men from the management of the Bank of Ireland to the great problems of overpopulation, competition for land, and improvidence of landlords. Committees were appointed to manage petitions to Parliament, to provide for a Catholic burial ground, and to devise means to open Protestant corporations to Catholics. Finally, all this clamor was being carried to the provinces by the newspapers, to attract the attention of Irish peasants even in the remotest farm lands. The latter, reading or having read to them the fiery tirades of O'Connell and Sheil, constituted an audience as large and potentially tremendous as that in the rooms over Coyne's was small and actually insignificant, an audience awaiting that yet undiscovered bond which would give them an interest in the new venture.

They had not long to wait. Just ten months after the first meeting O'Connell devised an expedient which completely transformed the nature of the body. Every Catholic in Ireland was to be called upon to enroll himself as an associate member by subscribing the monthly sum of one penny, to be known as the Catholic Rent. "By a general effort of that kind, the people of England would see that the Catholic millions felt a deep interest in the cause, and that it was not confined, as is supposed, to those styled 'agitators.' " [8] The Rent plan,[9] for its novelty, its daring, and especially on account of the bitter denunciation of English rule in Ireland with which O'Connell seasoned it, alarmed the fainthearted. Nicholas Mahon, a wealthy Catholic merchant, begged O'Connell, in mercy to the people, not to press a measure "that might involve the Catholics of Ireland." [10] But such precisely was O'Connell's aim. And he was soon rewarded by the public interest which his project aroused. All during February 1824 lively debate on the measure occupied

7. Goulburn to Peel, Nov. 16, 1823, BM, PP, 40329, fol. 223.
8. Report of meeting of Jan. 24, 1824, ISPO, CAP.
9. For a fuller consideration of the Rent scheme see below, Chapter 4.
10. Meeting of Feb. 28, 1824, ISPO, CAP.

the association and attracted an unusual attendance of over fifty members and spectators. When the plan was submitted to an aggregate meeting the Dublin Catholics once again crowded Townsend Street Chapel, to greet O'Connell with enthusiastic cheers when he rose to exhort them, in words of Byron which at subsequent rallies he overworked almost to the point of absurdity:

> Hereditary bondsmen, know ye not
> Who would be free, themselves must strike the blow?

He went on to extol the American Revolution as an example of rights won by external pressure on England. In Ireland they had been blamed for being agitators. He thanked God for being one. Whatever little they had was gained by agitation, while they uniformly lost by moderation.[11] The oration was impressive, and the scene memorable to at least one person in the audience:

> I attended that meeting, . . . The edifice was dark and gloomy; and shortly after the chair had been taken, the dense crowd that filled the aisle and galleries excluded the scanty light of a closing winter's day. About four o'clock the entire scene became obscure, while the introduction of one solitary light, placed upon the secretary's desk, gave a solemnity to the proceedings which was most impressive. When O'Connell ceased, the sharp and penetrating tones of Shiel [*sic*] issued forth from the same obscurity, and he delivered that brilliant oration which was subsequently published as "Speech on Plato and Dr. Magee." The project of the Rent was adopted, and several persons throughout the country volunteered to act as collectors, according to the plan arranged in the printed report, and during the following assizes county meetings were held in many parts of Ireland, at which the project was agreed to be put in operation, and a mode of communication with the Association arranged.[12]

The beginning of the Rent marks the transition of the Catholic Association from a small club into a mass movement. With the Rent scheme the organization in Dublin shot out roots into the soil of Ireland, to provide countrymen everywhere with a diet of political food as universal and as staple as the national potato. The

11. *DEP,* Feb. 28, 1824.

12. Thomas Kennedy, "Reminiscences of a Silent Agitator," requoted from C. M. O'Keefe, *Life and Times of Daniel O'Connell* (Dublin, 1863–64), *2,* 325.

project of small, general contributions, as the undersecretary at Dublin Castle, William Gregory, remarked, was "the most efficient mode that could be devised for opening direct communication between the popish Parliament and the whole mass of the Catholic population." [13] Gregory's superior, Goulburn, noted uneasily the progressive tendency of the association "to organize the whole country and to place themselves at the head of that organization." [14]

Before a month had passed after the aggregate meeting Catholic lawyers on their spring circuits, with the aid of two thousand priests, small shopkeepers, and traders, were carrying the Rent project to the country towns, organizing county, city, and parish meetings, and developing a pattern that was to become common during the next five years. The largest chapel in the town was the setting; a peer or the local pastor, sometimes the bishop, presided; petitions were adopted setting forth specific instances of oppression, committees appointed to manage the Rent collection, resolutions passed expressing confidence in and thanks to the Catholic Association, the chief agitators, and the local clergy; and for a climax O'Connell, Sheil, or some other of the grand orators denounced for an hour or two England's perfidy. In the evening the more prominent local gentlemen sat down to a public banquet with their Dublin guests, rose to a long list of exuberant toasts, and applauded strenuously another round of extravagant philippics. The newspapers noted thirteen county conventions and many more town and parish meetings in 1824, whose effect was soon evident. In the autumn grievance letters and Rent returns, many of them the work of the parish priests and their curates, began to pour into Dublin. Hitherto the clergy had held back. Now not only did they preside at local meetings and supervise Rent committees; many of them, with the approval of their bishops, began also to correspond with the association.

The change in the scope and force of the movement was a dramatic one. The association had to hire a permanent clerk and two secretaries to handle its fast-mounting correspondence; attendance at the weekly meetings passed the hundred mark; and the rooms over Coyne's proving too small, members and spectators moved into new quarters, the picture gallery of the Royal Arcade on Usher's Quay. About three hundred and fifty people were present for the first meeting there on October 16, 1824; the following week

13. Gregory to Peel, April 11, 1824, BM, PP, 40334, fol. 87.
14. Goulburn to Peel, Oct. 27, 1824, *ibid.*, 40330, fol. 148.

there were five hundred; and on October 27, as the editor of the Dublin *Evening Post*, a pro-Catholic paper, noted proudly: "All the avenues to the Picture Gallery were crowded to excess. The place reserved for Spectators presented a dense and almost impassable mass of beings of all creeds and opinions. Beyond the railing there were [*sic*] an unusually large number of the Catholic Clergy, together with many Protestant Gentlemen and Ladies. At three o'clock, Mrs. and the three Misses O'Connell entered the room. They were received with three distinct and enthusiastic rounds of applause."[15]

The crush of the crowd was so great that a temporary gallery at the end of the room gave way, and, to add to the confusion, an attempt was made to break up the meeting. While the pro-secretary for the Rent was reading a letter from the country he was interrupted by shouting outside both doors of the room. Several members, O'Connell among them, went to the members' entrance and tried to quiet the hecklers, but to no avail. The uproar increased, and under persistent hammering the door crashed inward amid a splintering of glass and a chorus of shrieks from the ladies. Their escorts rose gallantly and eagerly to the occasion, with a zest for battle, indeed, that prompted the intruders, a mob led by Trinity College youths, to beat a hasty retreat. The excitement convinced the members that they should move once again, and in November they took up new and what proved permanent quarters in the Corn Exchange, where without any previous expectation they found a guard in the coal porters, whose stand was just opposite, quite sufficient to frighten off belligerent young Orangemen. O'Connell often afterward declared that it was the Dublin coal porters who saved the agitation and thus "carried" emancipation.

The Corn Exchange proved ideal for the purposes of the association. Here was a great room, an office for the secretary, a committee room, a drawing room, and a tap room, while the hotel adjoining the Exchange could be leased as a sort of club for the members. The great room, an oblong hall surrounded by benches and arranged nearly in the same manner as the House of Commons, was larger by far than their previous places of meeting. Yet at times it also could not accommodate the crowds, who on one occasion, numbering over six hundred members in addition to hundreds of spectators, filled the hall and even the lobbies at all within hearing of the speakers.[16] The room, as a fastidious foreign traveler observed,

15. *DEP*, Oct. 28, 1824.
16. Meeting of Feb. 2, 1825, ISPO, CAP.

was "as dirty as the English House of Commons"; here also every man kept his hat on while speaking; here also there were good and bad orators, but certainly less dignified manners than there.[17]

The more spectacular business of the association was transacted at such meetings. The members debated topics ranging from the protests of rack-rented Tipperary peasants to the complaints of Irish convicts in Botany Bay, the abuses of the Established Church, the conduct, public and private, of officials in the Irish and English governments, of the King and his brothers, debates in Parliament, and the general state of Ireland: taxes, education, agrarian secret societies, the lack of poor laws and of public libraries, the number and disposition of the army and the police. Equally important work was done behind the scenes. At informal meetings, in committees, and at dinner parties, frequently at O'Connell's house in Merrion Square, a junto of leaders discussed and formulated policy, prepared resolutions, and gathered material for debates. While at first the committees were little more than nominal affairs, with O'Connell, Sheil, and one or two others doing most of the work, when the association expanded suddenly in 1824 they became more active and extensive, preparing and forwarding petitions to Parliament, collecting facts to support the claims of the petitions, framing resolutions for aggregate meetings, drafting addresses to the people, arranging legal aid for the peasantry, considering the grievance letters of forty-shilling freeholders, promoting the registration of freeholds in preparation for elections, and watching over the police. Besides these temporary bodies there were standing committees for finance, correspondence, education, grievances, burial grounds, and the administration of justice; and when the association adjourned during the summer months interim committees sat weekly. In its committees as in its public sessions the association, although it had no regular presiding officer [18] and no distinct government and opposition benches, was acting like a parliament.

In addition to its weekly sessions the association summoned occasional aggregate meetings in Dublin to pass on important measures like the Rent project and to adopt annual sets of petitions to Parliament and addresses to the King. Held in one of the larger city churches, these conventions attracted larger crowds than could

17. "A German Prince" (H. von Pückler-Muskau), *A Tour in England, Ireland, and France in the Years 1828 and 1829* (London, 1832), *2*, 117–118.

18. A chairman was nominated to preside at each meeting. There was, however, a permanent secretary with three professional clerks to care for minutes, correspondence, petitions, and accounts.

attend at the Corn Exchange. The audience readily accepted a predetermined procedure of business and adopted resolutions by acclamation. Even the order of speeches was fixed days in advance. But the whole affair, having the air of a popular assembly, gave convincing proof of the enthusiasm and unanimity of the people. Such aggregate meetings, coupled with the regular sessions at the Corn Exchange, struck alarm in members of the Protestant ascendancy. Seeing their privileged status imperiled by this democratic colossus, they disclosed the anxieties of their class in angry letters like the following to the chief secretary:

> The existence and proceedings of an assembly, openly, aye and successfully too, arrogating to itself . . . direction of three-fourths of His Majesty's subjects in this country, usurping upon His Majesty's prerogatives by the issue of Proclamations, upon the functions of Parliament by the levy of taxes, with all its close and open Committees, having the whole Romish Priesthood zealously engaged in carrying its measures into execution, and thus presenting a chain of organization far more prompt and effectual than the regular Government of this, or perhaps of some other countries can command, . . . an assembly such as this, establishing its regular sessions at the very seat of Government . . .[19]

From the provinces came equally disturbing reports. At Rathkeale, in Limerick, the chief constable noted that the proceedings of the association were closely followed by the people, frightened the loyal part of the community, and induced in the Catholics an "arrogance and pride at their numerical strength, as well as the money they are likely to command."[20]

Robert Peel, the home secretary, received many such letters forwarded from Ireland. They induced him to write to his friend, John Leslie Foster, M.P. for Louth, to request the latter's confidential opinion of the changed state of affairs. Foster replied: "The Catholic Association is a subject on which I have more difficulty in approaching to a decision than any other you might mention. So lately as the spring of this year it was so perfectly contemptible that Government might be excused for supposing it was on the point of dying a natural death. Its present prosperity has been most unexpected and perhaps in a great measure accidental.

19. The Earl of Clancarty to Goulburn, Dec. 5, 1824, ISPO, SCP, 445/2624/30.
20. W. Smith to F. Blackburne, Nov. 13, 1824, *ibid.*, 445/2619/47.

It is impossible to rate too highly its present influence. . . . The organization is complete." [21]

Another confidant of Peel, through Sir Robert Inglis, evangelical M.P. for Dundalk, as intermediary, was the Protestant bishop of Limerick, John Jebb. The Bishop, living in the overwhelmingly Catholic Southwest, an opponent of emancipation yet widely respected for his lack of rabid party bias, penned fearful descriptions of the growth of discontent. Only three short years ago a priest had assured him of O'Connell's insignificance among the people of Limerick: "But how stands the matter now? Throughout all parts of Ireland the Catholic Association is omnipotent; its mandates are respected as much as the Acts of Parliament are contemned. In any district or parish the Catholic Rent needs only to be proposed, and it is hailed with acclamation. . . . There is what we of this generation have never before witnessed, a complete union of the Roman Catholic body. . . . In truth, an Irish Revolution has, in great measure, been effected." [22] Sir Henry Parnell, M.P. for Queen's County, whose opinion was even more trustworthy owing to his sympathy for the Catholic cause, corroborated the judgment of Bishop Jebb. Parnell, viewing the association with apprehension of a serious commotion, thought it particularly noteworthy that this was the first time means had been found of combining into one body, with a common object, the highest and lowest orders of the Catholic clergy and laity with the demagogues who had promoted every previous agitation; the chapels in the country were becoming regular debating halls.[23]

The mobilization of the Catholic masses and the virulence of the association were now the subject of universal attention and comment in Ireland. In England Cobbett was extolling the Irish leaders; Bentham subscribed £5 to the Catholic Rent; and the English Radicals generally, expecting O'Connell to link emancipation with parliamentary reform, took heart. Tories attacked the association as a hotbed of radicalism, while the Whigs held high hopes that the Irish problem might wreck Liverpool's ministry. The Whig *Morning Chronicle*, reprinting full reports of the Dublin meetings, commented: "The organization which has been effected in Ireland is of too formidable a nature to be put down by half measures; and the Minister must be a bold man that would

21. Foster to Peel, Nov. 10, 1824, BM, PP, 40370, foll. 23–24.
22. Jebb to Inglis, Nov. 19, 1824, *ibid.*, foll. 187–189.
23. Goulburn to Peel, Nov. 20, 1824, *ibid.*, 40330, foll. 207–208.

plunge Ireland into another Rebellion, for the sake of riding his old hobby." [24]

Lord Liverpool's government did not resort to half measures. From the beginning it had kept close but fruitless watch on the proceedings of the new organization. O'Connell and Sheil, astute lawyers, had avoided any grounds for prosecution or suppression. Finally, as an ultimate resort, Henry Goulburn gave notice in the House of Commons, on February 4, 1825, of intention to bring in a bill outlawing political societies in Ireland of longer duration than fourteen days. Goulburn's bill passed quickly. But before it became law the Irish agitators dissolved their organization. And they did so with an ominous defiance. O'Connell challenged ministers to frame a statute capable of stifling their protest:

> But I am told we are to have a parliamentary interference for suppression. Well, should they be displeased at the formation of this room, or our meeting in it, why we can build another; if they object to the denomination we have given ourselves, why we can change it with that of board, or committee, or even directory. If they prohibit our meeting, surely they cannot prevent our assembling to dine together. This Association is the creature of the Penal Code, and as long as Catholic disabilities exist, so long must some organ have its being through which to convey our complaints, to proclaim our grievances and to demand their redress.[25]

It was almost a year before O'Connell was able to justify such bravado. First he had to overcome a personal setback.

Early in 1825 a deputation of the Irish leaders crossed to England in hope of being allowed to defend their association now threatened by Goulburn's bill. Denied permission to plead their cause before the Bar of the House of Commons, they had, nevertheless, an opportunity while in London to consult frequently with parliamentary advocates of emancipation. In a significant example of a policy that was to become familiar later in the century in matters relating to Ireland, the blow of Goulburn's act was to be eased by the balm of an emancipation bill. O'Connell himself was accorded a major role in drawing up the terms of Sir Francis Burdett's Catholic relief bill which followed immediately upon Goul-

24. London *Morning Chronicle,* Oct. 23, 1824.

25. Speech of O'Connell, Jan. 8, 1825, in John O'Connell, ed., *The Select Speeches of Daniel O'Connell* (Dublin, 1854), *2,* 469.

burn's act. In the course of the negotiations he agreed to a fateful compromise: emancipation was to be followed by two other measures intended to ease its passage and consequently dubbed the "wings." The one provided state payment of the Catholic clergy; the other raised the electoral franchise in Ireland so as to disqualify forty-shilling voters. The latter wing, especially, brought down a whirlwind of protest around O'Connell's head. English reformers condemned him for betraying the interests of the people.[26] In Ireland a rapidly risen anti-wings party, composed of a minority of association members, political radicals, or personal antagonists of O'Connell, taunted him with his statement of only a few weeks previously that, "We are collecting the Rent for the benefit of the people; for them we are bound to seek protection and redress." [27] Disfranchisement seemed scarcely a measure for the protection of the people.

Burdett's bill did pass the Commons, only to flutter into abrupt oblivion in the Lords after a vehement "so help me God" from the heir apparent, the Duke of York. Emancipation seemed as remote as ever; Goulburn's act now prevented the Catholics from forming a permanent political association; and wingers and anti-wingers were at each others' throats. To restore confidence in himself O'Connell set about creating a new organization. Goulburn's act had a loophole. It was still possible to constitute a society to manage such portion of their affairs as had no relation to redress of grievances or any alteration in the existing laws, while everything connected with petitioning and political matters could be reserved for separate and aggregate meetings of less than fourteen days' duration. Thus O'Connell, in a typical instance of double talk, inaugurated the New Catholic Association for the purpose of promoting "public peace and harmony," encouraging "a liberal and religious system of education," conducting a census of the Catholic population, promoting a liberal and enlightened press, and pursuing public charity "and such other purposes as are not prohibited by the said statute of the 6th Geo. IV, chap. 4." [28]

But the work proceeded slowly.[29] Throughout the summer Dublin dozed in a silence so novel that Goulburn reported to Peel: "The

26. E.g., Joseph Hume in a speech in the House of Commons, May 9, 1825. Hansard, *Parl. Debates*, 2d Ser., *13*, 461–466.

27. *DEP*, Feb. 10, 1825.

28. *DEM*, July 15, 1825.

29. The vote for members of a committee to form a new association indicated the loss of prestige suffered by O'Connell. His name was sixth in the tally of votes and preceded on the list by that of Nicholas Mahon, a leader of the anti-wing faction.

general opinion is that there will be very little done in the way of mischief until after the circuits or even until the opening of the law courts in November . . . quiet is good for O'Connell's embarrassment at present."[30] The quiet of the metropolis was haunted by the twin specters of Goulburn's act and the wings. The New Catholic Association was a timid one compared with the old.[31] On one occasion it adjourned in haste upon hearing a rumor that the police intended to disperse it. It was now necessary to hold two meetings a week, one of the association on Saturdays and a "separate" meeting on Wednesdays, at both of which the attendance was once again less than fifty. But in the provinces the people were assembling still in county, town, and parish, and now for the first time in provincial meetings. In 1825 such gatherings proved that O'Connell was still as popular as ever with the masses, despite the heckling of the anti-wingers.

Three of the four provinces, Munster, Leinster, and Connaught, held the first of a series of annual conventions that were to become a prominent feature of the agitation.[32] In subsequent years the larger provincial towns competed for the honor, and the profit, of playing host to the crowds; preparations were made months in advance; the pomp and bustle of the assembly, frequently coincidental with the excitement of the local fair, attracted farmers from all parts of the province; and the proceedings became the subject of conversation for months afterward. The provincial meeting of Connaught in 1825 at Ballinasloe was typical. An old, bleak, partially ruined but spacious church provided the setting; before the altar on a crude platform sat about two hundred country gentle-

30. Goulburn to Peel, July 22, 1825, BM, PP, 40331, fol. 109.

31. The government reporter who attended the meetings noted that the members "were acting with a degree of caution that was particularly remarkable" and that the association was attracting mainly "clerks in distilleries and breweries." Meetings of July 15 and Aug. 6, 1825, ISPO, CAP. The Protestant archbishop of Dublin, William Magee, wrote to Lord Colchester on Aug. 5, 1825: "It happens indeed that there is nothing to communicate but the one great miracle, that we are quiet. For several years I have not witnessed the appearance of so much tranquillity as this country presents at this time. . . . Our great agitators are at this time on circuit. This, and the serious divisions existing amongst the leaders, afford us a respite from turmoil. When the demagogues, civil and ecclesiastical, have shaken hands, and a plan of operations has been fixed on, we may then have something more to talk of. One extraordinary proof of the degree of quietism to which the minds of the commonalty have lately been brought is, that the Archbishop of Dublin is allowed to walk abroad unmolested by rude expressions or menacing looks." Lord Colchester, ed., *The Diary and Correspondence of Charles Abbot, Lord Colchester* (London, 1861), *3*, 402.

32. In Ulster, with its large and hostile Presbyterian population, the Catholic Association was never so strong as in the South.

men, in the gallery on the right the more well-to-do farmers and townspeople, in that on the left their womenfolk; well-ordered but wild-looking peasantry filled the body of the church. The proceedings, begun after the most distinguished person present had been called to the chair and a secretary appointed, continued for almost five hours, with thirty resolutions and a petition, prepared the day before, being proposed and unanimously adopted. The main attraction was the speeches accompanying each resolution, and to a visitor unacquainted with and apprehensive of the eloquence of the men of Connaught they came as a pleasant surprise; the rustic orators expressed themselves with "warmth and facility"; but they were outshone by Sheil, whose hour-long display of histrionic pyrotechnics dazzled the audience. When he finished, "hats were waved over every head, and a piercing cry, the expression of joy among the Irish, shook the chapel to its very roof." [33]

Elsewhere in Ireland O'Connell and his cohorts of the Corn Exchange were arousing similar fervor, among people who carried their speeches home to market towns, country villages, and plowland cabins and thus set the pattern for thousands of less polished addresses which in turn were repeated from memory in the pubs, outside the chapels of a Sunday morning, and around the winter hearths. It was a type of oratory scarcely appealing to the fastidious. One pamphleteer, for example, turned his wit to a ludicrous summary of the formula adopted by the rural demagogues:

> As an infallible recipe for acquiring popularity with the great body of Irishmen of the present day, I should advise a public speaker to deal largely in gross adulation of the people, dwelling, especially, on those very perfections in which they are known to be most deficient; then to launch forth, in excessive lamentations, over the destitute condition of the "poor oppressed creatures"; thirdly, to bestow a plentiful measure of the coarsest personal abuse and invective on their opponents by name; and, fourthly, that a general tone of jesting and buffoonery should season the entire effusion. If among all this, be occasionally introduced references to Julius Caesar, St. Patrick, Nebuchadnezzar, and Brian Boru, the oration is perfect.[34]

33. Duvergier de Hauranne, *Lettres sur les élections anglaises et sur la situation de l'Irlande* (Paris, 1827), pp. 157–163. Translation mine.

34. Anonymous, *Letters to a Friend in England on the Actual State of Ireland* (pamphlet, London, 1828), pp. 157–163, RIA, Haliday Pamphlets, Vol. 1438.

The summer, autumn, and winter of 1826 heard many orations basically true to the above caricature. It was a year of general elections, with more than the usual spate of bombast. Yet ears as far away as England turned toward one immeasurably fateful hustings in the South of Ireland; and eyes blinked in astonishment as the Catholic forty-shilling freeholders of Waterford, in complete disregard of the hitherto sacrosanct orders of their landlords, rallied to the polls to return a pro-Catholic candidate to Parliament.[35] Thereupon O'Connell made an explicit recantation of his compromise on the wings and announced a revival of the Catholic Rent for the purpose of protecting the rebellious freeholders from eviction by their irate landlords. Moreover, the Waterford election evoked from the peasantry everywhere resolutions of determination to imitate the lesson in the next parliamentary elections. There were meetings in twenty-eight of the thirty-two counties. Westmeath met for the first time in ten years, Wicklow in fifteen, Tyrone in fourteen; in Leinster, King's County was the only one as yet unconvened.

Still the agitation failed to recover the pitch it had reached in 1824. During 1827, when Canning, long an advocate of emancipation, succeeded Liverpool as prime minister, the Irish leaders purposely adopted a moderate tone. Even after Canning's death in August they held to the hope that his political principles might be acted upon by Lord Goderich. Consequently the year 1827 saw only eight county meetings, and Sheil wrote worriedly to O'Connell:

> We should not hide from ourselves; the public mind is beginning to cool. The reason is, I think, this. When Peel and Dawson and our decided antagonists were in office, the Catholics were exposed to perpetual affronts which kept their indignation alive. The Priests especially were held in constant ferment. But now that Lord Lansdowne is in, we say to each other, "What a pity that our friends in the cabinet cannot do us any service," and convinced that they cannot we "take the will for the deed." In this view it would be almost better for us to have our open enemies than either our lukewarm and impotent advocates in power. . . . It behoves us therefore to make double exertions, and I shall not, you may rely on it, be deficient in my efforts. . . . Our

35. See below, Chapter 6, pp. 94–96.

> great object should be to bring the Priests into efficient and systematic action.[36]

Toward the end of the year Sheil's promised efforts seemed to be bearing results. The country meetings in the autumn, organized by the local priests, were numerous. Goulburn's act had nearly run its course: its two years expired in March 1827, and it remained in operation only until the beginning of the next session of Parliament. The old Catholic Association could then be revived.

The first days of the new year gave signs in Ireland of the approaching storm.[37] All excuse for moderation vanished when Goderich resigned and Wellington and Peel, high Tories and "Protestants," returned to office. On January 13 the peasantry assembled in simultaneous meetings in about two-thirds of the 2,500 parishes of the island. In Dublin alone, O'Connell boasted, over 100,000 attended meetings, while in the country he estimated, quite extravagantly, the number at close to five millions. He challenged the government to bring together such vast multitudes.[38] Denouncing Wellington and Peel, he threatened that if they tried to suppress the association he would evade any law they could devise:

> If they pass an Act, preventing any three men from meeting to discuss Catholic affairs, we will take off our gloves, and hold up our hands in the street, declaring that we are not speaking on Catholic affairs (cheers). We will talk of them at dinner, if they prevent us from speaking at our meals, we will proclaim a fast day, and in prayer we shall talk of Catholic politics. We will speak of them, whilst we sip our tea and coffee. I defy them to prevent us—if they prevent us from talking politics, why we will whistle or sing them (loud cheers). We shall implicitly submit to the letter of the law—but that shall be the extent of our obedience.[39]

Not only did the King's Tory ministers not attempt to enact new legislation; they recognized the futility of renewing Goulburn's act. By the end of July the association was able to drop the *New* from its title and to resume all its old functions. It now had ten thousand regular members; its weekly income amounted to over £2,000; and it began again its invasion of the jurisdiction of Dub-

36. Sheil to O'Connell, Sept. 30, 1827, UCD, O'C P.
37. The state of Ireland in 1828 is described in detail below, Chapter 8.
38. *DEP,* Jan. 15, 1828.
39. *Ibid.,* Feb. 19, 1828.

lin Castle, not only by sending down to the country its lawyer members to prosecute Orangemen and defend Catholics in the courts but also by setting up its own arbitration boards among the people. And once again an election provided the necessary stimulus. Early in 1828 O'Connell introduced into the association a resolution calling upon the Catholic electorate to oust any Irish M.P. who supported Wellington's administration. The famous Clare election in July put the resolution to the test. O'Connell, who as a Catholic could not take the qualifying oaths, was returned to Parliament in another stampede of rebellious freeholders. The crisis mounted rapidly. In the predominantly Catholic South of Ireland the peasantry, intoxicated with their newly discovered power, were assembling in huge open-air meetings and semimilitary processions, while in the Protestant North emissaries from the association were touring the countryside, organizing meetings and thus risking a clash between the mobs that accompanied them and the Orangemen who sought to bar their way.

Throughout the island ultra-Protestants were gathering in Brunswick clubs to outdo the Catholic Association in belligerence. A young Irish Protestant, returning to his studies at Cambridge after spending the summer holidays at his home in Clare, noted in his journal as he passed through Dublin: "The state of political agitation into which this country has been thrown by the intemperance of the ultras on both sides of the question exceeds description. All other topics are uninteresting now; we hear and speak nothing but politics. The very cabin children, that run out in their rags to stare at the passing traveller, cry 'High for O'Connell!' while perhaps a rustic politician within reads aloud with note and comment from some Catholic journal the speeches of the orators of the Corn Exchange to an agitated circle of hereditary bondsmen."[40]

While the Irish undergraduate was on his way across the Irish Sea to Holyhead an equally observant Englishman, Thomas Creevey, who had made the same crossing a few weeks previously, but in the opposite direction, in order to see Ireland "during the operation of this crisis," attended the Leinster provincial meeting at Kilkenny. Disappointed perhaps in failing to be an on-the-spot witness of another Irish rebellion, Creevey was, nevertheless, impressed by what he saw at Kilkenny:

40. Entry of Oct. 21, 1828, Journal of G. H. Ross-Lewin, MS, in the possession of Professor John Wardell, the Old Abbey, Shanagolden, County Limerick.

> The meeting was in an immense Catholic chapel, which was crowded to excess. A great portion of its interior was covered with a platform for the speakers and the gentlemen interested in the business. It being known that Lady Duncannon was coming, we were met by a *manager* at the chapel door, who told her a place was reserved for her upon the platform. . . . There were women without end in the galleries. I was my lady's bottle-holder and held her cloak for her the whole time; not that she wanted my assistance, for I never saw such pretty attentions as were shewn her all the day. . . . You can form no notion of the intense attention paid by the audience *of all ages* and of all degrees to what was going on; . . . On the floor of the chapel, in front of the platform, the commonest people from the streets of Kilkenny were collected in great numbers; and if a publick speaker in the midst of his speech was at all at a loss for a word, I heard the proper word suggested from five or six different voices of this beggarly audience. . . . Yet a better behaved and more orderly audience could not possibly have been collected.[41]

Creevey was surprised by the size of the meeting and the discipline of an Irish mob. The effect was even more impressive when one considered that what was happening in Kilkenny was being repeated throughout Ireland.

By the end of 1828 the majority of Irishmen looked, for the real government of the country, not to Dublin Castle or to Westminster but to the Corn Exchange, to a political body that had developed within six years from a small club of about sixty persons into a central directory at the head of fifteen thousand regular and over three million associate members.[42] Ireland appeared on the brink of another rebellion. At least it seemed so to the Duke of Wellington. Taking counsel of his lieutenant, Peel, the Iron Duke decided upon one of his strategic retreats. He wrung from the King permission to introduce as a government measure a reform which, as leader of the high Tories, he had consistently opposed—unqualified emancipation.

41. Sir Herbert Maxwell, ed., *The Creevey Papers* (New York, E. P. Dutton & Co., 1904), *2,* 182–184.

42. *DEP,* Feb. 28, 1829.

# 3. *Demagogues and Priests*

The original members of the Catholic Association included one viscount, the younger son of a baron, two baronets, a knight, a Carmelite friar, nineteen barristers, twelve attorneys, three editors of newspapers, one surgeon, eleven merchants, and ten landed gentlemen—sixty-two members in all. The figures are illuminating. By far the largest single group was that of the thirty-one lawyers. Outnumbering, with the aid of the other professional men, the peers and gentry by three to one, they formed the core of the movement. Yet in another respect the proportion is misleading. The lone Carmelite, although he remained for six years virtually the only priest who participated regularly in the Dublin meetings, was but a token representative of the large body of clerics who, once the association caught the imagination of the people, provided throughout the island its most energetic leadership.

At the head of the Catholic population of Ireland stood a remnant of aristocracy and landed gentry who, led by the premier Catholic peer, the Earl of Fingall, had been the directors of the boards and committees that secured the first Catholic relief acts, but whose conservatism and timidity had lost them in the 1790's control of the movement to bolder, more vigorous spokesmen, prosperous merchants like John Keogh and, later, impatient young lawyers like Daniel O'Connell. In the spring of 1823, on the invitation of O'Connell and Sheil, the peers and gentry again came forward. The plan of the Catholic Association seemed innocuous enough, and their presence, so they hoped, would keep O'Connell, who lately had threatened a junction with the English Radicals, to a moderate course. Consequently Lord Killeen, heir to the Earl of Fingall, and Sir Edward Bellew presided alternately for the first month at the association's meetings. But true to the Fingall family motto, *Festina lente*, Killeen soon found the lawyers setting too fast a pace. When O'Connell insisted that, instead of adhering to the old practice of sending an annual and fruitless petition to

Parliament, the association should detach specific grievances from the general catalogue and expose them to the British Empire and the world and, horror of horrors, "bring the Catholics to act with the Reformers of England," [1] the peers and gentry, gaining no support for their motion that all passages not relating to emancipation be stricken from their petitions,[2] retired from the association. They did not return until almost a year later, and then only because their absence was isolating them from every other segment of the Catholic population. By that time many noblemen and gentlemen, both Protestant and Catholic, and even some members of Parliament were subscribing to the Catholic Rent, as Goulburn noted worriedly: "The subscription on the part of the Roman Catholic gentry is also not confined to the violent. . . . Although Lord Fingall, Sir Edward Bellew, and others stated privately their disapprobation of the Association, they did not conceal that they did not dare set themselves against it." [3]

The main function of the reconciled peers and gentry was to lend prestige to the movement. The Irish peasantry, a title-loving people,[4] now had a high-sounding name, evocative of proud memories, to grace the chair at their public meetings. Years later O'Connell remarked that after 1824 only one Catholic nobleman had held aloof: Lord Southwell "was the only Catholic of rank or fortune who did not join in the struggle for Emancipation . . . We brought over before 1829 every other Vetoist, every other nobleman, every other Catholic." [5] After the failure of their initial efforts to temper the tone of the association, the peers and gentry wisely left the business of policy and debate to men who spoke out more bluntly and rashly, to lawyers like O'Connell and Sheil.

For the first half of the 19th century the public life of Ireland revolved around one man, Daniel O'Connell. Even the most casual

1. *DEP,* June 10, 1823.

2. The passages to which they objected contained pleas for a reform in the temporalities of the Irish church establishment, better regulation of juries, and disfranchisement of rotten borough corporations. Meeting of Feb. 27, 1824, ISPO, CAP.

3. Goulburn to Peel, Oct. 27, 1824, BM, PP, 40330, foll. 145–151.

4. The Irish peasantry, habituated to servility, affected a sometimes ludicrous reverence for their "betters." Thackeray, traveling in Ireland in 1842, was disgusted by their cringing attitude: "Why are they so ready to go down on their knees to my lord? A man can't help 'condescending' to another who will persist in kissing his shoestrings. They respect rank in England—the people seem almost to adore it here." W. M. Thackeray, "The Irish Sketch Book," p. 84, *The Works of William Makepeace Thackeray* (ed. de luxe New York, 1904), *15*.

5. O'Connell to Thomas Drummond, Sept. 25, 1837, NL, O'C MSS.

glance at the newspapers of the day is sufficient to reveal his Gargantuan stature in the eyes of Irish and English alike. Idolized or despised, he never failed to command attention. Born in 1775, the son of a small landlord in Kerry, O'Connell was called to the Irish Bar in 1798, after spending about a year and a half in Catholic colleges on the Continent and two years at Lincoln's Inn. Perhaps it was his religious training at Louvain, St. Omer's, and Douai, perhaps a more deep-seated loyalty bred in the bones of a wily Kerryman by ancestral devotion to an outlawed creed. Whatever the reason, the young student managed to survive a brief period of skepticism while in London, where he gave almost as much time to Voltaire, Rousseau, Paine, Godwin, and Bentham as he did to his "Coke on Littleton," and to emerge a convinced Catholic. But a rare sort of Catholic for his day, a Catholic Radical. Bentham did not lose completely to Bellarmine and Bossuet; they shared a sincere, if sometimes truculent, devotee.[6] The eighty-year-old patriarch of British utilitarianism acknowledged himself highly pleased when O'Connell wrote to him in 1829: "I avowed myself on the hustings this day to be a 'Benthamite,' and explained the leading principles of your disciples—the 'greatest happiness principle' —our sect *will* prosper. I begin my parliamentary career by tendering you my constant, zealous, and active services in the promotion of that principle." [7]

The disciple held to the promise. No doctrinaire, in fact rather more than a confirmed Benthamite in sometimes pushing his

6. During 1828 and 1829 Bentham and O'Connell carried on a steady correspondence, begun when the former wrote to express his gratitude for O'Connell's identifying himself as "an humble disciple of the immortal Bentham." Subsequent letters of O'Connell were addressed to "Benefactor of the Human Race" and "Respected and Revered Master," while Bentham replied, buoyantly and impetuously, with salutations like "Liberator of Liberators" and "Dear, honest, supremely public-spirited, truly philanthropic, consistent, persevering, self-devoting Friend." In one of the letters O'Connell revealed the inspiration for his Catholic Radicalism: "I am convinced that no one individual, in modern times, approaches in any degree to the practical and permanent utility of Bentham. . . . I belong to a religion which teaches the merits of good works; and I am quite a sincere votary of that creed. Besides the pleasure of doing good, and the gratification which a light heart feels even at the attempt to be useful, there is—I hope I say it without any tinge of hypocrisy—a higher propelling motive on my mind. There is the stimulant, I hope, of religious duty and spiritual reward. There are many who would smile at my simplicity. And the *liberaux* of France, who hate religion much more than they do tyranny, would sneer at me. Yet it is true. I do look for a reward exceedingly great, for endeavouring to terminate a system of fraud, perjury, and oppression of the poor." O'Connell to Bentham, Oct. 6, 1828, in John Bowring, ed., *The Works of Jeremy Bentham* (Edinburgh, 1843), *10,* 602–603.

7. O'Connell to Bentham, July 30, 1829, *ibid., 11,* 20.

utilitarianism beyond the limits of political consistency, he was yet proudly sensible of being the herald, in Ireland at least, of a new type of democratic policy. In Parliament after 1829, although occasionally dallying with the Whigs, he attached himself to the Radicals, to become a vigorous proponent of such favorite Benthamite schemes as sweeping reorganization of the legal system, codification of the law, abolition of tithes, of sinecures, and of grand juries, radical amendment of the subletting and libel laws, and parliamentary reform.[8] He supported the abolition of slavery within the empire and condemned the institution as it existed in America. Reason and justice, he asserted, demonstrated also the right of every man to freedom of conscience,[9] equally the right of a Protestant in Italy or in Spain as of a Catholic in Ireland. Thus he favored repeal of the Test and Corporation acts against dissenters and the admission of Jews to Parliament. Indeed, the amalgam of his Radicalism and his Catholicism gave rise to the conviction that his own church, doing well to adapt herself to the trend of the world toward democracy, should be grateful for what he regarded as one of the blessings of the French Revolution of 1830, complete separation of church and state.

The same revolution illuminates another aspect of O'Connell's thought. He is often quoted as stating that no political objective was worth a single drop of human blood. Indeed, his conviction of the supreme efficacy of moral force, of legal, constitutional, and peaceful methods, deriving something from his personal experiences of the Reign of Terror on the Continent and of the Rebellion of 1798 in Ireland and from his early reading of Godwin, as well as from Catholic teaching, imbedded in him a deep respect for constituted authority and a sincere attachment to the Throne. Yet he praised the French rebels of 1830, their predecessors the Greeks, and their successors the Belgians and the Poles, sent one of his sons in 1820 to fight in the army of Simón Bolívar, and in his own agitations at home employed constantly the threat of physical force, the policy of calculated risk.

In 1823 O'Connell, at the age of forty-eight, although not yet the "Liberator" or, as many Englishmen preferred to salute him, "the king of the beggars," was the most prominent member of the Irish Bar and a hero to the Catholic masses, the first national leader

8. O'Connell's proposals went beyond the Reform Act of 1832 to include suffrage for taxpayers and the secret ballot.

9. Speech of O'Connell, Feb. 23, 1814, J. O'Connell, *Select Speeches*, *2*, 6.

whom they could follow wholeheartedly since Sarsfield.[10] Unlike Grattan, Flood, Tone, and Emmet, he was not of the Court, the Government, Parliament, or the Protestant ascendancy. He could assert proudly that he was "only the fourth in descent from a lady who was concealed forty-eight hours in a garden and the bloodhounds passed four times within twenty yards of the spot where she lay." [11] But the boast was scarcely needed to identify him as one of the native Irish. His very appearance proclaimed his ancestry: a big man, six feet tall, with a head of copper curls, bright blue eyes, blunt, irregular features—a typically Irish face it was called. To see him in the streets, on his way from a trial at the law courts to an association meeting at the Corn Exchange, shouldering his umbrella like a pike and flinging out one factious foot before the other, with a broad-shouldered, rolling, self-confident gait, was to recognize a man who had sworn to free all "hereditary bondsmen." A judiciously selected Dublin jury would have found the very gestures of this "broguing Irish fellow" evidence of democratic principles and high treason by construction. The swagger, the cockiness, the vulgarity of the man! Here was something new and native in a modern Irish leader, something reminiscent of the devil-may-care impetuousity of the Gael.

If his mere appearance inspirited his countrymen, O'Connell's oratory was calculated to shame them out of their helotry. He had a voice magnificent in power and melody. From the platform of a vast open-air meeting, "you'd hear it a mile off," said an Irish peasant, "and it sounded as if it was coming through honey." Since O'Connell usually spoke extemporaneously, few of his speeches come down to us as he gave them. One such, neither rewritten nor repolished, was delivered in 1843 on the subject of repeal of the Union:

> My first object is to get Ireland for the Irish (loud cheers). I am content that the English should have England, but they have had the domination of this country too long, and it is time that the Irish should at length get their own coun-

10. O'Connell's patriotism was closer to the Anglo-Irish tradition of Grattan and Flood than to the romantic, doctrinaire nationalism which came into vogue only in the 1840's with the Young Irelanders, who turned for their inspiration back beyond Georgian Ireland, ruled by English-speaking Whig landlords and productive of Swift, Berkeley, Sterne, Goldsmith, and Burke, to the Ireland of high kings and Gaelic septs.
11. Speech of O'Connell, Oct. 23, 1828, NL, CA MSS.

THE LIBRARY
STRANMILLIS COLLEGE
BELFAST

> try—that they should get the management of their own country—the regulation of their own country—the enjoyment of their own country—that the Irish should have Ireland (great cheers). Nobody can know how to govern us as well as we would know how to do it ourselves—nobody could know how to relieve our wants as well as we would ourselves—nobody could have so deep an interest in our prosperity, or could be so well fitted for remedying our evils, and procuring happiness for us as we would ourselves (hear, hear). Old Ireland and liberty! (loud cheers). . . . The labourer, the artizan, and the shopkeeper would be all benefited by the repeal of the union; but if I were to describe all the blessings that it would confer I would detain you here crowding on each other's backs until morning before I would be done (laughter). In the first place, I ask you did you ever hear of the tithe rent charge (groans). Are you satisfied to be paying parsons who do not pray for you (no, no). . . . What I want you to do is, for every one of you to join me in looking for Repeal. As many of you as are willing to do so let them hold up their hands (here every person in the immense assemblage raised his hands aloft amidst loud and continued cheers). I see you have ready hands, and I know you have stout hearts too. But what do I want you to do? Is it to turn out into battle or war (cries of no, no)? Is it to commit riot or crime (cries of no, no)? Remember "whoever commits a crime gives strength to the enemy" (hear, hear, and cheers). . . . I want you to do nothing that is not open and legal, but if the people unite with me and follow my advice it is impossible not to get the Repeal (loud cheers and cries of "we will").[12]

On such occasions O'Connell's tumbling eloquence ranged the scale of pathetic appeal, savage invective, rough humor, bitter sarcasm, sublime declamation. From his meetings the audience would carry home dozens of stories and jokes on their inveterate enemies, the Orangemen. Even strangers were quite as profoundly moved as the wild-looking Irish countrymen. A French traveler noted the effect:

> It is especially in the midst of the people that O'Connell shows his complete self. Known personally to the Irish peasants, and living with them for a part of the year, he has

12. Edmund Curtis and R. B. McDowell, eds., *Irish Historical Documents, 1172–1922* (London, Methuen & Co., 1943), pp. 269–274.

> something of their manners, their language, and their accent. You should see him in a chapel in Munster, his cravat loose, his waistcoat unbuttoned. He boasts of the beauties of Ireland, the delights of her valleys, the loveliness of her hills, and above all the incontestable superiority of her inhabitants over the rest of the earth: and if by chance he should touch on "the children of your bosom and the wives of your affection," tears of joy sparkle in every eye. . . . O'Connell is of the people. He is a mirror in which Ireland sees herself complete, or rather, he is Ireland herself.[13]

In personifying his country O'Connell embodied not only the more appealing characteristics of the Irish people, their sentimentality, their imaginative romanticism, their generosity, hasty enthusiasm, and ready wit; he shared their cunning, the trickery ingrained in them through long years of hatred for lawful but alien authority, the vindictiveness with which they sometimes regarded each other as well as their Sassenach lords, the vanity which made every Irishman a descendant of kings. Often betrayed by his undisciplined temper, he could be pettily spiteful toward insubordinate followers, while toward political opponents he was unsparing in the coarsest scurrility. Wellington and Peel were "filthy state apothecaries," "a stunted corporal," "spinning-jenny Peel," "Orange Peel," and the English aristocracy, "pigs with soaped tails." [14]

The apathy of his audience and his fierce desire to rouse them from national abasement help to explain such vulgarity. But much of it was due to a smarting sense of personal injustice. Recognized as the ablest member of the Irish Bar, O'Connell was compelled to stand aside in his stuff gown and watch fellow barristers, inferior in talent and achievement, don their silk. In 1825 while in London

13. de Hauranne, *Lettres,* pp. 178–179. Translation mine.

14. O'Connell was the victim, indeed, as well as the perpetrator of savage invective. The London *Times* described him as

> "Scum condensed of Irish bog!
> Ruffian, coward, demagogue!
> Boundless liar, vile detractor!
> Nurse of murders, treason's factor!"

But the *Times,* Nov. 26, 1835, was merely returning measure for measure. Even the intercession of Bentham, with "Dan, Dear Child—put off, if possible, your intolerance," was effective only in causing a sudden coolness between master and disciple. Bentham to O'Connell, Nov. 7, 1829, J. Bowring, *Works of Bentham, 11,* 26. But to his wife O'Connell acknowledged his weakness. Referring to his son he advised: "Maurice *did* make a good speech, but he should not imitate his father's faults by being so personal." O'Connell to his wife, Feb. 22, 1825, in W. J. Fitzpatrick, ed., *The Correspondence of Daniel O'Connell* (London, 1888), *1,* 100.

conferring with parliamentary leaders he confided to his wife: "The truth is, and I would not say it to another human being but you, I felt in our conversations that it was not difficult to exceed in intellect and sound views men of high names. . . . I felt how cruel the penal laws are which exclude me from a fair trial with men who [*sic*] I look on as so much my inferiors." [15] This brooding sense of oppression was offset, nevertheless, by a generous patriotism.[16] At times disheartened by the supineness of his countrymen, O'Connell would demand querulously: "How is it possible to succeed for a people who will not make a small sacrifice to the common cause?" But the answer came immediately, "redouble our exertions and . . . make by our own struggles the best compensation we can for the deplorable neglect of others. I am really astonished how any human being can tread this lovely green land and not feel his heart glow within him with the warmest anxiety to see her what she ought to be." [17]

Such a glowing, constant anxiety proved one of O'Connell's greatest assets as a popular leader. After wading through an exhausting agenda in the courts he would come in the afternoon to the association's rooms, there to make twenty short speeches independent of a major one on some important motion. A grievance letter from Tipperary, a Rent remittance from Galway, or a remark from another speaker brought him to his feet to convulse the meeting with laughter, to evoke deeper emotions with an anecdote of persecution, or to excite cheers of indignant pride with a fervid account of the "glories of Ireland."

Some members, indeed, resented what they considered, with justice, O'Connell's dictatorial manner, and as early as June 1824 the editor of the Dublin *Evening Post* warned: "Mr. O'Connell may be the Catholic Association, but he is not the Catholic Cause." [18] Not

15. O'Connell to his wife, n.d., probably 1825, O'Connell Letters, MSS in the possession of Col. Manners O'Connell FitzSimon, Newbliss, County Monaghan. Hereafter cited as O'Connell Letters to His Wife.

16. A fee book of O'Connell's for the years 1822–28 shows that his preoccupation with the Catholic Association cost him a sharp decline in professional income at a time when his fame as a barrister brought him his choice of briefs:

| | | |
|---|---|---|
| Fees for | 1822–£5,057 | 1826–£4,497 |
| | 1823– 5,157 | 1827– 4,868 |
| | 1824– 6,045 | 1828– 5,178 |
| | 1825– 3,893 | |

AHD, CP.

17. O'Connell to Edward Dwyer, secretary of the association, Sept. 16, 1827, *ibid.*

18. *DEP*, June 29, 1824.

content with carrying his main recommendations, O'Connell showed that tendency, attended with such pathetic results in his later agitation for repeal of the Union, of brooking no opposition, even in trivial matters, when he considered it, as he was too often prone to do, a challenge to his leadership. On at least three occasions he threatened never again to attend a Catholic meeting if his wishes were not followed.[19] Factious opposition explains such petulance. Jealousy, combined with Irish love of contention, prompted some members frequently to throw the assembly into an uproar with their bickering over personalities and rules of procedure. Although he was able almost always to silence the discordant minority with the persuasiveness of his oratory or to outvote them with the aid of a contingent of faithful supporters, O'Connell complained bitterly, and in a tone significantly autocratic: "I am often blamed for not having managed Catholic affairs so as to have attained Emancipation long since. Alas, how little the fault-finders know the species of material with which I have had to deal, the kind of persons who eternally clog every movement and who would prefer breaking my head to smashing the pates of five hundred Orangemen." [20]

Only once was there a possibility that O'Connell's head might be broken—when he agreed to the wings in 1825. How was he led into the blunder? Sheil gave a partial explanation:

> The moment we entered England I perceived that the sense of our own national importance had sustained some diminution. A man like Mr. O'Connell, . . . could with difficulty resist the intoxicating influence of so many exciting causes, and became a sort of political opium-eater, who should be torn from these seductive indulgences in order to reduce him to perfect soundness and soberness of thought. His deputation to England produced a temporary effect on him. As we advanced, the din of Irish assemblies became more faint; the voice of the multitude was scarcely heard in the distance as we entered the murky magnificence of Warwickshire.[21]

19. On one of the occasions O'Connell denounced a fellow member, William Bellew, for receiving a pension from the Irish Government and on this account objected to his appointment to one of the association's committees. Several members, disgusted by O'Connell's action, retired from the meeting, but upon his threatening to resign the others voted as he demanded. S. N. Elrington to the Magistrates of the Head Police Office, Dublin Castle, June 12 and 19, 1825, ISPO, SCP, carton 48.

20. O'Connell to Edward Dwyer, March 21, 1827, AHD, CP.

21. Requoted from C. O'Keefe, *Life and Times of O'Connell, 2,* 359–360.

In London O'Connell had occasion to confer with the friends of the Catholics in Parliament and to mingle with the more cautious, reserved, and ready-to-compromise English Catholics. He soon forgot Cobbett's warning: "I hope, sir, that you are aware that you are come into hell, and, of course, that you have devils to deal with." The genteel atmosphere of the lobby of the house and of dinner parties at the Duke of Norfolk's was far removed from the boisterous clamor of the Corn Exchange and Townsend Street Chapel. Flattered by the polite attention shown him, he appeared less the demagogue and more the politician, amenable to the compromise which seemed so essential, in the light of English party politics, if Catholic Emancipation was to pass the legislature. And he had been given to believe that emancipation was certain if accompanied by the wings. The very situation of the Irish electorate, he argued, gave ample justification for raising the franchise.[22] While the London negotiations were still in progress he wrote to urge the association to be silent on the issue until he returned to Ireland. His tactic seems to have been to prevent discussion until he could come home with a *fait accompli*. He knew that chagrin over the compromise would then be lost amid the universal satisfaction attending the removal of the last of the penal laws.

Although a few malcontents did attempt to raise the issue of the wings within the association, the majority voted a resolution of confidence in O'Connell. "Several applauded," noted the government reporter who attended the meeting, "but a colder feeling than usual seemed to exist towards that gentleman." [23] When O'Connell returned to Ireland the cold feeling became an icy blast. During the summer he went on four different circuits exclusive of his own, to Antrim, Newry, Galway, and Wexford, in an effort to recoup his popularity: his friends, wrote a government informer, "have a difficult task to persuade the people that he is honest." [24] But O'Connell himself was a master of persuasion. At the country meetings, witty, scurrilous, handsome, cocking his eye here and there to his "boys" as he strode to the platform, never disdaining a cruel jibe at his hecklers, grossly flattering his audience, and protesting

22. See the testimony of O'Connell before the select committee of the House of Lords on the state of Ireland, March 11, 1825, in *Parliamentary Papers* (1825), *9*, 163–164. O'Connell's argument was persuasive. Peel remarked: "Mr. O'Connell says, and I am not at all sure that he is wrong, raise the qualification and you strengthen the Roman Catholic influence." Peel to William Gregory, March 21, 1825, BM, PP, 40334, fol. 125.

23. Meeting of March 18, 1825, ISPO, CAP.

24. Information of "Q" in a letter from Goulburn to Peel, n.d., 1825, BM, PP, 40331, foll. 75–76.

the while that he had acted only for the good of "ould Ireland," he succeeded, with his lawyer's wiles, his evasiveness and ambiguity, in winning over potential and even actual rebels. Thus at Carlow: "We beat the Wingers out of the field. . . . The good sense, the good feeling of *my* poor people. May the great God bless them. They would not listen to the Wingers and their fantasies." [25]

Back in Dublin the wingers were less easily put down. They raised the question constantly, and gradually their clamor forced O'Connell to reverse his stand. He admitted he had made a barter in London through motives of expediency.[26] When the Waterford election showed the power of the forty-shilling freeholders he emphatically recanted. It was, indeed, typical of the man that his main consideration throughout was expediency. "To accomplish any particular object," observed Charles Greville, "he cares not to what charges of partial inconsistency he exposes himself, trusting to his own ingenuity to exonerate himself from them afterwards." [27] O'Connell's ingenuity was taxed by the effort to extricate himself from the wings difficulties. He did so by making full use of his talents as a manager and a mob leader. It was expedient to agree to the compromise in London and later to disavow it at home. In both instances he testified to his consistency on one score at least, his confirmed, if not always admirable, utilitarianism.

The wings controversy presented the sole occasion on which O'Connell's supremacy was seriously challenged. On all important issues and, indeed, on most minor ones he decided the course of the agitation. When the old association was suppressed he improvised a new one: "A gentleman who was standing on Tuesday night below the Bar of the House of Lords, and next to O'Connell when the division [on Burdett's emancipation bill of 1825] was announced told me that he heard him say, 'If that's the case, we must do it all over again.' " [28] O'Connell, for all his lawyer's tricks, his occasional truculence, his ruthless ridicule and penchant for personal derision, his vulgarity, and his dictatorial manner, was the dynamism behind the association, the leader above all others responsible for its success. He was great, as Balzac remarked, "because he incarnated a whole people." [29]

25. O'Connell to his wife, Dec. 17, 1825, O'Connell Letters to His Wife.

26. Meeting of Jan. 16, 1826, ISPO, CAP.

27. Entry of Dec. 20, 1828, in Lytton Strachey and Roger Fulford, eds., *The Greville Memoirs, 1814–1860* (London, Macmillan & Co., 1938), *1,* 225.

28. Mont. Cholmeley to Peel, May 19, 1825, BM, PP, 40378, fol. 135.

29. Requoted from Seán O'Faoláin, *King of the Beggars* (New York, The Viking Press, 1938), p. 69.

Yet the association was not a one-man affair.[30] Some of its most effective tactics were due to others, and with one of them, Richard Lalor Sheil, O'Connell shared national popularity as an orator. Sheil was the son of a Waterford merchant. He had been called to the Irish Bar in 1814, and though highly successful as an advocate, suffered the same religious disqualifications as O'Connell.[31] He was a small man, homely, fidgety, shambling in gait, reminding one more of the tailor just off his sewing table than of a fire-breathing demagogue. When he spoke from the platform, his voice shrill and rasping, it was said to be a mixture of grunts and screams, accompanied by sharp gestures, sudden jolts and shuffles. But his audience forgot all that within a very few minutes. An old farmer who attended Catholic meetings on many a hillside recalled that he "was not much to look at till he began to speak, and then you'd see genius coming out from him." [32]

A reputation for genius was something on which Sheil, with a little of the snob about him, prided himself; he enjoyed great popularity in both islands as a dramatist. His oratory was as flamboyant as his melodramas. When O'Connell spoke of emancipation being opposed in the House of Lords "by an old gouty bishop," Sheil referred to it as encountering "an episcopal array of orthodoxy and a united phalanx of bigotry." But the countrymen were as enthralled by his extravagance as by O'Connell's bluntness: "After a late brilliant and powerful speech of Mr. Shiel [*sic*], I asked an intelligent countryman what he thought best and most remarkable in the speech. 'Bad luck to the word good or bad, myself knew of what he was saying, but sure it was all for our side, and against the parsons; well, success to him, any how, he's a fine little man.' " [33]

Unlike O'Connell Sheil wrote out his speeches carefully and

30. While it is impossible to accept without qualification Lecky's judgment, in his *Leaders of Public Opinion in Ireland* (2d ed. London, 1871), p. 248, that Catholic Emancipation "was won by the genius of a single man," it is true that the Irish agitation which was responsible for that reform was due primarily to O'Connell. Gladstone remarked of him: "Almost from the opening of my Parliamentary life I felt that he was the greatest popular leader whom the world had ever seen." W. E. Gladstone, "Daniel O'Connell," *Nineteenth Century, 25* (Jan.–June 1889), 151.

31. Sheil was slightly envious of O'Connell's commanding position. Although he rivaled him in demagogic oratory, he affected to disdain boisterous public meetings and privately ridiculed O'Connell's plebeian rudeness. Sheil to William Curran, March 28, 1829, copy, BM, PP, 40399, foll. 106–107.

32. Lady Gregory, ed., *Mr. Gregory's Letter-Box* (London, Smith, Elder & Co., 1898), p. 39.

33. Anonymous, *Letters on the State of Ireland,* p. 32.

memorized them, but he seemed often to be carried away by the vehemence of his emotion, summoning all his lawyer's skill to keep his words, bordering on the very edge of sedition, within the law. To his friend, the poet Thomas Moore, he revealed something of his strategy as an agitator. Moore recorded in his journal:

> A good deal of talk upon the Catholic cause. Said I thought their best policy would have been, after the defeat last session, to have had one great meeting, to have let their feelings explode on that occasion as violently as they pleased, and after that to maintain a sullen and formidable silence, which (for the same reason that makes the government always apprehensive when the fellows are not drinking and breaking each others' heads at fairs) would have had ten times more effect in alarming their rulers than all the oratorical brawling in the world. Shiel [*sic*] said this would not do; there was but little public spirit in Ireland; they wanted continual lashing up; the priests were the only lever by which they could raise the people and they had now fully brought them into play.[34]

Much of the credit for bringing the priests into play was due to Sheil. He was the instigator of the association's census project, a scheme effective rather in re-establishing a regular correspondence with the parish clergy after the suppression of the old association than in securing any complete enumeration of the population. But the scattered census returns emphasized the numerical disproportion between Catholics and Protestants in various sections of the country and thus served, as did articles which Sheil wrote for a Paris newspaper, *L'Étoile*, as a highly successful propaganda device for drawing attention to the state of Ireland.

No other member of the association rivaled O'Connell and Sheil as mob leaders. Within the body there were only two or three good speakers and four or five working members to whom much of the detail of business was necessarily consigned. Foremost among the latter was Frederick William Conway, editor of the Dublin *Evening Post* and one of the ablest men connected with the Irish press. Conway, a Protestant, had long been an advocate of the Catholic claims, and in 1823 he became one of the earliest and most energetic members of the association. His was the idea of an education survey that first enlisted the cooperation of the Catholic clergy. Seldom

34. Entry of Jan. 2, 1826, in Lord John Russell, ed., *Memoirs, Journal, and Correspondence of Thomas Moore* (New York, 1857), *2*, 564.

on his feet in debate, he made his principal contribution in the routine business of committees and especially in circulating throughout the country, with the aid of Michael Staunton, editor of the Dublin *Weekly Register* and the Dublin *Morning Register*, full accounts of the proceedings of the agitators in their weekly meetings.[35]

Thomas Wyse, a well-to-do landlord of County Waterford, was not one of the original members. He did not join the association until 1826, and thereafter, although he frequently was seen at the Corn Exchange, he seldom participated in the debates. Aloof, cold, even haughty, he was repelled by the raucous atmosphere of the Dublin meetings and resented the despotic hold over the people exercised by Sheil and O'Connell. For the latter, especially, he ill concealed his dislike, deeming him invaluable, to be sure, as an agent for rallying the masses but dangerous should he continue to inspire in them nothing but blind devotion to a demagogue. Wyse, idealistically, looked rather to the political education of an intelligent, discriminating electorate. He was almost solely responsible for the Waterford election, which provided the association with a powerful new weapon.

At the opposite extreme from Wyse was John Lawless, "Radical Jack," the Don Quixote of the association, a wild-looking Irishman, but with a sort of rude dignity about him. His magnificent voice led one to expect something extraordinary when he rose to speak, as he was forever doing; "but the speech, which commences in an earnest tone, soon falls into the most incredible extravagancies, and sometimes into total absurdity. . . . He is therefore little heeded; laughed at when he rages like King Lear . . . The dominant party, however, use him to make a noise." [36] Noise-making was Lawless' forte. In his youth his well-known revolutionary sentiments had blocked his admission to the Bar; he had tried his hand at brewing; during the 1820's he was a journalist, editor of a Belfast newspaper, *The Irishman*, a staunch radical, friend of Cobbett, and convenient instrument of the association when it wished to

35. Conway played a dual role. At the same time that he took an active and extremely valuable part in promoting the agitation he was receiving secret service money from the Irish Government. "Permanent Charges on the Secret Service List," Aug. 1828, ISPO, OP II, 588L/670/9. He also furnished secret information to William Gregory, the undersecretary. On September 9, 1828, Gregory sent to Peel an unsigned letter from an informer whose address was 22 Rathmines Road, Dublin. Conway lived at that address in 1828. Gregory to Peel, Sept. 9, 1828, BM, PP, 40334, foll. 246–248. Gregory to Peel, Jan. 30, 1829, *ibid.*, foll. 271–273, encloses "a letter from an old correspondent" at the same address and initialed "F. W. C."

36. Pückler-Muskau, *Tour, 2,* 119.

attack the government. Lord Anglesey, viceroy in 1828, described him to Peel as a "determined republican without a guinea and of some nerve." [37] At the Corn Exchange Lawless showed himself one of O'Connell's most persistent hecklers, sniping at him on almost every issue, raising the question of the wings whenever possible, and frequently throwing the meetings into pandemonium with fierce statements of his radical opinions. In one respect, at least, he was more consistent than O'Connell, and more sincere: he urged constantly the necessity of demanding parliamentary reform. Had he proved more stable and rational there might have arisen within the association a healthy opposition to O'Connell. As it was, his violent and erratic nature discredited him in the eyes of most of his fellow members.

Although Dublin was the headquarters of the Catholic Association and the Corn Exchange the arena for its brawling orators, the four provinces of Ireland discovered the true source of its power. In the towns, villages, and plowlands of Munster, Leinster, Connaught, and, to a lesser degree, Ulster, the Dublin leaders perfected an island-wide organization of the people. And they did so, significantly, through a system ready to hand; in the Catholic clergy scattered in their parishes throughout Ireland, yet closely bound together by obedience to their bishops and by a common consciousness of their caste, they found invaluable allies.

Prior to the French Revolution the majority of the Irish clergy had been compelled by the penal laws to seek their theological training on the Continent. But in 1795, with the revolutionary wars disrupting the colleges in France and in the Low Countries, the Irish Government, at the insistence of Pitt, in a conciliatory mood and in an effort to secure the loyalty of the Irish priesthood, endowed from state funds a national seminary outside Dublin, Maynooth College. The effect of the measure, the reverse of what Pitt had intended, became apparent when the younger generation of Maynooth priests entered the parishes. The alumni of Douai, Louvain, Coimbra, and Salamanca had returned to their native land polished and conservative gentlemen; Lady Morgan noted amusedly the Louis-Quatorze bow of these Irish priests of the old school. But the new generation had never been out of Ireland. The sons of farmers and small shopkeepers, they retained the loyalties, the sense of oppression, and sometimes the uncouthness of their class. A hostile observer who visited Maynooth in 1824 remarked its influence on these men:

37. Anglesey to Peel, July 20, 1828, BM, PP, 40325, fol. 128.

> My late tour of inspection gave me full opportunities of comparing the Maynooth priests as a class with the foreign educated clergy, and O'Connell would have found in the latter but a rope of sand if he had been obliged to deal with such for his materials. But it is plainly Maynooth that has enabled him to construct his organization. The students who enter it are literally [word indecipherable] peasants. They leave it with as great an ignorance of the world as they brought into it, but they acquire in it an Esprit de Corps which it is impossible to describe, of which a taste for religious controversy and a keen anti-British feeling are the leading features. These are just the men to influence the people and to be led themselves by a bold demagogue.[38]

O'Connell himself admitted that the Maynooth priests were less anti-Jacobin than their older colleagues who had seen at first hand something of the French Revolution.[39] And one of the Catholic bishops, Dr. Doyle, warned:

> The Minister of England cannot look to the exertions of the Catholic Priesthood; they have been ill-treated, and they may yield for a moment to the influence of nature, though it be opposed to grace. This clergy, with few exceptions, are from the ranks of the people, they inherit their feelings, they are not, as formerly, brought up under despotic governments, they have imbibed the doctrines of Locke and Paley, more deeply than those of Bellarmin, or even Bossuet on the divine right of Kings; they know much more of the principles of the Constitution than they do of passive obedience.[40]

A few of the clergy considered Dr. Doyle's sentiments rash and unorthodox. But it is noteworthy that their public protest, in the form of a declaration of loyalty, was the work mainly of two Maynooth professors whose very names, de la Hogue and d'Anglade, betrayed their background. The document was popularly ridiculed as "the Sorbonne Manifesto" and laughed at by the Irish priesthood.[41] Maynooth was, indeed, fostering a new, insular, and na-

38. John L. Foster to Peel, Jan. 20, 1825, *ibid.*, 40372, foll. 154–155.

39. See O'Connell's testimony before the select committee of the House of Commons on the state of Ireland, March 4, 1825, *Parl. Papers* (1825), *8*, 120.

40. Public letter to Mr. Robertson, "The Conciliation of Ireland," London *Morning Chronicle*, May 18, 1824.

41. M. W. Savage, ed., *Sketches, Legal and Political, by Richard Lalor Sheil* (London, 1855), *2*, 188.

tionalistic spirit among the younger Irish clergy.[42] The garrulous Creevey when he visited the college in 1828 found there "three hundred and eighty precious blackguards . . . the men that are to guide and controul the whole Catholic population of Ireland." [43]

If the priests controlled the Catholic population, they were in turn subject to their bishops. It had not been so long before, in 1798, that an archbishop of Dublin, in sending a letter he had received to a member of the Irish Government, remarked humbly: "You will observe he styles me *Lord.* I do not assume that title nor do I wish to be addressed under it; but I cannot hinder persons from miscalling me." [44] By 1823, although the bishops no longer shrank from the title "Lord," the older and more conservative among them showed themselves still reluctant to enter the political arena, even when the goal of the popular struggle was religious as well as political. They were hurried along by a few bolder and more resourceful prelates who gave to the cleavage in the ranks of the lower clergy its counterpart among the hierarchy.

Two men clearly typified the old and the new schools: the aged and shuffling archbishop of Armagh and primate of Ireland, Patrick Curtis, and the young and vigorous bishop of Kildare and Leighlin, James Warren Doyle. Both prelates had been educated abroad, but Doyle had returned from Coimbra almost immediately after his ordination, to be consecrated a bishop in 1819 at the age of thirty-three, while Curtis had remained on in Spain to teach and later to become rector at Salamanca. When, through the influence of the Duke of Wellington, whose friendship he had gained during the Peninsular War, Curtis came back to his native land as primate, he was in his late seventies and more Spanish than

42. From a report of an informer, William Lyon, a Protestant, who had served on the faculty of Maynooth as a music instructor from 1805 to 1816, the government had a good idea of the sentiments of the majority of the Maynooth clergy. Lyon, posing as a Catholic, found the students and professors holding forth in private feelings and arguments hostile to the government. They regarded emancipation as an objective secondary to separation from England. Lyon also asserted that he had once given information to Lord Castereagh which led to a cut in the Maynooth grant from £13,000 to £9,000. Lyon to Peel, Feb. n.d., 1825, BM, PP, 40373, foll. 110–113. A priest of the Tuam archdiocese sent to his archbishop in 1824 letters he had received from some of the junior clergy who were participating in the agitation "to show Your Grace what a contrast between the sentiments of the young and the old." The Very Reverend James Duffy to Dr. Kelly, May 25, 1824, AHD, Archbishop Murray Papers.

43. Maxwell, *Creevey Papers, 2,* 192.

44. Dr. Troy to Mr. Secretary Marsden, Dec. 24, 1798, William J. Fitzpatrick, *The Life, Times, and Correspondence of the Right Rev. Dr. Doyle* (London, 1861), *1,* 493.

Irish. Cautious and retiring, he was slow to identify himself with patriotic causes. His junior colleague, on the other hand, exuding self-confidence and belligerence, had a genius for controversy.

In the autumn of 1823 Bishop Doyle published a pamphlet the very idea of which would have horrified a Catholic prelate a few years previously. Composed as an open letter to the lord lieutenant and entitled *A Vindication of the Religious and Civil Principles of the Irish Catholics*, it was recognized immediately, although signed merely "J.K.L.," as the work of James of Kildare and Leighlin. The *Vindication*, while it helped to inspirit the masses whom O'Connell was striving to rouse, shocked bishops of the old school. When the impetuous young prelate continued in an even more indiscreet and forceful vein in a public letter on "The Conciliation of Ireland," in which he warned the government that it could not depend on the Catholic hierarchy to prevent rebellion, the Archbishop of Armagh hastened to write to his friend Wellington. He reprobated Doyle's "eccentric and wild" letter and even promised the Duke that unless Doyle atoned for his offensive conduct the rest of the bench would disavow and silence him. In the same letter Curtis went on to say he had been watching the Catholic Association, whose leaders, when they appealed to him to approve some of their proceedings, he had rebuffed with a refusal to interfere in civil or secular affairs.[45]

His fellow bishops neither disavowed nor silenced Dr. Doyle. On the contrary, he rallied them to the Catholic Association.[46] Dr. Plunkett of Meath publicly welcomed O'Connell in the town of Navan and made him a guest in his house.[47] The association repeatedly praised Dr. Patrick Kelly of Waterford for his zeal in promoting the census project. At least three of the bishops reported to the association the names of the clergy in their dioceses with a view to collecting the Rent, and others publicly urged their priests to cooperate in the project.[48] Goulburn, in noting the event,

45. Curtis to Wellington, June 2, 1824, *Despatches, Correspondence, and Memoranda of Arthur Duke of Wellington* (London, 1867–80), *2*, 272–274.

46. Even from Peel the bishop drew a grudging tribute: "Dr. Doyle is a clever fellow. I have read a letter from him on the education of the Roman Catholics, giving, I dare say, a very inaccurate account of the state of education, but very ably written." Peel to Gregory, April 14, 1824, BM, PP, 40334, fol. 89.

47. Francis Hamilton to Gregory, March 4 and 7, 1824, ISPO, SCP, 443/2608/4 and 5.

48. Doyle, Coppinger of Cloyne and Ross, O'Shaughnessy of Killaloe, Kelly of Waterford, Sugrue of Ardfert, Keating of Ferns, McGettigan of Raphoe, Plunkett of Meath, Kelly of Dromore, and the coadjutor of Clonfert.

expressed fear that such episcopal approval "does give the Association an authority and a power which I did not think it likely to obtain and . . . which renders it more formidable than I have hitherto considered it." [49]

Archbishop Curtis followed in the wake of his bolder confreres. In a letter to the Duke he announced that he now sanctioned the agitation and had subscribed to the Rent, after having held back longer than the other bishops, so long, indeed, that his "fastidious and sullen apathy" had given grave offense to many worthy men. The association, he asserted, was necessary "for calling the attention of the people to the perilous situation in which their lives, property, and liberty were placed, at the mercy of a lawless, biggotted [*sic*], unrelenting faction." [50] Curtis' angry tone must have surprised himself, when he reconsidered it, no less than the Duke; the next day he wrote again to explain that although he did not see anything alarming in the principles of the Catholic Association, he hoped Wellington did not conclude that he approved "certain unguarded, petulant, rash, or insolent speeches" made there; he had often remonstrated with the leaders on that score and "particularly on their Utopian proposal of having the Parliamentary Union of both nations dissolved and the odious mention of making common cause with the English Radicals for obtaining a radical Parliamentary reform." [51] The Primate was playing a wily game, going along with his fellow bishops and yet toning down his actions to his high-placed friend. It was a less forthright course than that of Doyle, and one that led Peel to comment:

> If you have any *certain* information as to the moving spring of Dr. Curtis, pray send it to me in strict confidence. I have seen communications from this Dr. Curtis, not very recent ones, but communications made by him in the course of the last two years, which make me infer that there has been of late a great change in his character—none perhaps in his character, but in his conduct influenced by his speculations on passing events. He used to profess great alienation from the Roman Catholic agitators, lay and ecclesiastical. Now he seems, probably from his unmerited station only, a convenient tool in their hands.[52]

49. Goulburn to Wellesley, March 26, 1824, BM, PP, 37302, fol. 239.
50. Curtis to Wellington, Dec. 6, 1824, *Wellington Despatches, 2,* 361–364.
51. Curtis to Wellington, Dec. 17, 1824, BM, PP, 40306, foll. 97–98.
52. Peel to J. L. Foster, July 16, 1826, RIA, MSS Letters from Sir Robert Peel to John Leslie Foster, 1821–39.

Peel was quite correct. Curtis did prove a convenient tool, if only for the distinction of his rank as primate. The cooperation of Dr. Doyle, on the other hand, was an extremely valuable asset, for with his polemical writings he was fast showing himself the most capable spokesman of the hierarchy. "Dr. Doyle is the Pope of Ireland," remarked Sydney Smith, "and the ablest ecclesiastic of that country will always be its Pope." [53]

The Irish clergy were almost unanimously in sympathy with their native pope. At the initial meetings of the Catholic Association some members objected to O'Connell's proposal that the clergy be accorded *de facto* membership in the organization without having to pay the normal subscription. They had no wish to encourage a political priesthood and suggested that the clergy be welcomed as members but not entitled to vote. Despite the objection O'Connell's motion was carried, and the fears of the malcontents proved groundless. For the first year only a very few priests attended the meetings, and then only as spectators. Even after the introduction of the Rent, when they appeared in greater numbers at the Corn Exchange, only infrequently did they join in the debate or in the divisions. Their main function was performed not in Dublin but in the provinces, where, as one traveler noted, "the Association had no more active lieutenants." [54]

The parish priests circulated through the country over eight thousand copies of J.K.L.'s angry *Vindication*.[55] From their altars, where preaching in English and in Irish was more frequent and popular than in many Catholic countries, and in its enthusiasm and fervor similar to the evangelism of Methodist preachers in England, they did not hesitate in many instances to deliver passionate denunciations of their religious grievances and the political system which perpetuated them. A police report in 1824 described a typical example: the Reverend Mr. Keogh in his chapel in Gallagly condemned proselytizing Bible societies, the Orangemen, and

53. Article in the *Edinburgh Review* (1827), reprinted in *The Works of the Rev. Sydney Smith* (London, 1839), *2*, 411. The remark was a reference to the independent, insular spirit shown by the Irish hierarchy in some of their relations with Rome, as in 1814 when they refused to accept a Roman rescript approving the veto. In 1826 Thomas Wyse, in a speech before the association, declared: "I have heard Pope Pius VII state in a conference which I had with him that he found more difficulty in governing the Church of Ireland from its refractory disposition than all the rest of the Churches put together." Meeting of Jan. 26, 1826, ISPO, CAP, carton 1157.

54. de Hauranne, *Lettres*, p. 188.

55. Mr. Sugrue, Custom House, Dublin, to Peel, March 31, 1824, BM, PP, 40363, fol. 203.

the Established Church, and urged his parishioners to support the Catholic Association and its Rent; "in different parts of his discourse there was great applause by clapping hands, at other times much laughter . . . it appeared more like a mob assembled to hear an inflammatory speech than a congregation in the House of God." [56]

The clergy were also zealous collectors of the Rent. Vesey Fitzgerald, M.P. for Clare, reported to Peel: "Every parish in Ireland is in correspondence with the Board, in every parish they have their agent . . . and in the few instances where the priest has been either cautious or reluctant, a coadjutor of a more daring . . . spirit is sent to take the management out of his hands, and under the pretence of collecting the Catholic Rent, is on the spot to organize the people." [57] In some instances the priests collected the Rent by threats or even by force. Thus in Sligo depositions were taken against a Father Devins for striking a man who refused to subscribe, and the local inspector of police reported to Peel that he himself had been condemned in the newspapers as an intolerant bigot when the priests denounced him for having prevented his tenants from acting as collectors.[58] In Limerick a magistrate noted that in his barony the Rent had been systematized entirely by the clergy, who thereby increased their influence over the people.[59]

Had it not been for the cooperation of the priests the Dublin demagogues would have been far less successful in rousing the country. Sheil summarized the situation succinctly when he told Thomas Moore that the clergy were the only lever by which they could raise the people. Yet such a lever was a dangerous instrument. Because of his long identification with the peasantry through penal times, his supernatural, sacerdotal character, the ignorance and dependence of his flocks, the Anglophobia inculcated at Maynooth, and the coarseness which that seminary often failed to eradicate in its students, the parish priest, especially in country districts, enjoyed the power of a local despot. He could and sometimes did curse the cattle and the crops of insubordinate parishioners. He did, on occasion, descend like an irate Moses on his people gathered at the crossroads to listen spellbound, with characteristic Irish admiration for impassioned eloquence, to the grand language of an

56. Report from Crossley and Gallagly, Sept. 12, 1824, ISPO, SCP, carton 47. A similar occurrence in Limerick is described in another report, *ibid.*, 445/2619/51.

57. Fitzgerald to Peel, Jan. 24, 1825, BM, PP, 40322, fol. 119.

58. Colonel Irwin to Peel, Feb. 19, 1825, *ibid.*, 40373, foll. 217–218.

59. J. Lloyd, magistrate of Rathkeale, to Francis Blackburne, Dec. 14, 1824, ISPO, SCP, 445/2619/56.

itinerant Methodist preacher—to disperse them with a horsewhip! He denounced from the altar those of his congregation who defaulted in their payment of the Catholic Rent. His chapel often housed a boisterous political rally, while for his Sunday text he was not above taking the latest dictum of O'Connell. He and his fellows did in reality show themselves a very political clergy, in the provinces if not in Dublin, and much of their crudeness and petty tyranny is decidedly repellent.

Yet the accusation made at the time, and often repeated, that during the course of the agitation a landlord-ridden peasantry merely substituted clerical for lay masters, though it had some justification, overlooked an important consideration. The exchange was made voluntarily, in fact enthusiastically. The peasantry found their new riders a lighter weight, reining them in a direction they themselves had chosen. The clergy, although they acquired additional prestige as leaders, were, on closer inspection, essentially followers. During the veto controversy there had been indications that it did not pay to swim against the tide of popular sentiment. In 1814 on the door of one presbytery whose incumbent was suspected of favoring the veto and government pensions for himself and his class, angry parishioners had chalked the warning, "No congregation for Vetoist Priests," and in a country like Ireland, where the clergy depended entirely on the people for support, such a "boycott" could be disastrous.

Moreover, although with the flight of the Catholic gentry, the "wild geese," in the 17th and 18th centuries, the peasantry had become more and more dependent upon the clergy, they had also looked among their own class for leaders. And they often found them in agrarian secret societies, such as the Ribbonmen.[60] While the priests on the whole advised conformity to the law, however harsh, the agrarian leaders were rebels. Rarely did Ribbonmen and priests see eye to eye, and when they did come into conflict the former, despite threats even of excommunication, often emerged the stronger. In 1821 and 1822, for instance, when the island was suffering one of its periodic famines and the southern counties were in a state bordering on insurrection, it was evident from the failure on many occasions of their efforts to prevent agrarian outrages that the control of the priests over the peasantry was far from complete.[61] Two years later, when many of the clergy came forward

60. See below, Chapter 8.

61. "A Sketch of Some of the Measures of Lord Wellesley's Administration in Ireland," sent by Col. Meyrick Shawe to Sir William Knighton, Sept. 18, 1827, in

to join the Catholic Association, it was perilous for other priests, usually members of the old school, who remained neutral. A pastor of County Cork, appearing before a select committee of the House of Lords in 1825, testified that he had incurred hostility and been abused in the Cork *Freeholder* for not having collected the Catholic Rent; in an attempt to intimidate him the people threatened not to contribute to his fund for a new chapel.[62]

Within the association itself uncooperative clergymen were the subject of scathing rebuke. Sheil, in particular, was unrestrained in his criticism: "For the Catholic priest . . . who combines a high sense of religion with that just feeling of patriotism that becomes a citizen, I entertain a feeling that goes beyond respect . . . but for the priest who trafficks upon the word of God, for the priest who turns religion into a trade, for the priest who delves in Mount Calvary for gold, I entertain no respect." [63] Sheil went on to condemn a Father Murray, who failed to collect the Rent, as "a sacerdotal agriculturalist, a sycophant in a surplice, a consecrated grazier," language which would have scandalized an Irish politician of later date.[64] But in the Ireland of 1826 it met with "great applause." During the Waterford and Clare elections, especially, the priest who refused to campaign for the popular candidate found himself in a sorry state, as a certain Father Coffey of Ennis could attest. His cloth did not protect him from the jeers of the mob, from the epithet "Protestant priest," and from the loss of much of his dues. In addition he was not allowed to officiate in his chapels and was compelled to keep a curate.[65] Another pastor who tried in his parish to prevent unauthorized meetings and processions of the peasantry was besieged in his house by a mob of three hundred of his congregation. His plight led Lord Clare to comment, in a letter to the chief secretary: "It is clear the people neither mind the magistrates nor their priests, when they act in opposition to their wishes." [66]

Such refractory priests were the exception. The majority of the clergy threw themselves eagerly into the struggle. Especially

A. Aspinall, ed., *The Letters of King George IV, 1812–1830* (Cambridge, England, The University Press, 1938), *3*, 300–301.

62. Testimony of the Reverend John Keily, April 26, 1825, *Parl. Papers* (1825), *9*, 368.

63. Meeting of Oct. 21, 1826, ISPO, CAP, carton 1158.

64. The farmer priests were a real problem. Bishop Doyle maintained a steady opposition to them in his own diocese.

65. Entry of Oct. 17, 1828, Journal of G. Ross-Lewin.

66. Lord Clareto Lord Francis Leveson Gower, Sept. 22, 1828, BM, PP, 40326, foll. 65–66.

was this true of the younger, lower orders fresh from Maynooth who, encouraged by their superiors, entered for the first time as a body into political agitation. Indeed, some of their bishops led the way and in their zeal carried with them, however timorously, the Primate and other hesitant prelates. The clergy both followed and led the peasantry in the country and instead of losing, or at least weakening, their hold on the people by standing apart from the popular struggle, strengthened their control over the masses in Ireland.

This role of the clergy as prime agents of the Catholic Association outside the metropolis has been obscured by the predominance of lay agitators, especially O'Connell. The latter's primacy in the affection and adulation of the people has tended also to overshadow a small group of leaders who rendered him invaluable aid. Sheil was second to O'Connell in his ability as a strategist and in his popularity as a mob leader. Less concerned with the week by week details of meetings and committees, he nevertheless devised the census scheme, carried on an effective propaganda campaign in the foreign press, and was able continually to whip the huge country meetings into a frenzy of enthusiasm. Thomas Wyse was responsible for the first victory of the association in parliamentary elections. Frederick Conway placed the resources of one of Ireland's most influential newspapers at the disposal of the agitators. And John Lawless at the head of a faction of radicals, however eccentric, provided a stimulating resistance to the dictatorial tendencies of O'Connell. This handful of men made the association in Dublin a formidable instrument of political agitation. But it was the clergy scattered in their parishes to the wildest bogs of the island, imbued with a new, nationalistic fervor, and encouraged by their bishops, who made of the thing a mass movement. The demagogues created the agitation; their accomplices of the surplice and the stole blessed it; and the titles of a faded nobility made it respectable. But it was the coal porters of Dublin, as O'Connell jokingly suggested, and the plowmen of Tipperary who carried emancipation.

# *4. O'Connell's Penny-a-month Plan for Liberating Ireland*

THE measure responsible for making the association an organization of the people, rather than merely another coterie of Dublin agitators, was the Catholic Rent. When O'Connell first proposed the project, early in 1824, he described its possibilities in the most exuberant terms: it would provide a party chest of £50,000 a year and give to every Catholic in Ireland a stake in the enterprise. Yet it is doubtful whether O'Connell really expected such a success as the Rent did become. Certainly the majority of his colleagues did not. Some of them tried to shelve the plan; others ridiculed it; and O'Connell's son John recalled that as a boy he was mocked by his schoolmates for his father's fantastic "penny-a-month plan for liberating Ireland." [1]

The idea was not new. The Methodists had provided a remarkable example of the effectiveness of small, general dues in building up a campaign fund and in knitting together a widespread religious society.[2] A favorite scheme of Thomas Hardy, founder of the London Corresponding Society in 1792, the first organization led by and comprising workingmen in clubs all over the country, was that of penny-a-week subscriptions. Hardy's plan was never realized, but a similar one was put into practice in the Hampden clubs. Sir Francis Burdett and Major Cartwright intended their first club, founded in 1812, to be an upper-class body, with an annual admission fee of £2 and proof of owning or being heir to a landed estate. But the postwar economic crisis of 1816 stimulated popular interest in political radicalism; Hampden clubs multiplied rapidly; the subscription became a penny a week, based on the organizational

1. J. O'Connell, *Select Speeches, 2,* 286.

2. Brougham, arguing against suppression of the association in the House of Commons in 1825, referred to the Methodist example: "The collection of the Rent, too, . . . ought not to be stopped, because the Methodists collected money, and no attempt was ever made to prevent them so doing." Requoted from A. G. Stapleton, *The Political Life of George Canning* (2d ed. London, 1831), *2,* 127.

precedent of the Methodists; and the members came to be known actually as "Political Protestants." The Hampden clubs were suppressed by the acts of 1817 and 1819, before the scheme could be carried out on a grand scale.

In Ireland the very name, Catholic Rent, was venerable. It had been applied to subscriptions raised by the Catholics in the reign of James I.[3] In 1784, as O'Connell acknowledged when he proposed the plan, Lord Kenmare had suggested to Dr. Moylan, bishop of Cork, the levying of a rent of £1 yearly on each of the 2,500 parishes of the country to raise a fund for the struggle against the penal laws.[4] Nothing came of Kenmare's suggestion, but when the Catholic Committee of 1793 ceased to function, after having won the franchise, it had on hand £5,198 of which slightly less than one-half had come from public collections in Dublin and the rest from subscriptions in several counties and towns.[5] Again in 1811 the Catholic leaders voted to set on foot a general subscription; in the following year O'Connell recommended a two-penny rent which realized £79 in three Dublin parishes; and in 1813 the Catholic Board drew up a plan for the appointment of collectors to apply to every householder for ten pence or more.[6] The boards of 1811, 1812, and 1813 were short lived, and their projects were never thoroughly realized. Not until 1824 did Ireland, or England, see a program similar to that of the Methodists put into effect in the field of political agitation.

The association approved O'Connell's Rent scheme in a series of resolutions recommending the naming of a secretary and an assistant to manage the returns and open accounts with the parishes, nomination of from three to twelve collectors in each parish, publication of the names of subscribers in or near each Catholic chapel, and the appointment of a finance committee to manage the collection and expenditure.[7] The day after the aggregate meeting sanctioned the project and urged its adoption throughout the country O'Connell announced that forty-eight of the orphan charities collectors of Dublin had volunteered their services; three days later a letter from Waterford contained the

3. Testimony of the Reverend William Phelan before the select committee of the House of Lords on the state of Ireland, May 27, 1825, *Parl. Papers* (1825), *9*, 567. Phelan also mentioned a rent raised in the reigns of George II and George III.

4. Meeting of Feb. 4, 1824, ISPO, CAP.

5. Anonymous, *The Proceedings of the General Committee of the Catholics of Ireland, 1792–93* (pamphlet, Dublin, 1824), pp. 11–13, RIA, Haliday Pamphlets.

6. "Plan for Parochial Subscriptions," broadside, Oct. 26, 1813, AHD, CP.

7. *DEP,* Feb. 19, 1824.

news that eighty tradesmen there had formed an association to manage the Rent.

In the meantime the finance committee was busy sending printed copies of the Rent Report in broadside form, along with collectors' books, into the provinces; [8] O'Connell wrote to the Catholic bishops and received immediately from one of them, the energetic Dr. Doyle, a list of the parishes in his diocese; and the lawyers on their spring circuits were beginning to organize country meetings for the formation of local committees and bands of collectors. In each county a treasurer, secretary, and committee were appointed to arrange the details of collection, make monthly returns to the secretary of the association, and receive information from subcommittees, treasurers, and secretaries in the parishes.[9] By the end of June, with 200,000 copies of the Rent plan and 4,000 collectors' books in circulation, encouraging reports began to reach Dublin: land agents on country estates offered to collect subscriptions along with their regular land rents; the attorneys in the neighborhood of Thurles, where over 200 cases came annually before the petty sessions, arranged for the parties in each litigation to pay one penny to the Rent; farm laborers in Kilrush were giving up tobacco and snuff money; and at the market fairs the pig jobbers undertook to pay the "lucky-penny" that was allowed by the seller to every buyer of pork.

According to the general pattern followed in the country collectors volunteered their services, formed a committee, and divided the town or parish into districts which in turn were split into walks, in each of which two collectors made the rounds.[10] In some places the committee hired rooms, held weekly meetings, sent their reports and returns through their secretary or, more frequently, through the local pastor [11] to the association, and received the Dublin newspapers in which their remittances were acknowledged. In rural areas, especially where landlords showed themselves hostile, the collectors soon gave up making rounds and received the

8. The government reporter observed, on March 13, "great piles of paper in an inner room and in the Association's front room were two piles of Reports, one of them labelled '10,000 Reports.'" Information of S. N. Elrington, n.d. (probably March 13, 1824), ISPO, CAP.

9. Copy of the Rent Report and Instructions, ISPO, SCP, 445/2622/17.

10. In Limerick one large parish was divided into thirteen such walks with two collectors for each, one of whom received the money while the other registered the names of subscribers. *DEP*, June 17, 1824; Bishop Jebb to Sir Robert Inglis, Nov. 29, 1824, BM, PP, 40370, fol. 276.

11. Of the Rent received by July 17, 1824, one-third was paid by the clergy. *DEP*, July 20, 1824.

Rent instead at the doors of the chapel on a monthly Rent Sunday.

The first list of returns, £131 from County Cork, appeared in the Dublin *Evening Post* on July 6, 1824. Thereafter the *Post* and other metropolitan newspapers published weekly accounts of the Rent along with the text or summaries of the more striking grievance letters. When the association adjourned during the summer months its finance committee continued to meet weekly in order to prepare digests of the Rent returns for the newspapers; the letters accompanying the returns were read carefully and the more important of them, when published, served to advertise hundreds of local complaints.[12]

When the association reassembled in the autumn of 1824 even members who had derided the Rent as a "beggar's tax" were jubilant. They found 1,000 names on their roster; the weekly Rent averaged well over £300; and already £1,000 were invested in government bonds. And the Rent was becoming not only a source of much needed funds but also a cause of alarm to Castle officials. They recognized in it the ideal basis for an island-wide organization of the people. Peel, at the Home Office, admitted that he was studying with anxiety the progress of the Rent, which in itself might not be dangerous, although "the organization by means of which it is raised may be very formidable." [13] In Ireland the provincial inspectors general of police reported that the Rent was everywhere collecting: at Ballinasloe, for instance, in the chapel on Sunday morning, November 7, 1824, it amounted to £20, "and even the poorest gave silver." [14] A circuit judge of the southern district, returning to Dublin after holding court at Nenagh, informed the chief secretary: "The greatest activity still prevails in the collection . . . and a perfect system of treasurers and collectors is established everywhere; the previous office is generally filled by the priests, the latter by the farmers and shopkeepers, and exclusion from the chapels and denunciations from the altar are resorted to against unwilling contributors." [15]

12. One such letter, from a priest near Kilrush, "lying at the western extremity of the County Clare," stated that the parish contained 12,000 Catholics and only 7 Protestant families; the people were still in a wretched state as a result of the famine of 1822; they were overburdened by rack rents and exorbitant tithes and had no resident gentry or magistrates; they looked, therefore, to the association for protection and offered to forward their leases and other information. *DEP*, Oct. 5, 1824. Another letter gave grim details of the sale of a cottier's personal possessions for failure to pay tithe: "one cow, one bed, one gown, one pettycoat, and one apron." *Ibid.*, Nov. 3, 1824.

13. Peel to J. L. Foster, Nov. 2, 1824, RIA, Peel Letters to J. L. Foster.

14. Major General Warburton to Goulburn, Nov. 11, 1824, PRO, HO, 100/211.

15. Mansell Blacker to Goulburn, Jan. 1, 1825, ISPO, SCP, 447/2731/3.

Although in the majority of instances the peasantry paid their pence willingly, some, as the judge noted, had to be coerced. At the Skibbereen quarter sessions when the people were all examined as to their having contributed, a few replied that they had done so under orders from the priest, on threat of being denied admission to the chapel and being obliged to say their prayers outside.[16] Occasionally, also, the collectors resorted to intimidation and to violence, as noted in a report from a magistrate in Meath: "The only Roman Catholic in this neighborhood who [*sic*] I know of having refused paying the Roman Catholic Rent is a poor schoolmaster of the name of McLaughlin, and on the third night after his having refused to pay, the windows and door of his house were broken to attoms, although within half a mile of a Police Station, and he was cautioned to quit the country." [17] More usual than physical force was the threat of social ostracism or, if the recalcitrant were Catholic or even Protestant merchants, withdrawal of custom. Thus one Dublin tradesman complained to the police that two attorneys, collectors of the Rent, called on him for a sixpence contribution; when he declined one said to the other, "Put it down refused." Shortly thereafter the shop lost most of its Catholic patronage.[18]

Whatever the reluctance of some to subscribe, the Rent was more successful than even O'Connell had expected. He boasted that it had united the peers and the prelates, the peasants and the professions, the merchants and the manufacturers. And Bishop Doyle endorsed the project as "the most efficient measure ever adopted by the Catholic body." [19] By March 1825 the association had £13,000 invested; the Rent for the week ending March 16 totaled £1,840; and the country presented an alarming picture of united action. With the suppression of the old association in 1825 the Rent lapsed until the Waterford election in the following year. Then a new purpose appeared in the necessity of protecting the rebellious Waterford freeholders from eviction. O'Connell, heralding the event with his familiar "hereditary bondsmen" exhortation, urged the priests to resume their former roles: "Who will begin in his parish? Clergyman or layman, whoever he be, glory to him." [20] Overruling a suggestion that the old Rent be

16. Mansell Blacker to Gregory, June 21, 1824, among "Papers Presented by Command," *Parl. Papers* (1825), *9*, 6–7.

17. A. Tyrrell to Goulburn, Dec. 12, 1824, ISPO, SCP, 443/2608/22.

18. Police report, Dec. 7, 1824, *ibid.*, carton 47.

19. Doyle to Mr. Brennan, Oct. 18, 1824, Fitzpatrick, *Doyle, 1*, 363.

20. Letter of O'Connell to the Catholics of Ireland, *DEP*, July 11, 1826.

applied to the relief of the forty-shillingers, O'Connell wisely insisted on a new collection; he knew that the value of the system lay primarily not in the money itself but rather in the organization it cemented. Yet the Rent, despite its new-found motive, did not prosper as it had in 1824. The highest weekly total for 1826 was £473. In the following year, with another lull in the agitation, the weekly returns fell off sharply; usually the amount was less than £100; only once did it reach £300; and for a fortnight or two no receipts at all were to be found in the newspapers.

A new Rent campaign began with the simultaneous meetings of 1828. O'Connell devised a plan for Catholic churchwardens, two in every parish, the priest to name one, the parishioners to elect the other. Thus a constant communication would be established between the Corn Exchange and the provinces. The churchwardens received instructions to send monthly reports of the state of the Rent in their districts, the names of collectors, the number of registered and unregistered freeholds and the state of parties with a view to the next elections, the prevalence of evictions and the character of local landlords, the condition of education and any instances where tenants were made to suffer for refusing to send their children to proselytizing schools, the amount of tithes, church rates, and county cess. Moreover, the churchwardens would supervise the Rent collectors, publicize the first Sunday of each month as "Rent Sunday," and attend the Masses on that day to receive subscriptions.

The system of churchwardens was set in operation immediately. The Rent, which for the week ending January 19 was only £199, rose sharply seven days later, when 39 parishes had already appointed churchwardens, to £604. The number of letters from the country, mounting proportionately, demanded the services of a special secretary. Once again Peel recognized the danger signs, as he had in 1824. To Lord Anglesey, the viceroy, he wrote that he had learned that "the Association had not only appointed in each parish of Ireland . . . Churchwardens, but that at least in some parishes, and in those as part of a general system, twelve persons were nominated, standing in some relation to the Association. . . . the nomination was considered by my informant as connected with some scheme of general organisation of the Roman Catholic population." [21] Peel's forebodings and O'Connell's hopes, arising from the first promising response of the churchwardens, were premature.

21. Peel to Anglesey, April 7, 1828, in Earl Stanhope and Edward Cardwell, eds., *Memoirs by Sir Robert Peel* (London, 1857–58), *1*, 36–37.

What was needed was a stimulus such as that presented two years before in Waterford. And again fortune supplied it. The first word of O'Connell's intention to stand for Clare shot the Rent in one week from £68 to £1,602; a fortnight later it reached the highest weekly sum in its five-year history, £2,705.

When the Clare election fever subsided the Rent returned to an average level of £500. In the autumn it rose slightly as a result of the efforts of emissaries from the association in the North, where heretofore few Catholics had shown themselves rash enough to act as collectors and churchwardens in predominantly Orange districts, and the excitement attendant on tumultuous meetings and processions of the peasantry in the South. But the system was still imperfect, as O'Connell admitted at the end of the year when he announced that churchwardens were active in only half the parishes of the island. He proposed to remedy the defect by appointing five inspectors of the Rent in each county to act under one chief inspector named by the association; each of the thirty-two counties would be divided into five districts in which the inspectors would superintend the work of Rent collectors and churchwardens; and the inspectors would make monthly reports of their progress.[22] This latest innovation was never put to the test: within a few weeks the King recommended to his Parliament reconsideration of Catholic disabilities. The association voted its own dissolution, and with it passed the Rent.

At no time did the project reach the goal originally set by O'Connell, £50,000 a year. The grand total of the association's

22. The inspectorate was already prominent in Irish local government. In 1814 Peel, as chief secretary, had made a beginning of the latterly famous Royal Irish Constabulary by substituting a civil force of salaried constables, acting under specially appointed magistrates who were responsible immediately to the government, for the hitherto exclusively military patrols. This temporary and local measure developed into a national system with the appointment in 1822 of four inspectors general of police, one for each province, to supervise this special constabulary and magistracy. In England, although the Factory Act of 1802 and Peel's proposed factory legislation of 1815 provided for inspectors and although Bentham constantly propounded, as an essential feature of his system of centralized government, the necessity of inspectors to furnish full information to central departments and be the agency of their detailed control over local authorities, it was not until 1829 that "Peelers," the first prominent inspectors, made their appearance in the Metropolitan Police Force. Thereafter Bentham's preaching of the virtues of central control showed results in the appointment of official salaried inspectors to oversee the enforcement of the factory acts (1833), the whole system of poor law administration (1834), prisons (1835), and certain schools (1839). By 1840 four different sets of paid government inspectors were at work. See E. L. Hasluck, *Local Government in England* (Cambridge, England, The University Press, 1936) and Maurice W. Thomas, *The Early Factory Legislation* (Leigh-on-Sea, Essex, Thames Bank Publishing Company, 1948).

receipts from all sources during the six years of its existence was slightly under £58,000, and the highest yearly income was £22,700 in 1828.[23] There was nothing secret about the Rent; the returns were published in the newspapers, and the account books stood open for inspection. Lord Anglesey was, as usual, misinformed when he wrote, in answer to an inquiry from Peel in April 1828: "I do not believe it will be possible to discover what is the actual amount of rent received. Some assert that it is extremely exaggerated, whilst others contend that a vast deal more is collected than the Association acknowledge the receipt of." [24] Yet the lord lieutenant's suspicions suggest the concern the measure aroused. The funds and the regions from which they came formed an accurate gauge of the pitch of the agitation and the extent of the organization in the four provinces and the thirty-two counties.

Leinster in the east, Munster in the south, and Connaught in the west were the traditionally Catholic provinces, while Ulster in the north was Protestant. It is significant that the first Rent returns came from the extreme South, County Cork, and that Cork stood first in the total of county returns for the period before the suppression of the association in 1825. The £2,824 collected there were almost a third again more than came from the next county on the list, Dublin, with £1,952. Tipperary and the rest of the counties of Munster, Leinster, and Connaught followed, with Ulster at the very bottom of the list. Upon the revival of the Rent in 1826 Leinster gained and held first place, slightly ahead of Munster; Connaught, the poorest section of the island, was third, and Ulster again last. The system of meetings, committees, collectors, churchwardens, and inspectors never became so thorough in Ulster as it did elsewhere. From January to November 1826 seven of the northern counties, Antrim, Donegal, Fermanagh, Leitrim, Londonderry, Sligo, and Tyrone, made no return at all, and Down and Armagh together sent less than £20. The strength of the move-

23. The following estimates are based on a correlation of accounts found in the Dublin newspapers, the minutes of the association, and government reports of its proceedings:

| | | |
|---|---|---|
| to March | 1825 | £19,228 |
| " Dec. | 31, 1826 | 5,680 |
| " " | " 1827 | 3,640 |
| " " | " 1828 | 22,700 |
| " " | " 1829 | 3,712 |
| Interest on investments, etc. | | 2,617 |
| | | £57,577 |

24. Anglesey to Peel, April 13, 1828, *Peel Memoirs, 1,* 39.

ment lay in the South, in Munster and Leinster, and to a lesser degree in Connaught.

During the period before Goulburn's act £4,331 of the £19,288 collected went to defray the expenses of petitioning, the salary of a London agent, schoolbooks for Catholic institutions, and advertisements of meetings and resolutions published in the newspapers. The main item of outlay up to 1825 was the cost of prosecuting Orangemen and defending Catholics in the law courts. When the old association dissolved in 1825 it had £14,896 still on hand, invested in government securities. Almost all of the new Rent, begun in 1826, went to aid the forty-shilling freeholders, until the old uses of the Rent, precluded for a time by Goulburn's act, were revived in 1828.[25]

Thus did the pence of the peasantry succeed where for many years the pounds of the gentry had failed. And thus did the association acquire not only an ample party chest but, more importantly, control over a far-flung organization of the Irish people.

25. The minute book of the finance committee for 1828–29, in AHD, and a "File Book of the Catholic Association," at Darrynane Abbey, County Kerry, contain items of expenditure ranging from £3,800 paid to the Clare election committee to £10 paid to a piper whose bags were broken in the Waterford election.

# 5. *Grievances, Grievances*

UNDERLYING the structure of the Catholic Association and permeating all its activities was a common and universal sense of grievance. O'Connell and his cohorts by improvising constantly on the theme "Know your wrongs!" created at home a vast organization; and abroad, by using this theme as the motif of a far-flung propaganda campaign, they made the case of Ireland as well known, if not as spectacular, as that of the rebellious Greeks and the embattled American colonies of Spain.

In Ireland the leaders of the association educated the people to a realization of the nature, the causes, the immense variety, and the political remedy of grievances which, through long habits of subjection and inferiority, many Irishmen had come to accept as inevitable and against which, except for agrarian outrage in times of acute distress, as in 1822, and in areas with a tradition of lawlessness, like Tipperary, they knew no effective protest. Forgotten, under the weight of immediate oppressions, were the nobler aspects of Anglo-Irish rule: the great age of Grattan's parliament, the fidelity to the cause of equal rights displayed by Grattan and other liberal Protestants, the sincere and friendly efforts of viceroys like Fitzwilliam and Wellesley, the extensive canal system and the architectural grace of Georgian Dublin, the prosperity of the Catholic trading classes, the generosity of Englishmen in times of famine, as in 1817 and 1822 when they subscribed £750,000 in charity, and finally the neglect and later repeal of the greater part of the penal code. To the Kerry cottier these things meant little when he lamented the burden of rack rents paid twice over, of rates for the building and repair of Protestant churches, even to the payment of organist, tuner, choristers, and the cost of prayerbooks, of tithe proctors valuing potatoes by good years for the quantity, by bad years for the price, of public money voted for proselytizing schools, of the gross jobbery with which county cess was levied and squandered, of village tyrants dispensing a partisan justice from the bench, of armed Orangemen swaggering at county fairs while against Catholics the constabulary pursued rigorously the midnight search for arms.

The association now publicly and systematically canvassed these things and fulfilled, in addition, a promise made by a Dublin candidate in the election of 1822 to inform the people of "five hundred grievances which they had previously known nothing about." Sir Henry Parnell noted that the incessant efforts of the association were rendering the people "more keenly sensible of their political situation." [1] And Lord Cloncurry, an Irish Protestant patriot suspected of treason in 1798, informed Peel that the association was "looked up to by six millions of a despairing . . . population, destitute of employment, education, sufficient food, clothing, or habitation, subject to daily insult or injury from an irritated gendarmerie and a partial magistracy." [2]

The one great complaint that had been since 1800 the exclusive concern of the Catholics was their exclusion from Parliament and from almost all official life. In the administration of justice there were 257 posts, ranging from lord lieutenant down to subsheriff, from which they were barred by law; of 1,314 lower offices for which they were eligible they held in 1828 only 39. Moreover, 653 offices of civil rank or of honor, from seats in Parliament to officers of corporations, were closed to them, while out of 3,033 of minor rank to which they might aspire they held but 134.[3] Yet six-sevenths of the population were Catholics. The disqualification, to be sure, affected directly only the wealthier Catholics; it did not perturb the great mass of the peasantry for whom emancipation would mean no immediate change in status. But when it was linked with the manifold grievances of all classes, and even shown to be at the bottom of many of them, then the great measure took on a personal significance for even the rudest bog dweller.

One of the first Anglo-Irish institutions to feel the attack was the state church. For a specific and dramatic example of the abuses perpetuated by this top-heavy establishment the agitators seized on an incident that occurred in St. Kevin's churchyard, Dublin, in September 1823. Although the custom of Catholic priests reciting the *De Profundis* at the grave of their parishioners in the cemeteries (all of which were in Protestant hands) had long been

1. Parnell to the Duke of Buckingham, Nov. 25, 1824, BM, PP, 40357, fol. 271.
2. Cloncurry to Peel, July 2, 1823, *ibid.*, fol. 14.
3. These figures are based, with corrections by myself, on statistics in Wyse, *Historical Sketch*, 2, Appendix xxxv, cclxxxii–ccxc.

silently tolerated, the sexton of St. Kevin's on this occasion refused to allow the priest to proceed with the function. Immediately the association inflated the incident into a monstrous example of persecution. It was estimated that the fees paid by Catholics to the incumbent, clerk, sexton, bell ringer, and gravedigger in a single Dublin parish amounted to £2,000 yearly, while the aggregate annual tax imposed on Catholics for the right of burial within the city was £20,000. So great was the resultant hue and cry that the Protestant Archbishop of Dublin, unjustly blamed for the interference, complained angrily to the chief secretary that it constituted "a new state of things to have the heads of the Established Church, immediately under the eye of the Government of the country, held up to public contempt and execration by a set of popish priests." [4] It was, indeed, a novelty. Both priests and laymen were beginning to manifest a new self-assertiveness, a frightful belligerence.

Within the association the burial question touched off debates on the whole range of religious issues,[5] from a parasitic system of tithes and church rates to the incursions of evangelical reformers. The latter, undertaking with the sponsorship of English and Irish Bible societies an intensive campaign for a "New Reformation" in Ireland, were touring the country in 1824, distributing religious tracts and pamphlets, holding revival meetings, and preaching, along with fervid Bible sermons, violent attacks on popish creed and ritual. They were surprised to find O'Connell, Sheil, and other association orators, assuming now the role of lay apologists, invading their meetings and challenging them to public debate. The "New Reformation" soon degenerated into endless and frequently amusing religious controversy.[6] But religious animosity, as one observer reported to Peel, was never so intense: the speakers in the Corn Exchange were attacking the "New Reformation" and the establishment "at a time when we were all thunderstruck by Doctor Doyle's then alarming, but now comparatively moderate pam-

4. Archbishop Magee to Goulburn, Sept. 27, 1823, copy, BM, PP, 40329, fol. 157.

5. The Established Church was in an extremely vulnerable position. It was only with difficulty and at the cost of £500 from the secret service fund, approved by Liverpool and Peel, that Goulburn was able in 1824 to prevent publication by the disgruntled Dean of Raphoe of a manuscript describing accurately the disposal of church patronage in Ireland for the past forty years, a history "which would reflect infinite discredit on the Church and much on the Government." Goulburn to Wellesley, May 11, 1824, BM, WP, 37302, foll. 261–262.

6. One of the debates, held in the Dublin Institution in April 1827, lasted six days and was reported in detail in the Dublin newspapers.

phlet."[7] In addition to Bishop Doyle's writings another publication was serving to embolden the Catholics. The priests, not hesitating to accept as an ally the importer of Tom Paine's bones, were circulating among the people and strongly recommending from the altar Cobbett's shoddy *History of the Protestant Reformation*, cheap editions of which had consequently a phenomenal sale in Ireland.[8]

Attack on the Established Church[9] and on the "New Reformation" was but one phase of the strategy. Another source of vexation and insult was to be found in the Orange Order, a Protestant secret society founded in 1795, with flourishing lodges throughout the country. July 12 and November 14 were traditional days for the Orangemen to dress the statue of King William in College Green, march in procession through the towns and countryside, and at their banquets in the evening drink to "the glorious, pious, and immortal memory of the Great and Good King William." Had the celebrations been limited to such solemnities they might have been harmless enough. But frequently the Orangemen carried arms, and almost always their demonstrations ended in factious riots and even loss of life. In the North especially, although the prudent Catholic eschewed the streets on the twelfth and the fourteenth, there were often enough of the foolhardy to assure a clash. The association denounced the Orangemen and their organization, O'Connell in particular taking great delight in exposing the secrets of the order, their warrants from central to district lodges, their certificates, books of rules, and explanations of signs and pass-

7. Vesey Fitzgerald to Peel, Jan. 24, 1825, BM, PP, 40322, fol. 121. Fitzgerald was referring to J. K. L.s' *Vindication*, 1823.

8. "I went into three of the principal Catholic booksellers [in Dublin] this day and it was absolutely like a mob pressing to the galleries of a theatre and Scully (who [*sic*] Cobbett calls his own bookseller here) told a friend of his in my hearing that he was at that moment writing to London for ten thousand copies by return of the mail and that he had no doubt of requiring ten thousand more." G. G. Gordon to Peel, Jan. 5, 1825, BM, PP, 40372, fol. 39. Accounts of the popularity of Cobbett's *History* in the country are found in the Reverend John B. Wallace to Peel, Feb. 14, 1825, and Col. John Longfield to Peel, Feb. 15, 1825, *ibid.*, 40373, foll. 130–131 and 142.

9. The attack was not constant. At times O'Connell tried to tone it down for fear of antagonizing even liberal Protestants. But in a letter to his wife he stated his true position: "I am decidedly of opinion that tithes should be abolished." O'Connell to his wife, March 25, 1825, O'Connell Letters to His Wife. Bishop Doyle was more outspoken. In a public letter he declared: "I think the Church Establishment must fall sooner or later; its merits in Ireland are too well known." J. K. L., *Letter to Lord Farnham*, Feb. 6, 1827 (pamphlet, Dublin, 1827), p. 3, RIA, Haliday Pamphlets.

words. He was well aware of the eagerness with which his coreligionists awaited his ridicule of their most inveterate enemies. That the Orangemen constituted the ultrafringe of the ascendancy party and a society condemned by the more moderate Protestants, Peel among them, was a distinction which the average peasant did not bother to make.

One of the principal institutions in Ireland for the education of the poor was the Kildare Street Society, named for the street in Dublin where it had its headquarters. The society had been founded in 1811 to promote "mixed" schools in which poor Catholics and Protestants should be educated together, where, according to theory at least, only the general principles of Christianity would be taught. O'Connell himself was a member of the society until 1820, when he resigned because the system, although supported in part by an annual government grant of £30,000, had become, under a provision of its constitution for the reading of the Scriptures "without note or comment," an instrument of proselytism. In March 1824 a member of the House of Commons declared that the Kildare system had rescued the Irish Catholics from the "thick and palpable darkness" of schools run by the priests. Immediately seizing upon the charge as slanderous, the association condemned the Kildare Street Society, its schoolmasters, and its state grant, and welcoming the opportunity of making allies of the priests, enlisted their aid in undertaking a survey of Catholic education. In addition it allocated part of the Rent to the aid of Catholic schools. The diatribes of the Dublin leaders struck a responsive chord in the country. Detailed accounts of the sufferings of tenants abused by their landlords for not sending their children to the Kildare schools began to pour in from local Rent secretaries and from the clergy.

The letters kept before the attention of the country another grievance which bore heavily on a particular group within the population, the lawyers. O'Connell noted that during the last thirty years not one Catholic barrister, although eligible, had been promoted to a situation of honor or emolument.[10] Lord Wellesley, indeed, urging on Peel the policy of showing some distinction to the Catholic Bar, pointed out that while he was prevented by law from making any of them king's counsel, he would like to give at least one a patent of precedence. He had the support of Canning for his recommendation. But the King objected strongly,

10. Meeting of May 22, 1824, reported by S. N. Elrington, PRO, HO, 100/213.

and Peel discouraged the proposal on the grounds that it might appear a timid concession to the violence of the association.[11] It was probably too late anyway for such a limited sign of benevolence. The association was already taking within its purview and daily attacking the abuses of the whole system of administering justice in Ireland: the packing of juries, the negligence of the constabulary, the partiality of judges and especially of magistrates.[12] It was sending down from the metropolis barristers to defend Catholics and to prosecute Orangemen in the courts,[13] discussing at length the reports they remitted to the Corn Exchange, and publishing them in the newspapers and in pamphlet form for circulation through the country.[14]

In addition to canvassing religious and political grievances, such as the abuses of the Established Church, the Bible societies and their "New Reformation," the Kildare Street schools, the Orange Order, and the judicial system, the Irish leaders exploited, for their propaganda value, more basic ills of their country. On the surface was the grim spectacle of a dense, improvident, wretchedly poor, and traditionally anarchical population. In the 1820's the density of population in Ireland was greater than that of any other European country.[15] In 1821, the year of the first complete census,[16] the population of the island was 6,846,949, with a density of 365 per square mile, while that of Great Britain was 14,391,631, with a density of 210.8 in England and Wales and of 86 in Scot-

11. Wellesley to Peel, June 20, 1824, and Canning to Peel, June 27, 1824, *ibid.*, 100/210 and 211.

12. In 1829 the solicitor general of Ireland complained to Peel of the corruption of the Irish magistracy; it was appointed, he said, "by Englishmen who know as much of Ireland as they do of the heart of Africa." H. Doherty to Peel, n.d., 1829, BM, PP, 40326.

13. Vesey Fitzgerald described one such intervention to Peel, Jan. 24, 1825, *ibid.*, 40322, foll. 117–118: the Catholic press was used for days before to prepare the people; an association barrister with his agents came down to prosecute; every Catholic magistrate, some of whom had never before been seen at a sessions, every priest for miles around, and a huge crowd of people "such as I never saw on such an occasion" attended the court. Fitzgerald remarked that Peel had the facts of the case: "I only allude to it to mark the changed demeanour of the Popish body."

14. The avowed purpose of one such pamphlet was "to show that a Catholic, even under an upright judge, has little or no chance of justice in party disputes." Randall Kernan, *Report of the Trials of Certain Individuals . . . of Fermanagh on 6 August, 1824* (Dublin, 1824), RIA, Haliday Tracts, 425/9. Kernan, a Catholic barrister on the Northwest circuit, reported trials for both the association and the government.

15. William Forbes Adams, *Ireland and Irish Emigration to the New World from 1815 to the Famine* (New Haven, Yale University Press, 1932), p. 4.

16. A rough estimate in 1813, based on an incomplete census under the Act of 1812, placed the population at 5,395,856.

land.[17] Of the almost seven million Irishmen slightly less than six million were Catholics.

The association challenged these figures. O'Connell insisted that the census of 1821 was known to have been imperfect: in Mayo alone during the famine of 1822 the number of persons who received relief exceeded by 30,000 the stated population of the county. If the census of the other counties was deficient in proportion, the population of Ireland was above eight millions.[18] Although figures based on applications for relief would scarcely be a fair challenge to the census statistics, Sheil proposed that they attempt to prove O'Connell's assertion, as an expedient to overcome in 1825 the stifling effect of Goulburn's act, the plague of the wings controversy, and the disappointment resultant from the defeat of Burdett's relief bill: "Forty-eight non-contents [in the House of Lords] have produced seven millions of malcontents. That we are malcontents, they admit—that we are seven millions, they deny. What, then, is to be done? Let there be a census of the Catholics of Ireland. 'Do not dress your slaves in a peculiar garb,' said a Roman statesman, 'lest they should learn their own strength.' "[19]

The census did not reveal the full strength of the Catholics or come near to proving O'Connell's and Sheil's allegations. It was never completed. On August 12, 1826, after the project had been in operation ten months and despite frequent complaints of its neglect, there were returns from only 41 of the 963 unions of parishes. By the following December the number amounted to 141, of which 64 were from Munster, 42 from Leinster, 20 from Connaught, and 15 from Ulster. Even as late as June 1828 there were only 273 returns, representing but one-fifth of the kingdom. Thereafter the census was forgotten in the excitement of 1828.[20] Yet the census figures, inconclusive as they were, when read in the association and summarized in the press, made good propaganda. A

17. *Parl. Papers* (1822), *14*, 738, and *15*, 542. In 1949 the population of Ireland, North and South, was approximately 4,315,000 to Britain's 48,767,000.

18. Meeting of Feb. 4, 1824, ISPO, CAP.

19. *DEM*, June 10, 1825.

20. The last summary of the census to be published was as follows:

| | *Catholics* | *Not Catholics* | *Ratio* |
|---|---|---|---|
| Munster | 839,708 | 39,047 | 21.5 to 1 |
| Leinster | 438,625 | 40,985 | 11 to 1 |
| Connaught | 284,354 | 13,087 | 21.75 to 1 |
| Ulster | 177,515 | 80,656 | 2 to 1 |

None of the great towns and only one parish in Dublin were included in these returns. *DEP*, June 24, 1828.

typical letter, from the pastor of Ferrier and four other parishes, revealed that although there were 7,270 Catholics to only 18 Protestants in his district, the former were obliged to build churches and to pay tithes and church rates for the cure of souls of the 18.[21] Letters such as this, emphasizing specific examples of religious disproportion, were impressive reminders of the disqualifications and grievances of the majority of the people.

An even more fundamental problem was the land. Ireland is an island of twenty million acres, of which thirteen and a half million, in the 1820's, were fertile soil. Much of the rest, bog and hill land, was capable of being reclaimed but neglected by improvident landlords and by tenants who would have been forced to pay higher rents had they tried to improve it. Agriculture, the dominant industry, supported 80 per cent of the population, unevenly distributed over the good lands of the island, an important fact which much of the contemporary talk about overpopulation failed to consider. In 1815 Ulster contained 368 persons per square mile of arable land, which in Ireland meant acreage fit for either tillage or grazing; Munster and Connaught 320; and Leinster 255.[22] A high proportion of the best soil of the country, that of Leinster, was given over to large grazing farms, especially after 1815 when the postwar drop in grain prices was more rapid than that of Irish meat. After 1815, also, the population of the western counties, tilling some of the poorest land of the island, increased faster than that of other parts. There, as a report of a railway commission noted in 1838, the "division of land into small farms, and their subdivision into portions, continually decreasing in extent with each succeeding generation . . . was the immediate cause of the rapid increase of the population." [23] From 1821 to 1831 this multiplication of small tenures enabled the population of Donegal to rise by 20 per cent, Mayo by 24 per cent, Galway by 23 per cent, and Clare by 24 per cent,[24] to constitute a great mass of peasantry of whom the railway commission noted: "Poverty and misery have deprived them of all energy; labour brings no adequate return, and every motive to exertion is destroyed. Agriculture is in the rudest and lowest state. . . . The country is covered with small

21. Meeting of Feb. 25, 1826, *ibid.*, Feb. 28, 1826.

22. Adams, *Ireland and Irish Emigration*, p. 5.

23. "Report of the Railway Commission, July 11, 1838," p. 295, in R. Barry O'Brien, *Thomas Drummond, Under-Secretary in Ireland 1835–1840* (London, K. Paul, Trench & Co., 1889), pp. 289–311. This report, ordered by Drummond, is one of the best sources for the condition of pre-famine Ireland.

24. *Ibid.*, p. 299.

occupiers, and swarms with an indigent and wretched population."[25]

Throughout the island the peasantry, dependent on the land, subsisting on the potato, or, as in Munster and Connaught, on a very inferior species of the same root called the lumper, subject to perpetual poverty[26] and to periodic famine and fever, existed at the sufferance of exacting landlords and their agents, "deputies of deputies of deputies" as Chesterfield called them. In England the landlords let farms; in Ireland they only let land, raw land unimproved and uncared for, exhausted, unmanured, and improperly drained, from which half-starved cottiers pulled snatch crops and thus speeded the process that drained the fertility of the country. The average produce of the soil in Ireland was not much above one-half the average produce in England, while the number of laborers employed in agriculture was, in proportion to acreage under cultivation, more than double: five to two.[27] And unlike the system in England, Irish property involved little responsibility.[28] The small farmers, having lost all tenant right except in Ulster, could be evicted, as they were in many instances immediately after the post-war drop in grain prices in 1817 and the elections of 1826, because their rents were normally, through a custom called the "hanging gale," common through most of Ireland, from six months to two years in arrears.

Absentee landlords added to the burden.[29] The same John Jebb, bishop of Limerick, who complained so often to Peel of the danger of the Catholic Association, stated that from his section of the country alone £300,000 were annually withdrawn by absentee proprietors, while £150,000 left the neighboring County Kerry. He

25. *Ibid.*, p. 291.

26. Sir Walter Scott, after touring Ireland in the summer of 1825, noted: "There is much less exaggerated about the Irish than is to be expected. Their poverty is not exaggerated; it is on the extreme verge of human misery: their cottages would scarce serve for pig-styes, even in Scotland, and their rags seem the very refuse of a rag-shop, and are disposed on their bodies with such ingenious variety of wretchedness that you would think nothing but some sort of perverted taste could have assembled so many shreds together." Entry of Nov. 20, 1825, *The Journal of Sir Walter Scott* (New York, 1890), *1,* 1–2.

27. "Report of the Railway Commission, 1838," p. 306.

28. "In England the Poor Law, while it tied the laborer to his parish, secured him subsistence even though he had no land or no employment. Ireland had no Poor Law, and the landless man, outside the cities, was forced to beg, steal, or starve." Adams, *Ireland and Irish Emigration,* pp. 16–17.

29. See *ibid.* for a corrective to George O'Brien's overemphasis of the role of the absentee landlords in his *The Economic History of Ireland from the Union to the Famine* (London, 1921).

lamented the existence of a system bearing so heavily on an exhausted peasantry: it was "a calamity beyond our grasp or comprehension; . . . The reality of wide-spread suffering which it has been my lot to witness, is so vast and overwhelming, that I am afraid to calculate, and yet more unwilling to imagine, its extent." [30]

The affliction witnessed by the Bishop, although perennial, was especially shocking in time of distress following a general slump in agricultural prices or failure of the potato crop. Coincidental in 1817 and 1818, the two brought acute suffering to the whole island. Four years later when the potato crop was again short, the resultant famine was confined to Munster, Connaught, and County Donegal. From 1823 to 1825 excellent harvests of grain with a rising market for it in England brought economic revival, but even in the former year fear of famine was widespread on account of the scarcity of potatoes.[31] In 1826 the shock of the money quake in England reached across the Irish Sea and combined with a long drought to produce not only idle mobs in the streets of Dublin but starvation and typhus once again in the provinces.[32] This monotonous chronicle of recurrent depression, famine, and fever reached its appalling climax in the period from 1846 to 1848 when, through death and emigration, the population of Ireland fell from eight to six and one-half millions. But even before the great famine staggered the conscience of England on the Irish question, the Devon Commission of 1842 had exposed the injustices of the landlord system and the lack of industries and of a healthy economy in Ireland to support the rapidly growing population.

In the 1820's few men appreciated the basic nature of the land problem in relation to the misery of the Irish peasantry. At least no one offered a serious solution. Certainly the leaders of the association did not. O'Connell himself, in Kerry, was an improvident landlord; Thomas Wyse, in Waterford, had his fields overrun and his corn destroyed by irate tenants whom he had evicted; and in general Catholic proprietors were proverbially as exacting as Protestants.[33] But indirectly the association did emphasize the extent of the evil. The thousands of letters addressed to it from the country, while serving to call attention to the more flagrant

30. Speech of Bishop Jebb in the House of Lords, June 10, 1824, *Parl. Debates*, 2d Ser., *11*, 1140.

31. Goulburn to Peel, Nov. 7, 1823, BM, PP, 40329, foll. 199–201.

32. Goulburn to Peel, July 25, 1826, *ibid.*, 40332, foll. 65–70.

33. Patrick Murphy to George Canning, Nov. 28, 1825, *ibid.*, 40311, foll. 160–161.

abuses of individual landlords, aroused an expectation among the peasantry that some settlement of the land question would follow as an immediate result of emancipation.[34] A vain hope! More than half a century was to pass before any adequate attempt was made to deal with the problem. The Irish leaders of 1828, absorbed with readily perceptible religious and political issues, exploited economic grievances merely for their propaganda value. As with overpopulation and the land, so too in matters of emigration and the lack of poor laws they adopted no constructive policy. Emancipation was to be the panacea, or at least the prelude to a solution of all the ills of Ireland. Nevertheless, the persistent and emphatic refrain of the agitation was grievances. In improvising on the theme the association aroused more concern for the Irish question, with its many facets, than it had received at any time since the Union.

The most effective instrument in this propaganda campaign was the newspaper press. For six years the metropolitan and the provincial journals made the proceedings of the popish parliament the most impatiently awaited news throughout the island. Early in 1824 Peel observed that it was the publicity given the association by the newspapers that countervailed "the insignificance of the members." [35] Later, when the body was no longer contemptible, Wellington and Peel, in an exchange of letters, agreed that in the press lay the real mischief; there would be no chance of peace in Ireland so long as the newspapers were allowed to report seditious speeches. What could be done? One dared not assail the Irish press openly, for it was already more restricted by taxation and the necessity of bonds and sureties than the English. But since it was vulnerable in its responsibility after publication for libels on the government and things Protestant, Wellington toyed with the idea of appointing a special representative to examine carefully every newspaper printed in the sister island.[36] Nothing came of the idea: it was put forward in 1828, too late. Yet in the exchange of letters Peel made one quite discerning remark: the peasantry had a sort of mystical reverence for the printed word; they were convinced of their grievances by seeing them in print. Observers closer

34. J. Norcott to Goulburn, Feb. 17, 1825, ISPO, CSORP, 1118/11421. Norcott reported that in County Cork the lower orders imagined that after emancipation they were "certain of being independent, inasmuch as the lands of this country . . . is [*sic*] to be equally divided with them."

35. Peel to Goulburn, April 14, 1824, copy, BM, PP, 40330, fol. 35.

36. Wellington to Peel, July 20 and Nov. 5, 1828, *ibid.*, 40307, foll. 162–166, and 40308, fol. 52; Peel to Wellington, Nov. 3, 1828, *Wellington Despatches, 5*, 207–209.

to the scene corroborated the home secretary's analysis. Maj. George Warburton, inspector of constables for Connaught, when asked by a select committee of the House of Commons on the state of Ireland what was the source of the demagogues' power over the people, replied: "One of the characteristics of our people is, that whatever they see in print they believe; . . . and I have heard many of them say, 'I saw it in a book' as a reason why they implicitly believe what they asserted." [37] A colleague of Warburton, Major Willcocks, inspector for Munster, likewise testified that the newspapers kept the lower orders "in a state of irritation . . . for they are very fond of getting a newspaper read amongst them." [38]

The police officers exaggerated neither the credulity of the peasantry nor their delight in seeing their grievances and the names of their villages, their local committees, and their rent collectors in the columns of the newspapers. Every week, sometimes four times a week or more, when the papers came down from Dublin the usual cries that met the post were, "What of the Association? Is there anything from Dan or Sheil?" In some places a group of tradesmen or farmers subscribed to one of the metropolitan papers, passed it from hand to hand, or read it aloud to their neighbors. In many parishes Rent committees and collectors and later the churchwardens hired reading rooms where "the disaffected" collected at night to hear the papers read and where "everything bad is agitated." [39] A priest of County Clare noted: "Wherever the newspaper is read, on a Saturday or Sunday, the young and the old will attend there, standing round the reader *erectis auribus;* the dance-house, or whiskey-cabin, cease to have any charm for them whenever they can have a paper." [40]

The newspaper press served the association not only as a means of rousing and organizing the people but also as a potent weapon to intimidate their opponents. Vesey Fitzgerald complained to Peel in 1825 that already magistrates shrank from doing their duty "from terror of the press"; [41] a landlord in County Sligo reported that when he forbade his tenants to be collectors of the Rent, the association denounced him "in their prints as an intolerant bigot"; [42] and shortly after the Clare election the Clare *Sentinel*

37. *Parl. Papers* (1825), 7, 140–141.
38. *Ibid.*, 117.
39. Tompkins Bruel to Major Warburton, Feb. 6, 1829, ISPO, SCP, carton 51.
40. Letter of the Reverend Mr. Murphy read at meeting of Nov. 17, 1824, *DEP*, Nov. 18, 1824.
41. Fitzgerald to Peel, Jan. 24, 1825, BM, PP, 40322, foll. 123–124.
42. Colonel Irwin to Peel, Feb. 19, 1825, *ibid.*, 40373, fol. 218.

brazenly threatened: "We have been collecting the names of those proprietors who have commenced persecuting their tenants for voting, at the late election, honestly and fearlessly by their country. Should the system continue, we will place them alphabetically in our columns, but not without note or comment." [43] The *Sentinel*, a violently pro-Catholic journal, was scarcely more partisan than the rest of the newspapers. None of them could afford to be neutral on the Catholic question.

At the head of the Irish press were the newspapers of Dublin. With a population in 1821 of 227,335 the city was the metropolis of Ireland and the second largest in the British Isles. Since its press had a tradition of bitter faction politics, it is not surprising that its seventeen newspapers quickly chose sides, eleven roundly condemning the popish parliament, six extolling it—almost all with a reportorial slant and editorial scurrility worthy of Cobbett in his *Political Register*. The proportion was almost two to one against the association. But it was offset by the fact that two of the pro-Catholic papers, the *Evening Post* and the *Freeman's Journal*, were among the three most widely circulated journals in the country. Both triweeklies, they had a joint circulation of 588,000 copies for the year 1821.[44] The former, edited by F. W. Conway, carried the fullest accounts of the association's proceedings, even to the point of printing actual minutes of meetings to which Conway had access and which as temporary secretary he sometimes recorded. The reports in the *Freeman's Journal* were slightly more condensed. Michael Staunton, likewise a member of the association, edited the *Morning Register* and the *Weekly Register*. The latter, containing a weekly summary of the transactions at the Corn Exchange, was for this reason, as well as for its intemperate tone and its radical politics,[45] especially popular with provincial Catholics, among whom it was regularly distributed by the local Rent committees. In 1828 the churchwardens received 6,000 copies of it every week.

Of the eleven Dublin papers more or less hostile to the agitation the most prominent was the *Evening Mail*, a triweekly begun in 1823 by leaders of the extreme ascendancy faction to oppose the pro-Catholic policies of Lord Wellesley. The *Mail's* circulation

43. Clare *Sentinel*, July 18, 1828.

44. Arthur Aspinall, *Politics and the Press c. 1780–1850* (London, Home & Van Thal, 1949), p. 140. This book contains a valuable treatment of the Irish proclamation fund (pp. 134–147) and aid given to the association by the press (pp. 319–323).

45. The *Weekly Register* reprinted copious selections from Cobbett's articles.

of 315,000 copies for the year 1824,[46] mainly attributable to the popularity it enjoyed among the Protestant landlord class for its bitter denunciations of O'Connell as "shallow-headed . . . blackest-hearted man on earth" and his organization as a "permanent school for the inculcation of rebellion, bigotry, and falsehood,"[47] far surpassed that of the other anti-emancipation journals, notably the *Patriot*, *Correspondent*, and *Saunder's News Letter*, all government organs.

The so-called government papers, supported in large part by Dublin Castle through grants from the secret service fund to their editors and annual allowances for the insertion of official proclamations and advertisements, maintained at best a dubious loyalty to their patron. Much to the annoyance of the chief secretary in Ireland and the home secretary in England, they published the proceedings of the association almost as fully as did the Catholic papers. As early as November 1823 Peel protested to Goulburn: "Surely the Government Papers as they are called in Ireland (I suppose from doing mischief to the Government) need not publish the debates of the Catholic Board . . . Studious silence upon all that concerns the board would be the best policy."[48] Goulburn agreed with Peel. But so long as any other papers printed the speeches of the agitators and "while there is an eager desire in all persons to read them," he doubted whether it would be useful to prohibit the *Patriot*, *Correspondent*, and *Saunder's* from reporting "what many of their readers look for with anxiety."[49] On at least two other occasions, in 1824 and 1826, Peel complained again of the conduct of the government papers, especially the *Patriot*. Goulburn promised to keep a sharp eye on the latter but admitted that it would lose the little sale it had if it stopped catering to popular curiosity; in desperation he confessed that he had often thought it would be better to have no government papers in Ireland and would have got rid of them were it not for his desire to keep control over the press for government in the future.[50] Finally Peel summed up the whole discouraging situation when he observed that a moderate and judicial paper would have no readers. Ireland was divided into two acrid factions, both of which were following the course of the agitation with the keenest interest, the Catholics

46. Aspinall, *Politics and the Press*, p. 140.
47. *DEM*, Jan. 3, 1825.
48. Peel to Goulburn, Nov. 14, 1823, copy, BM, PP, 40329, fol. 217.
49. Goulburn to Peel, Nov. 16, 1823, *ibid.*, fol. 223.
50. Goulburn to Peel, Jan. 9, 1827, *ibid.*, 40332, foll. 254–255.

to gloat over the latest diatribes of big Dan and little Sheil, their opponents to shudder at the audacity and insolence of the demagogues.

The association well realized what an important ally it had in the press. It reserved in its meeting rooms a special section where every convenience was given reporters and where, after the inception of the Rent scheme, most of the metropolitan papers had a representative. It arranged its days of meeting and frequently the speakers wrote out in advance their major orations so that the proceedings might reach the country as quickly as possible. And what was more appealing to Dublin publishers, the association had a sort of "proclamation fund" of its own from which it contributed liberally even to the government papers for the insertion, as advertisements, of its resolutions and those of the country meetings. Provincial newspapers also, in return for reprinting reports from the Dublin papers and for their own accounts of local meetings, enjoyed increased circulation and a share of the association's patronage.[51] Some provincial editors were in a curious position. At the same time that they showed themselves active supporters of the Catholic cause they also were in receipt of government funds. Thus in an official record of payments made to newspapers by the Irish Government for the year 1827, five of the twenty-four non-Dublin journals listed received money also from the association.[52] The Waterford *Chronicle* was a notable example: it obtained £18 from Dublin Castle in the same year that it urged the Catholics to make an assault on their "great enemy, the Church." [53] It was such duplicity on the part of both Dublin and provincial editors that disgruntled Goulburn and Peel in their efforts to manage the Irish press.

The printed word as a propaganda weapon was not limited to the columns of newspapers. Pamphleteering, especially, was a popular pastime and medium of controversy in Ireland, to which

51. It is impossible to determine exactly the amount of money distributed by the association to the Irish press. Fragmentary records, such as checks, receipts, and a minute book of the finance committee for 1828–29 which I have found in AHD, CP, and a file book of the association in Darrynane Abbey, provide evidence for a total of £1,478 spent in 1827–28, but large gaps in the records indicate that three times this amount is probable, a figure comparing favorably with the sum spent by the government for the same purpose. In 1827, out of an annual parliamentary grant of £5,000 for the Irish proclamation fund, £3,705 were paid to 30 newspapers throughout the country. "Account of payment to sundry newspapers for the year ending 5 January 1828," ISPO, CSORP, 1231/1676.

52. *Ibid.*

53. Waterford *Chronicle,* March 13, 1827.

the rise of the association gave a powerful stimulus. In the virulent pamphlet war that developed the Catholics, on account of their organization and their funds, had the advantage.[54] They had also a formidable champion in "J. K. L.," whose caustic public letters appeared in pamphlet form, frequently at the expense of the association, and were circulated widely by the clergy. Moreover, Cobbett's three-penny pamphlets, as well as his *History of the Protestant Reformation*, were so popular that it was rumored the association employed him at a salary of £600 yearly.[55]

In addition to the polemics of Cobbett and Bishop Doyle, the association published as pamphlets for free distribution or at most for a few pence a copy the proceedings of the more important Dublin and country meetings, the reports of its lawyers who prosecuted Orangemen and defended the peasantry in the courts, and the major speeches of its orators. And in handbill and poster form it sent through the country its Rent Report of 1824, addresses to the people, condemnations of persecuting landlords, and proclamations on the occasion of elections. In the streets of some provincial town it was not uncommon to see placarded in bold type, side by side with those of Dublin Castle, the proclamations of the popish parliament, while inside many a rustic cabin one might find tacked to the mud wall tattered excerpts from the orations of O'Connell and Sheil.[56]

Another medium of propaganda employed to marvelous effect, one whose importance has been frequently overlooked, was the ballad. In lyrical Ireland, clinging to the romantic tradition of its bards and recalling wistfully their eulogies of kings long dead, the strolling singer as he wandered in rags through market town and country lane, with a symbolically decrepit harp or fiddle, was still a revered figure.[57] At the fairs, the petty sessions, the markets, the weddings and the wakes, the crossroad dances, his songs in praise of "Our Dan," "Little Sheil," and the other grand men of Dublin were the delight of the peasantry. Often carrying his ballads in his head, sometimes in his pocket on a dirty scrap of paper,

54. As early as November 1823 Peel requested Goulburn to send him the pamphlets "which have been fortunate enough to meet with the approbation of the Board." Peel to Goulburn, Nov. 13, 1823, copy, BM, PP, 40329, fol. 211.

55. Arthur Meadows to Peel, Feb. 14, 1825, *ibid.*, 40373, fol. 126. The rumor was false.

56. F. W. Conway to F. L. Gower, Sept. 27, 1828, copy, PRO, HO, 100/223; Lieutenant Colonel Hill to Peel, Nov. 22, 1824, BM, PP, 40370, fol. 163.

57. See Gerard Murphy's chapter on "The Gaelic Background" in Michael Tierney, ed., *Daniel O'Connell, Nine Centenary Essays* (Dublin, 1949), pp. 1–24.

wherever he raised his voice he was sure to gather an audience. They listened attentively to songs like "Granu Weal's Praises of O'Connell":

As Granu sat musing one day under a shade
Of a spontaneous oak, on the banks of Lough-Lein,
To think which of her Sons, the most honours had gain'd,
Arrah faith, 'tis O'Connell, says Granu Weal,
    Sing bubbaroo, didderoo, Granu Weal,
    Bubbaroo didderoo, Granu Weal,
    The Catholic Rent to pay we'll not fail,
    Drink good health to O'Connell, says Granu Weal.

Britannia may boast of a Fox or a Pitt,
And John Bull he may laugh, 'till his sides they do split,
But to such competitors, I never will yield,
When I speak of a Coppinger, O'Gorman and Sheil.
    Sing bubbaroo, didderoo, Granu Weal
    Bubbaroo didderoo, Granu Weal, etc.[58]

The association printed many such ballads as handbills and broadsides; countless others were the improvisation of the itinerant bard. Of the former only a few remain.[59] Yet it is probable that they aroused the emotions of the peasantry as strongly as did the rantings of the orators. Certainly they helped to sustain enthusiasm in the intervals between provincial, county, and parish meetings. Moreover, in an extempore song or between the lines of a printed one, ideas and hopes might be conveyed which could never appear on paper or be spoken from the political platform. Thus:

If I would run faster, than mastiff or beagle,
I'd find out two birds that I love, . . .
The one is the black bird, the other the eagle,
The Scotch and the Irish man's darling,
As Calledon's plains I'll range and I'll wander,
Ballymoreen and Lord Morneux's domain,
It is Waterloo I'll search through, with Flanders,
To find out my eagle, that noble commander,
We'll drink to his memory, that great Alexander,
On Patrick's day in the morning.

58. "Granu Weal's Praises of O'Connell," handbill, BM, PP, 40370, fol. 278.
59. A number of them are preserved in the BM, PP.

O, charming Louisa, now cease to lament thee,
Your spirits come cheer, it's near five and twenty,
When freedom once more on our shore we'll have plenty,
Though of it six ages defraud'd,
Fly not from your Eagle, away to Vienna,
To kiss his Royal Beak, or break the magic spell,
For of truth we are told, by old Pisterinia,
The Royal line of David, said he's in Sardinia,
We'll conduct to old Erin the Eagle of Helena,
Victorious, some glorious fine morning.[60]

Of such songs, with their cryptic allusions to the Jacobite pretender, to Napoleon, to one Pastorini and his prophecies of 1825 as the year of Catholic deliverance, Bishop Jebb, speaking for alarmed Irish Protestants, noted: "These ballads are listened to, and bought up, with great avidity. The itinerant minstrels, by way of interlude, haranguing the people after each stanza with much vehemence and gesticulation and inciting them to nothing short of rebellion. Several have been taken up both in Cork and in this city [Limerick] in the very act." [61]

It is difficult to assess the role of these crude ballads in relation to that played by other forms of propaganda. The speeches of O'Connell and Sheil, the newspapers, the pamphlets, and the placards, by stimulating discussion around the village pump, the church door, and the winter turf fires, educated the peasantry to an acute awareness of political issues. But the songs of the ballad-mongers appealed directly to their emotions. And significantly, the refrain was no longer merely a plaint for the faded glories of Tara and Brian Boru. The bards now sang of the Corn Exchange and of O'Connell.

Although one of the original purposes of the Catholic Rent was the conversion of the no-popery majority of Englishmen by means of the press, the expectation proved futile. Most of the British newspapers, and all of the London ones with the exception of the Whig *Morning Chronicle*, the *Examiner*, the *Globe and Traveller*, and Cobbett's *Political Register*, all of which published sympathetic reports of the association's meetings taken from the Dublin papers, were hostile. The Tory government organ, the *Courier*, was violently abusive; the *Times*, although it supported the Catho-

60. "A New Patrick's Day in the Morning," handbill, *ibid.*, 40370, fol. 166.
61. Jebb to Sir R. Inglis, Nov. 29, 1824, *ibid.*, 40370, fol. 276.

lic claims, condemned the association; and even the *Morning Chronicle* catered to popular taste with sarcastic articles on the creed and political practice of Catholic countries on the Continent. The London agent employed by the association, Eneas MacDonnell, spent much of his time in writing long letters which frequently appeared in the *Morning Chronicle* and even occasionally in the *Times* and the *Courier*. The association sent the pro-Catholic Dublin journals to various newsrooms, inns, and coffeehouses in England and often inserted its resolutions in the London papers. On at least one occasion, indeed, the Irish leaders made a vigorous effort to gain sympathy through the press. In February 1825 Cobbett wrote to O'Connell to suggest the following strategy in connection with a proposed "Address of the Catholics of Ireland to the People of England":

> But, pray send us your promised address. . . . I think it can be circulated all over the country without any expense to you, if your agent arranges well; . . . Let fifty copies of it be printed (very correctly) on slips of paper, and sent over to him. He ought instantly go in person and deliver one copy to each daily paper in London, apprizing the editor of each that he has done this with regard to all the daily papers. They will all publish it; they must; if they should not . . . you shall see what a game I will play with the vagabonds! . . . ten of each of the daily papers containing the address should be ordered before hand by the agent . . . he should send them . . . to my shop in Fleet Street. Thence I will have them dispatched to every country newspaper in England and Scotland. . . . I cannot conclude without beseeching you to be bold in your address to us. For God Almighty's sake do not suffer your thought to be castrated! . . . The people are *now* just in the mood to hear you. The King trembles at the brewings of the French and the Holy Alliance. Hit the thing hard while it is soft.[62]

The association did hit the thing hard. In its address it even included a veiled threat of rebellion if emancipation were withheld. But the effort proved futile. In spite of Cobbett's optimism few of the English papers printed the address; and the firebrand of Fleet Street himself within a month's time was attacking O'Connell for his compromise on the forty-shilling franchise.

62. Cobbett to O'Connell, Feb. 12, 1825, UCD, O'C P.

Notwithstanding such scant assistance given to the Irish cause by English editors, O'Connell and his organization did have able spokesmen in the British press. Francis Jeffrey, Sydney Smith, and Henry Brougham made the *Edinburgh Review* an advocate of the association, and the most popular poet of the day, Thomas Moore, showed himself a powerful ally. Moore, an expatriate Irishman whose verse, especially his *Irish Melodies*, had won him a wide public, never quite approved the rabble-rousing methods of the Dublin demagogues. He was, nevertheless, in sympathy with their aims. In 1824 he published *The Memoirs of Captain Rock*, an angry indictment of the penal laws, a code the rigor of which helped, if not to justify, at least to explain the terrible outrages perpetrated by the followers of "Captain Rock," "Captain Moonlight," and other mythical deliverers to whom the lawless Irish peasantry secretly swore devotion.[63] The book gave greater energy to the exertions of the Catholics; it embarrassed their opponents; its facts were recognized and indisputable; its irony was keen and bitter. Moore was no Swift; he hesitated to identify himself completely with the movement.[64] But his pen did help to make the Irish question more of a reality, at least, to his English readers.

Awareness of an Irish problem was not confined to the British Isles. News of the struggle for emancipation reached eastward across England and the Channel to the Continent and westward over the emigrant lanes of the Atlantic to America, in both worlds to arouse sympathy and assistance.

At the outset of the movement in Ireland O'Connell, with characteristic exuberance, advocated propaganda in every coffeehouse in Europe, a grandiose scheme for which the association never developed any adequate program. But its debates were translated into French, German, and Italian and did appear frequently in the foreign press. Travelers in Ireland, the Duc de Montebello, M. Duvergier de Hauranne, the Marquis de Dalmatie, and a Prussian prince, H. von Pückler-Muskau, published letters and reports describing what they saw in Ireland and comparing it with the

63. Lord John Russell, an intimate friend of Moore, wrote to him on the appearance of *The Memoirs:* "Success! Success! Your Captain is bought by all the town, extravagantly praised by Lady Holland, deeply studied by my lord, and has given all the Orangemen the jaundice with spleen and envy." Russell to Moore, April 1, 1824, in Rollo Russell, ed., *Early Correspondence of Lord John Russell* (London, T. F. Unwin, 1913), *1,* 237.

64. In 1828 Moore informed Sheil that on account of the hostility of the London *Times* toward O'Connell in the Clare election, he was withdrawing all connection with that newspaper; he desired, however, that the matter should not be publicly mentioned. Sheil to O'Connell, Aug. 6, 1828, UCD, O'C P.

contemporary struggle for independence of the Greeks. As a result English tourists on the Continent, when they boasted of the glories of Britain, were taunted with the oppression and misery of Ireland.

Some of the French newspapers, especially, openly championed the cause of the disaffected Irish. O'Connell, in July 1824, stated that he looked to the patronage of the Paris press to inform Europe of the state of Ireland, and in November of the same year he read a letter from a Mr. George Ivers in Paris offering to insert pro-Irish essays in a newspaper there, for whose proprietor he translated articles, and in four other papers. Ivers boasted of influence also with the press of Madrid, Vienna, St. Petersburg, and Rome, and recommended that the association appoint an agent in Paris.[65] O'Connell publicly scouted the suggestions as involving the sort of secrecy it was his express intention to avoid. Nevertheless, articles on Ireland soon began appearing in the French Government organ, *L'Étoile*. The first praised the association and censured English journalists, particularly those of the *Courier*, who at the same time that they condemned brutal treatment of Negro slaves advocated harsh measures in Ireland.[66] The article was the beginning of a series of attacks on England for her Irish policy in which *L'Étoile*, reviewing the history of oppression of one island by the other and comparing it with that of the Spanish colonies, asserted that rebellion in Ireland could be more easily justified.

Such insolent meddling was a source of some concern and irritation to English ministers. The *Courier* bristled at the arrogance of "interloping Frenchmen." But it could not well deny many of the facts presented in *L'Étoile* or its accurate description of the state of affairs in Ireland, so accurate, indeed, as to arouse suspicion about the authorship of the articles. An Irishman living in Paris wrote to Peel in 1825 that he had seen Sheil there recently in a reading room and suspected the little Irishman to be the source of the mischief.[67] The surmise was more than justified: Sheil not only supplied information to *L'Étoile;* he was, as he later admitted, the author of the articles.[68]

*L'Étoile* was joined by two other Paris newspapers in devoting space to the Irish question. *Le Globe* published in serial form "Lettres sur les élections anglaises et sur la situation d'Irlande" by

65. Meeting of Nov. 24, 1824, ISPO, CAP.
66. Reprinted in *DEP,* Dec. 18, 1824, from *L'Étoile* of Dec. 10, 1824.
67. M. Burke to Peel, Nov. 14, 1825, BM, PP, 40383, fol. 41.
68. *DEP,* Jan. 30, 1827.

Duvergier de Hauranne, a young French journalist strongly sympathetic, as a result of a tour of Ireland in 1826, toward the Catholics. *Le Journal du Commerce,* frequently drawing from events in Ireland the moral that France should oppose intolerance and bigotry, went to the length of referring to the English and Irish peers who opposed emancipation as "Anglican Jesuits"! But the sympathy of part of the French press was not the only aid the association received from the Continent. From Paris, Bordeaux, Dieppe, Tours, Harfleur, Lisbon, Brussels, Aporto, and Rome came contributions to the Rent, sent by Irishmen living abroad, the descendants in many instances of the "wild geese," their foreign friends, and sometimes by small societies founded to promote the Irish cause.[69]

The story of Irish grievances traveled also to America, and in the new world, already peopled by Irish emigrants, the struggle had its reverberations. One of the most active proponents of Irish causes in the United States was John England, a Corkman who had come out to America in 1820 as bishop of Charleston, South Carolina.[70] From his adopted country the Bishop corresponded frequently with the leading agitators and aided them concretely by encouraging the formation of American associations calling themselves the Friends of Ireland or the Friends of Civil and Religious Liberty. Such bodies were established in Charleston, New York, Baltimore, Washington, Augusta, St. Louis, Philadelphia, Boston, Norfolk, Savannah, Brooklyn, and Utica, and by instituting a Catholic Rent of their own were able to forward over $6,000 to the association in Dublin. In addition to money they sent addresses of sympathy and encouragement, the first of which in 1824, from the Friends of Ireland in New York, urged the Irish leaders to include in their demands universal suffrage and separation from England. The letter touched off a debate in the association that ended in a vote of thanks to the New Yorkers, not for their advice but merely for

69. On February 2, 1829, a committee of English, Scottish, and Irish residents of Paris was formed to collect the Catholic Rent, and a meeting of French gentlemen was held soon thereafter for the same purpose. *Ibid.,* Feb. 10, 1829.

70. Bishop England's Anglophobia did not escape the notice of the English and Irish governments. In 1826 Goulburn thought it of sufficient importance to pass on to Peel the rumor that, "The first vacancy on the Roman Catholic bench is to be supplied by Dr. England from America, a man of all others most decidedly hostile to British interests, and the most active in fomenting the discord of this country by inflammatory letters from Charleston." Goulburn to Peel, Sept. 13, 1826, Parker, *Peel, 1,* 419. The event apprehended by the chief secretary narrowly escaped realization: Bishop England refused several Irish dioceses including the metropolitan see of Cashel.

their expression of sympathy. The advice was too republican even for the Irish agitators. Subsequent addresses from America were more discreet in tone; arriving in Dublin at the rate of five or six a year, they merely expressed the hope that Irishmen might soon enjoy the same blessings of civil and religious liberty cherished by Americans.

Similar societies were set up outside the United States. Meetings held in Nova Scotia, Newfoundland, Montreal, Quebec, the West Indies, and South America likewise resulted in addresses of encouragement and about $1,000 in Rent. Wherever the vanguard of the 19th-century migration of the Irish had already penetrated, there the expatriates manifested concretely the ties that bound them to a nostalgically ideal but actually wretched island.

The echoes of the Irish struggle from America and from the Continent, although they helped to inspirit Irishmen, served at most only to irritate the British Government. But they were signs of the proportions the Irish question might well assume and the embarrassment that would confront England if she should refuse to settle the most obvious of Irish problems, the religious, let alone the more fundamental ones of the land and political autonomy. At home in England the propaganda of the association made little impression on a public no longer prone, indeed, to the malevolence of Gordon riots but still thoroughly suspicious of popery in all its manifestations. In Ireland, on the other hand, the movement owed its strength to the universal, constant, and acute awareness of grievances which the association aroused in a menacing but hitherto mute and unorganized peasantry. It did so through the newspaper and the pamphlet, and with those crude bardic ballads that thrilled with pride, fervor, and melancholy an emotional people.

# 6. *The Low Slang of a County Election*

The purposes of the propaganda campaign conducted by the association were to create and to hold together at home a national organization and abroad, especially in England, to sway public opinion. The former aim was achieved; the latter was not. But the failure was incidental. Had the majority of the British people abandoned their no-popery tradition, their conversion would have been neither necessarily nor immediately reflected in an unreformed Parliament, where one of the chief impediments to emancipation lay.

Of the nineteen years from 1805 to 1823, only six passed without a debate on the Catholic claims in the legislature,[1] and of the six new parliaments within the period only the short-lived, one-year Parliament of 1806 was totally silent on the issue. The question came to a vote sixteen times in the years from the Union to 1823: in the House of Commons all but three of thirteen pro-Catholic resolutions and motions for committees were defeated, while of three Catholic relief bills [2] two passed the Commons only to be thrown out by the Lords. By 1823, although the upper house was still opposing concession to the Catholics by majorities of from thirty-nine to forty-two, in the lower the cause was gathering strength.

The traditional form of communication with Parliament was by petition, the palladium of the constitution, a right, unlike that of public meeting, with which neither Pitt nor Eldon had ventured to meddle.[3] The Hampden clubs had been as free to indulge in their simultaneous petitions as had the earlier Wyvillian county associa-

1. 1806, 1807, 1809, 1814, 1818, 1820.
2. 1813, 1821, 1822.
3. Only once, by the Act of 1661 against tumultuous petitioning, was the right curtailed. The act made it unlawful to solicit more than twenty signatures to a petition for alteration of the laws concerning church and state unless three magistrates or the majority of a grand jury agreed to the petition. It also forbade the presenting of a petition by a company of more than ten persons.

tions their monster ones. The same freedom existed in 1823, and under it the Irish leaders set about inundating both houses of Parliament with all sorts of importunities. They did not presume that their pleas would sway any appreciable number of legislators. But they did hope that their persistence would at least provoke debates and in so doing draw attention to their cause, a function, indeed, which such an astute politician as Francis Place had asserted, respecting a reform petition from the electors of Westminster in 1828, was the main value of petitioning:

> It was a matter of indifference to a large body of the electors what the House did with the Petition, and many wished the House to reject it, as then another meeting would be held. What was most desired was a wrangle in the House. Everybody knew that, so far as the House alone was concerned, it was useless to petition it; no Petition had ever been entertained as it should have been; none had ever been taken into consideration; no part of the prayer of any Petition had ever been granted. But the House was the best vehicle through, or by which the people could be addressed, and a wrangle in the House when reported in the newspapers was sure to fix the attention of the people on our proceedings.[4]

Previous to 1823 the petitions of the Catholics had been limited in most instances to a simple prayer for emancipation. The association introduced a bolder policy: "No act of oppression should occur from the Giant's Causeway to Cape Clear, but they should drag it before Parliament."[5] During the six years of the agitation Catholic meetings petitioned *for* a general investigation of the state of Ireland, better administration of justice, reform in the temporalities of the Established Church, abolition of church rates, payment of tithes in kind, emancipation of Protestant dissenters in England, poor laws for Ireland, state aid to Catholic education, abolition of the paving board, and repeal of the Act of Union, the Subletting Act, the Vestry Act, Goulburn's act suppressing the association, and the law prohibiting priests from marrying Protestants to Catholics. They petitioned *against* the Orange lodges, government patronage of the press, the packing of juries, rotten borough corporations, the violation of the Treaty of Limerick of 1691, the monopolies and malpractices of corporations and

4. BM, Place MSS, 27,850, p. 218, requoted in Henry Jephson, *The Platform, Its Rise and Progress* (New York, Macmillan & Co., 1892), *1*, 263–264.

5. O'Connell at a Dublin parish meeting, July 30, 1824, *DEP*, July 31, 1824.

corporate towns, and the annual parliamentary grant to the Kildare Street Society.

When the association was only a year old one of its members noted that already the number of petitions forwarded to Parliament was nearly five to one compared with those sent by previous Catholic boards. Even so, they were not, it appears, so numerous as they might have been. Although O'Connell annually proposed flooding Parliament with more than one hundred and fifty petitions on the first day of the session, with five or six more to be presented on each day following, the plan was never fully realized. In 1826 the petitions were purposely delayed in Ireland so as not to provoke a no-popery cry in England in an election year, and in 1827 only about two hundred reached Westminster. The greatest number came in 1828 and 1829. In the former year over one thousand petitions were sent from as many meetings throughout the country, and in 1829 the number was about seventeen hundred to each house of Parliament.[6]

Many of the petitions were forwarded through the association to prominent parliamentary supporters of emancipation: Plunket, Brougham, Burdett, Joseph Hume, Thomas Spring-Rice, Sir John Newport, and Lords Grey, Holland, Donoughmore, King, Lansdowne, Clifden, and Darnley. Others were sent directly by secretaries of local meetings to their county M.P.'s.[7] The association assisted the country meetings by sending down from Dublin ruled paper and detailed instructions for the drafting of the petitions.[8] By 1829 a formal routine was developed whereby three or four models of a general petition for emancipation and of particular ones for relief from local grievances were dispatched to the parish priests, who would select an appropriate one and either appoint some person to take the ruled sheets from house to house or announce from the altar a special Sunday when a table with pen and ink would be set up outside the chapel door.[9]

The petitions succeeded in provoking debates in Parliament, pro-Catholic resolutions in the House of Commons in 1827 and

6. Not all the petitions were presented in Parliament. In 1829 only 1,923 petitions, from Ireland and England, were presented in favor of the emancipation bill, while 4,534 were tabled against it.

7. In 1828, by March 29, 609 petitions were sent through the association and 250 directly by local secretaries, *DEP*, March 29, 1828.

8. In January 1827 the secretary of the association sent to the parishes 775 papers for petitions with ruled spaces for 450,000 signatures. *Ibid.*, Jan. 18, 1827.

9. A circular letter of instructions for framing petitions to Parliament, Jan. 1, 1829, in Wyse, *Historical Sketch, 2,* Appendix xxxiv, cclxxvii–cclxxxi.

1828, and emancipation bills in 1825 and 1829. They also bore fruit in another way. In 1828 about 100,000 Irish Catholics signed a petition for repeal of the Test and Corporation acts. In the following year the Protestant dissenters of England returned the favor: when opponents of the government's emancipation bill of 1829 tried to raise a storm of protest against the measure, the "General Body of Dissenting Ministers of the Three Denominations," after defeating a motion to remain neutral, adopted a resolution in favor of emancipation, and throughout the country dissenters petitioned Parliament to pass the bill.[10]

Besides attempting to influence legislators by means of petitions, the Irish leaders, following the example of the colonies within the empire, maintained a London agent to watch over their cause in Parliament. To the post they appointed, in October 1824, one of their own number, Eneas MacDonnell, with instructions to communicate with the friends of the Catholics in both houses concerning the management of petitions, furnish them with information on difficult points in the Irish debates, cooperate with the leaders of the Catholic body in England, watch over the press of London and the provincial towns in an effort to refute attacks on emancipation, and report periodically to the association on the progress of the cause within and outside Parliament. MacDonnell took his job seriously enough, sending long controversial letters to the English newspapers, calling frequently at the offices of the *Morning Chronicle* and *Globe and Traveller* and at Cobbett's shop in Fleet Street with advertisements and articles, negotiating with the English Catholics to be prompt with their petitions, attending Irish debates in the Commons for three or four hours a night, carrying on a sort of petty diplomacy with Burdett, Plunket, Brougham, and other patrons of the cause, and sending verbose public letters back to Dublin in which he recommended specific, and usually impractical, courses of action. He also carried on a private correspondence with O'Connell to keep the latter posted on the latest political gossip in London, as during the ministerial crisis of February 1827 when, in a letter revealing something of his activities, he wrote:

> I think we should not express any sentiment as to the new cabinet till we know something more than is at present known; and least of all should we meddle with Canning, who is a very slippery gentleman and might throw us overboard,

10. Of 909 petitions presented in the House of Commons in 1829 in favor of the measure, 96 (11 per cent) were from declared Protestant dissenters.

as would suit his convenience . . . I have some petitions ready to place in different hands on Friday, and think it better to hold them till after the discussion on the Corn Bill on Thursday. I mean, if possible, to put forward some young members on the occasion. I am in correspondence with the Bishop of Norwich and his son the Archdeacon. They have got a petition signed already by 83 ministers on our behalf.[11]

Although MacDonnell's prediction in regard to Canning proved well founded, his letters to the association and to O'Connell were more often filled with solemn fooleries. An officious, troublesome sort of person who rather overestimated his own importance, he flattered himself with such an air of intrigue while in London that his Dublin colleagues never gave him their complete confidence. This was especially true of O'Connell who, finding in MacDonnell the potentialities of another Lawless, suggested him for the post of London agent mainly to remove his factious presence from Ireland.[12] Yet MacDonnell did prove of some use in laying first-hand information on the state of Ireland before parliamentarians like Burdett and propagandists like Cobbett.

On a few occasions the leaders of the Catholic body were heard in person in England as well as through their petitions and their agent. In 1824 and 1825 select committees of both houses of Parliament, appointed to inquire into the state of Ireland, summoned witnesses from many parts of the sister island, whose testimony on such matters as the growth and influence of the association, the Catholic Rent, elections, the condition of the peasantry, and the prevalence of agrarian crime did much to emphasize the proportions of the Irish problem. Early in 1825 O'Connell, Sheil, and five of the Catholic bishops appeared before the committees. Their evidence, especially that of the bishops on the theology and the political constitution of their church, although widely published through the country, did little more than elicit a spate of petitions against the Catholic claims and of letters of protest and contradiction directed to Peel at the Home Office. But while members of Parliament remained unconverted, many of them were impressed at least by the capability of some of the Irish leaders, notably O'Connell and Bishop Doyle. These Irishmen did not carry on their

11. MacDonnell to O'Connell, Feb. 27, 1827, UCD, O'C P.

12. O'Connell had long distrusted MacDonnell. A letter to Edward Hay in which he refers to MacDonnell as "the pliant Trojan" is dated July 27, 1817. Fitzpatrick, *Correspondence of O'Connell, 1,* 49.

persons a bloody shillelagh and could, indeed, be sober, even respectable men. Yet the witnesses before the select committees, the work of the London agent, and even the petitions proved that Parliament was not to be swayed, in any appreciable measure, by such methods. A more convincing argument was needed, and it came to hand almost accidentally.

Under the terms of the Act of Union Ireland was represented in the House of Lords by twenty-eight temporal peers, elected for life by the general body of Irish peers, and by four bishops who were replaced by the same number in rotation every two years. These lords consistently voted against emancipation in the proportion of two to one. In the Commons the ratio was more favorable to the Catholics. Of the one hundred Irish members, sixty-four of whom sat for counties, thirty-five for boroughs, and one for Trinity College, slightly over one-half were pro-Catholic, while the remainder either voted against concession or refrained from taking part in divisions on the question.[13] While none of these might be a Catholic, the majority of the electorate whom they represented, especially in the counties, were of that religion.

The Irish Catholics, unlike their English brethren, had been admitted to the franchise in 1793, a franchise remarkably liberal for the time: any freeholder the annual value of whose rental could be sworn to be forty shillings was entitled to vote in the counties. In Ireland this was actually equivalent to household, or rather cabinhold, suffrage, and in the 1820's there were over 100,000 forty-shilling freeholders registered as voters. With their great numerical preponderance over twenty- and fifty-pound freeholders these forty-shillingers were in a position to play a crucial role in elections, if ever they should rebel against the control of landlords who had created and could as easily destroy them. To the latter the votes of obedient tenants had been a source of power in local elections ever since 1793, and at the time of the Union when the number of seats was cut drastically by the dissolution of the Irish Parliament, the value of those that remained increased proportionately.[14] Seats acquired an added importance, also, from the official patronage usually distributed by county members. The forty-shilling freeholders were, therefore, precious political pawns, and in the period since the Union their numbers had grown con-

13. These proportions are based on analysis of the lists of voters on the Catholic question in 1821, 1822, 1825, 1827, and 1828 as found in the *Parl. Papers.*

14. In 1800 the government paid £15,000 per seat to the owners of boroughs disfranchised at the Union, when seats sold for £2,000 for the duration of a parliament

siderably, especially in areas of contested elections where it was to the interest of rival landed families to multiply them indiscriminately.[15] But they were likewise a potential source of disaster if ever their masters' power over them should be challenged, if ever they should refuse to be herded to the polls, sometimes by the very cattle drivers of their proprietors.[16]

The power of the landlords was successfully challenged in Waterford in 1826 and in Clare two years later. Both these elections have been generally accepted as one of the most significant aspects of the agitation in Ireland from 1823 to 1829 and as the first instances of rebellion of the forty-shilling freeholders. The former half of the judgment is true; the latter is not. The dates of the weakening of landlord control can be pushed back beyond 1826.[17] In the general election of 1818 the forty-shillingers of Wexford had disobeyed their landlords' instructions and returned, after a contest lasting twenty-one days, a liberal member for the county. Elsewhere, also, in Leitrim, Sligo, Armagh, Drogheda, and Cork City, the freeholders had been mobilized, usually by the priests, to support pro-emancipation candidates, and in Leitrim and Sligo they defeated the landlords. An even more dramatic contest occurred in the County Dublin by-election of 1823, just a few weeks before the founding of the association. The Catholic leaders formed a committee to campaign for Henry White, the son of a wealthy Dublin merchant, against Sir Compton Domville, the ascendancy candidate. O'Connell and the future demagogues of the Corn Exchange harangued the mob on the hustings and went the round of the chapels on the seacoast to canvass the freeholders, great numbers of whom were fishermen. So successful were their efforts that within a few days the hitherto absolute proprietors of the county found themselves destitute of influence; they looked on in amazement as their tenants, sent in droves to the booths to vote for Sir Compton, heeded rather the exhortation of O'Connell to "remember Ireland" and were set down on the tallies of Henry White.

15. In Donegal, Westmeath, Wexford, Galway, Leitrim, Clare, Cork, and Waterford the number doubled; in Meath and Tipperary it tripled, and in Londonderry quintupled.

16. O'Connell, in defending his compromise on the wings, declared he had witnessed forty-shilling freeholders in Clare brought in by scores to the hustings and reckoned, according to the state of the poll, at so much a head. In Cork he had seen two thousand brought in to vote against their conscience for an Orange candidate. *DEP*, Dec. 2, 1825.

17. Most historians date the process from the elections of 1826. Adams, *Ireland and Irish Emigration*, pp. 138–139, gives 1824, but what he is referring to is comment on the Dublin election of 1823. There are earlier examples.

It seems extraordinary that these elections, especially the Dublin one, did not suggest to O'Connell and his cohorts a potent weapon which they had almost to hand and which, with keener prescience, their opponents viewed as particularly disturbing. In October 1824 Goulburn wrote to Peel: "Whenever an election shall take place the people will be placed in opposition to their landlords and such members only returned as shall please the Association." [18] But the chief secretary credited the Catholic leaders with more political foresight than they actually demonstrated. They did occasionally threaten to unseat hostile members of Parliament; O'Connell at a Galway meeting in April 1824 condemned Irish members who, while giving an idle vote for appearances' sake in favor of the Catholic claims, supported the Tory government on every other measure. He warned them that an election was approaching.[19] In September of the same year Conway, in the *Evening Post*, advised voters to ask candidates not if they supported emancipation but whether they had promoted the Catholic Rent.[20] These at best were idle threats. The stimulus for a realistic program of interference in elections came eventually from outside Dublin, from a county thirty miles to the south.

In Waterford, a constituency with forty-one Catholic voters for every Protestant, Thomas Wyse and an election committee had, since August 1825, been developing plans to overthrow the supremacy of the Beresfords, the most powerful family in Ireland in patronage and influence, monopolizers of half the representation of the county for over seventy years, and staunch opponents not only of the Catholic claims but also of liberal Protestants like the viceroy, whose pro-Catholic sympathies they abhorred.[21] Wyse and his committee spent well over £10,000 in systematically canvassing the freeholders of the county to disregard the instructions of their landlords and thus defeat one of the sitting members, Lord George Beresford, who had held the seat for twenty years, by casting their

18. Goulburn to Peel, Oct. 27, 1824, BM, PP, 40330, fol. 150.
19. *DEP,* April 6, 1824.
20. *Ibid.,* Sept. 21, 1824.
21. In 1822 Wellesley had been publicly insulted in a Dublin theater by an Orange extremist who tossed an empty bottle into the royal box, aimed ostensibly at the viceregal head. The ultra-Protestants had done little to hide their satisfaction over the "Bottle Incident," and in Waterford the Beresfords tried to prevent a public meeting called to adopt an address of sympathy to the lord lieutenant sponsored by Wyse. Their action, coupled with their persistent snubbing of Wyse's French wife, the daughter of Lucien Bonaparte, provided personal motives for Wyse's determination to humble the family. Wyse, *Historical Sketch, 1,* 262–263.

votes for Villiers Stuart.[22] The Waterford committee received little cooperation from the association in Dublin. O'Connell, indeed, publicly expressed a hope that eight hundred new freeholders recently created by the Beresfords would not enable the family to tighten its grip on the county, but he declined, rather coolly, to help Wyse obtain financial aid from the Catholic Rent, which since the dissolution of the old association was in the custody of Lord Killeen. And although O'Connell himself was qualified to vote in Waterford, he made no effort to register in the constituency.[23] He still asserted that the forty-shilling franchise was an impediment to the Catholic cause.[24] Even when reports from the South of a strong popular trend toward Stuart began to reach Dublin in February 1826 the association merely passed a half-hearted resolution requesting the Waterford freeholders to demonstrate their independence. Mild as it was, the resolution encountered opposition from some members on the ground that it would involve the association in a quixotic experiment.

If they were slow to appreciate the fateful possibilities of the situation, the Dublin leaders did finally realize that the thorough preparations of Wyse and his committee gave promise of overthrowing what had hitherto been considered an impregnable monopoly. On June 13, just ten days before the election, they published a stirring address to the Waterford electors urging them to vote for Stuart. And on the same day O'Connell announced his intention of going to Waterford to act as Stuart's counsel. Excitement rose to a fevered pitch. Under the cold eyes of their landlords orderly forty-shillingers, heeding rather O'Connell and the priests, cast their votes for Stuart. There was none of the rioting ordinarily characteristic of Irish elections; the butchers of Ballybrisken patrolled the streets to keep the peace; there was strange lack of drunkenness. In all respects it was a novel election and, to the police who looked on idly, a startling one. Maj. Richard Willcocks, in charge of the extra force of constables summoned to Waterford in

22. The Waterford election organization comprised a general committee in the county town with branch committees in every barony and two local agents who made weekly reports to the baronial committees which in turn reported to the general committee. Each parish priest, local agent, and baronial committee had their registry book which was handed in a week or two before the election. A certain number of the committee were deputed to address each parish in the chapel on the eight Sundays preceding the election. *Ibid., 1,* 285–288.

23. O'Connell to Wyse, Oct. 14, 1825, in Fitzpatrick, *Correspondence of O'Connell, 1,* 112.

24. *DEM,* Dec. 2, 1825.

expectation of bloodshed, sent almost daily reports to the under-secretary at Dublin Castle. In each of them he had to admit that the profoundest peace prevailed, in spite of the fact that he had never witnessed in all his experience such party spirit, with the Catholics all wearing green handkerchiefs, sashes, cockades, and ribbons, flying green flags in all parts of the city, accompanying Stuart to and from the hustings with a band clad in green, listening to an inflammatory speech from O'Connell each day before the close of the poll, and everywhere insulting the Beresfords: "The constant cry is 'High for Stuart. Down with Lord George. Down with the Protestants.' This is to be heard in every part of the city and I may say all through the county." [25]

The polling ended with Lord George withdrawing from the contest. He had but 528 votes to 1,357 for Stuart and 1,424 for Power, the other sitting member for the county and a pro-Catholic in politics. Even after Power and Stuart had been declared elected there were over 700 freeholders still waiting to vote for them. The rout was staggering. To the great landed interests of the county the whole fiasco appeared a daring encroachment on the rights of private property. One proprietor wrote dazedly:

> . . . men who in the year 1798 with exemplary loyalty assisted me to keep Rebellion out of these parishes, and in the last year resisted to a man the payment of the Catholic Rent, although called upon by the priests from the altar to contribute, have been now compelled to bow to this Popish Inquisition . . . . none but my five Protestant tenants have been polled out of this large estate, and Lord Doneraile who has upwards of an hundred, has not been able to bring to the poll more than his seven Protestant tenants, and I understand all the remainder have polled against him, as have even Lord Waterford's own tenants.[26]

The Waterford triumph had long been prepared through the foresight and persistence of Thomas Wyse and with little encouragement from the Dublin leaders. The latter now realized with chagrin that if similar efforts had been made throughout the country in the general election of 1826, the phenomenon might well have been multiplied on a grand scale. As it was, a few other counties did take heart almost at the last minute from the news of what was happening in Waterford.

25. Willcocks to Gregory, June 23, 25, and 26, 1826, ISPO, OP II, 588zz/918
26. Letter of John Palliser, no addressee, June 24, 1826, *ibid.*

In Louth when a retired barrister, Alexander Dawson, came forward to announce himself a "Catholic" candidate, the news, for its suddenness and audacity, created an even greater sensation in Dublin than did the first word of Stuart's running for Waterford. For over half a century two prominent Louth families, the Jocelyns and the Fosters, had divided the representation of the county between them. In 1826 they expected an uncontested return of their protégés, the sitting members, Mathew Fortescue and John Leslie Foster, both opponents of emancipation. Dawson was an upstart with neither great wealth nor connections; he stated he would not bear any of the expense and must be returned through popular contributions; the ordinary preparations had not been made; and he declared his intention only ten days before the election. Immediately the Catholics set to work. The association issued proclamations exhorting the Louth electors to imitate those of Waterford; Sheil came down as counsel for Dawson; Archbishop Curtis dispatched a pro-Dawson circular to all his priests; lay committees were formed in the parishes to raise subscriptions; and the priests preached politics in their chapels and visited every parishioner who had a vote. When the contest ended Dawson headed the poll with 862 votes to 552 for Foster and 547 for Fortescue.

Foster, who had entered the contest with five-sixths of the electorate promised to him by their landlords, explained the result in a hasty letter to Peel:

> Very many Protestants were forced to vote against me by the threats of assassination or having their houses burnt. . . . When the poll commenced all the priests of the county were collected and distributed through the different booths, where they stood with glaring eyes directly opposite to the voters of their respective flocks as they were severally brought up. . . . At the close of the election the Catholics threw in their votes to the other Protestant candidate merely to get me out, but they were a little too late in the mancuvre and matters ended. . . . the tenantry [are] sullen and insolent. Men who a month ago were all civility and submission now hardly suppress their curses when a gentleman passes by. . . . I begin to fear a crisis of some kind or other is not far distant.[27]

Due allowance must be made for Foster's resentment, his sense of humiliation, and his natural desire to justify to Peel the near loss

27. Foster to Peel, July 8, 1826, Parker, *Peel, 1,* 409–412.

of his seat. Yet his estimate of priestly influence is scarcely exaggerated. In Louth as elsewhere, although their interference for the most part was limited to harangues on the dire spiritual effects of voting against one's conscience, the priests glared, threatened, and intimidated. They showed themselves a very political clergy. Nevertheless, it is an exaggeration to lay the result, as did the landlords of Louth, to a sordid piece of priestly jobbery and coercion, especially when one considers that the great issue in Louth, as elsewhere, was the vote of the member of Parliament on the emancipation question, that the Catholic tenant who obeyed his landlord's orders acted contrary to conviction, that the distress warrant was employed on the one side quite as menacingly, if not as effectively, as the cross on the other, and that the great majority of the Catholic freeholders, enthusiastically following their clergy, did not hesitate to lampoon and ostracize any priests who remained neutral.

In contrast to the angry astonishment of Foster, the mood of the almost equally surprised Catholics was jubilant. Archbishop Curtis expressed it in a private letter to his fellow prelate, Daniel Murray of Dublin:

> Your Grace was in doubt of Mr. Dawson's triumph at Louth; but before this arrives, you will know it has been more complete than any other in the kingdom. So much so, that if another liberal candidate had been started with him, they could easily have ousted both Foster and Fortescue, the former of whom has been returned merely because the Catholic electors did not oppose him. Which boon, it seems, was granted by Shiel [*sic*] to the humble and urgent entreaty made to him and party publicly on the hustings by Counsellor North, brother-in-law to Foster, who, under pretence of indisposition, absented himself. I hope you may be able to tell me as much of your County Dublin Election.[28]

The Archbishop of Dublin was, indeed, able to report equally favorable news. In the metropolitan election, although there occurred no grand revolt of the freeholders and O'Connell complained of the slavish voting he saw at the booths, the liberal candidates, White and Talbot, were both successful. In Monaghan, Henry Westenra, with the support of the Catholics, unseated Colonel Leslie, whose family had long dominated the county; and in Cork City John Hely Hutchinson defeated the ascendancy candidate, Gerard Cal-

28. Curtis to Murray, July 2, 1826, AHD, Murray Papers.

laghan, 1,020 to 969, in a close race said to have cost Hutchinson's uncle, Lord Donoughmore, £15,000. Elsewhere, too, in Westmeath and Armagh, liberal candidates were returned, and Archbishop Murray was able to report: "The elections for the New Parliament have been favorable to the Catholic Cause." [29]

The elections, except for Waterford, being fought almost on the spur of the moment, were marked in many instances by the disorder and violence typical of contested elections in Ireland, when an express might be sent up to Dublin for both polling books and pistols. In Cavan, where many freeholders also voted "contrary to the wishes and entreaties of their landlords," the affair was "noisy and violent." [30] From Galway the inspector of police reported that "yesterday has passed off rather more tranquil—there was only one house demolished and one man's skull fractured." [31] And in Monaghan: "The people have been fired on. Magistrates have headed the military and acted in a most unbecoming manner . . . One man is at the point of death and others desperately wounded." [32] But more impressive than the rioting and bloodshed in Galway and Monaghan was the lack of violence, the good order and sobriety of the Waterford freeholders. There the election stood forth as a foreboding sign of what could be achieved by patient preparation and thorough discipline. If the example proved contagious, as the landlords of Monaghan, for instance, feared it would, "we apprehend [it] must ultimately terminate in these people . . . sending forward the representatives for many, if not the greater number of the counties in Ireland." [33] A prospect which led Peel to remark, on learning the results of the Irish elections, ". . . a darker cloud than ever seems to me to impend over Ireland, that is if one of the remaining bonds of society, the friendly connection between landlord and tenant, is dissolved." [34]

But for the Catholic Association the cloud was far from dark. The elections provided just the stimulus needed by a waning agitation. O'Connell at last acknowledged unambiguously his error in having agreed to the disfranchisement of the forty-shillingers; the

29. Murray to Dr. Blake, agent of the Irish bishops in Rome, July 7, 1826, Bishop's House, Newry, Blake Correspondence.

30. Major D'Arcy to Gregory, June 22, 1826, ISPO, OP II, 588zz/915.

31. Major Warburton to Gregory, June 28, 1826, *ibid.*

32. Lord Rossmore to Wellesley, June 24, 1826, *ibid.*

33. "An address of consolation to Col. Charles Powell Leslie on being turned out as M.P. for Monaghan, by the Landed Proprietors and Gentlemen of the County of Monaghan," June 29, 1826, NL, Add. MS E2.

34. Peel to Sir George Hill, July 16, 1826, copy, BM, PP, 40388, fol. 66.

association resolved to exert all its energies in the next elections in Tyrone, Donegal, Derry, Wexford, Cavan, Sligo, and King's County; and the Rent was revived for the purpose of protecting the rebellious freeholders of Waterford, Louth, and Monaghan from the vengeance of their outraged proprietors.

Immediately after the elections the Dublin *Evening Mail* advised landlords that since it was the Protestant lords of the soil who had created the freeholders, it was they who could unmake them. The hint was barely necessary. Within two weeks after the last freeholder had cast his vote, letters from the country began arriving at the Corn Exchange complaining of evictions already under way. The association riposted with countermeasures. In Waterford and other centers of revolt protective associations were formed to transmit information on cases of local persecution to Dublin for publication and to serve as relief boards for the distribution of the new Catholic Rent. By September 1827 these local bodies had spent over £5,000 sent down from the metropolis to aid evicted tenants,[35] in addition to probably one-half again as much raised locally. While the funds dispensed by the protective associations helped to ease the distress of freeholders whose leases were suddenly called in, the odious publicity given individual cases dissuaded most landlords from adopting a policy of wholesale evictions. At the provincial and county meetings of 1826 and 1827 impoverished forty-shillingers like "honest Anthony Hearn" and "Harry Mills, this village Hampden" were brought to the platform to take a bow and to tell of their persecution by relentless landlords, personal histories which were published throughout the country by the Catholic press to the accompaniment of fierce denunciation.

Defense of the freeholders was also the pretext for another innovation. In July 1826 O'Connell announced a plan for an Order of Liberators, in imitation of a society founded by Simón Bolívar in South America. Qualification for membership would be the performance of acts of distinctive service to Ireland, such as the independent votes cast in the recent elections. The liberators would deter the peasantry from joining secret and lawless societies, conciliate all factions among them by preventing feuds and riots at markets and fairs, protect the freeholders, promote the regis-

35. The total spent up to Sept. 22, 1827, after which date there were only isolated cases of eviction, was £5,402, distributed as follows: Waterford £2,500; Louth £1,168; Meath £775; Monaghan £566; Cavan £243; other counties £150. *DEP*, Sept. 25, 1827.

tration of their holdings, and in general organize a perfect system in preparation for the next elections. The members of the fraternity would be ranked, according to the value of their acts of service, as liberators, knights of the grand cross, and knights companion, and wear a special uniform with a handsome medal of the order.[36] Although O'Connell took his plan quite seriously, unlike most of his improvisations it did not prosper. The majority of the Dublin leaders, led by the more self-conscious Sheil, found the sight of big Dan in his green finery and huge medal, or in the blue frock, yellow vest, and white trousers which he had originally recommended as a uniform for all association members, slightly preposterous. The Grand Knight of the Liberators could not persuade them to join in such pomposity, although in the provinces he did find some satisfaction in pontificating at occasional "chapters" of the order after High Mass in the chapels. As an effective organization, the liberators, for all their color, were a failure.

Success, on the other hand, attended the association's general program of protecting the freeholders. Thereby the prestige of the body was considerably enhanced and the spirit of independence so recently demonstrated in Waterford, Monaghan, and Louth perpetuated, a spirit that was to rekindle sooner than expected. Meanwhile the next general elections seemed remote, possibly seven years distant should the present Parliament run its full course, and during the lull of 1827 the association developed no general system of preparation for the next contest. The Order of Liberators made only rare and feeble attempts to secure a full registration of freeholds. In January 1827 when one of the speakers at the Corn Exchange proposed the formation of a central committee with subordinate societies to supervise registration, his plan was shelved as probably illegal.

Still the lesson of 1826 was not completely forgotten. It was recalled and repeated in July 1828 in the famous Clare election.[37] O'Connell, a Catholic, was returned to Parliament. Two years earlier John Leslie Foster, shortly after his narrow escape in the Louth election, had warned that if the franchise were not raised in Ireland, "you would have at least sixty Catholic members, and such Catholics! Sheil for Louth and O'Connell for any southern county he might choose." [38] Now O'Connell was threatening that the Catholics would return seventy candidates at the next general

36. *DEP*, July 8, 1826.
37. The Clare election is described below, pp. 156–160.
38. Foster to Peel, Nov. 6, 1826, BM, PP, 40389, f. 266.

election, and the Munster provincial meeting of August 1828 passed an ominous resolution urging all Irish members to assemble in Dublin one month before the opening of the session to discuss and agree on combining to press certain measures on Parliament. The resolution, although neglected, was a significant foreshadowing of what was to happen later in the century with the formation of a vexatious Irish party in the House of Commons.

Meanwhile the agitators were preparing for future elections. They used the Rent once again to aid freeholders evicted on account of their votes in Clare, and O'Connell warned, "If any man persecutes the forty-shilling freeholders, I implore those who hear me to find out and transmit to me an account of what judgment, debts, and incumbrances affect the estate of that man." [39] Election pledges were devised to be submitted to all candidates for Parliament: that they would not support the administration of Wellington and Peel until after total, unqualified emancipation, and that they would promote every measure of parliamentary reform, especially the broadening of the franchise and shorter duration of parliaments. Refusal to give the pledges would incur the "direct and active opposition" of the Catholic Association of Ireland.[40] The association also turned its attention to the registers of voters. One member noted that O'Connell's majority of 1,075 in Clare would have been 3,000 but for a defect in the rolls.[41] The forty-shillingers were not used to registering at their own expense. They did not know how to fill out the affidavits, and the matter was usually taken care of by the landlord or his agent.

For the development of a thorough system of registration Thomas Wyse had proposed, early in 1827, the formation of county "Liberal clubs." Once again he received little encouragement from the Dublin leaders, many of whom resented the importance Wyse had gained by his successful management of the Waterford election. O'Connell in particular, always suspicious of any challenge to his primacy, discouraged the project and tried to substitute for it a patently imitative one of his own for "County clubs." Wyse persisted and after the Clare election drew up detailed proposals for the organization of Liberal clubs throughout the country.[42] What the movement lacked, he suggested, was a well-digested system of political tactics; the association, despite fre-

39. Speech of O'Connell, July 3, 1828, in "Proceedings of the Clare Election," p. 338, MS, ISPO, SCP, carton 50.

40. Meeting of Aug. 4, 1828, Minute Book of the Association, AHD, CP.

41. Meeting of Sept. 18, 1828, NL, CA MSS.

42. See Wyse, *Historical Sketch, 1,* 342–347.

quent provincial and county meetings, at best only temporary stimulants, was too much Dublin and too little Ireland; it should, rather, stand at the head of permanent county, city, and parish societies, of which the clergy, the churchwardens and Rent collectors, and the more substantial farmers and merchants would form the nucleus. The Liberal clubs would be active political centers, diffusing information about local grievances, putting down secret and illegal societies among the peasantry, registering freeholds, and in general educating the people, through the press and public meetings, to an intelligent awareness of political issues. The system would, in effect, produce capable and self-reliant local leaders rather than mere rustic counterparts of the demagogic orators of the Corn Exchange, and by fostering enlightened laymen it would "free the Catholic clergy from the heavy yoke of politics." [43] Wyse also proposed the circulation through the clubs of a "Political Catechism," a sort of textbook containing, in imitation of the religious catechism so familiar to the people, simple questions and answers dealing with the history of the penal laws, the abuses of English government in Ireland, justification for such a body as the Catholic Association, and a summary of the liberties of British freemen to which the Irish Catholics aspired. He set about compiling the manual himself.

Lack of support from O'Connell, hardly surprising in view of some of the implications contained in Wyse's statement of the purposes of his project, and the lateness of the hour combined to prevent any effective launching of the Liberal clubs. Wyse completed and published his catechism [44] only a few weeks previous to the Catholic Emancipation Act of 1829, which was followed by another measure raising the franchise in Ireland and thus wiping out most of the electorate for whom the book was intended. His scheme, nevertheless, was a good one. What if it had been realized? Would the Irish electorate have become a more resourceful and discriminating body, less blindly devoted to personalities? Would other native spokesmen have arisen to offer a healthy opposition to O'Connell's demagogic and sometimes irresponsible leadership?

The pressure brought to bear on legislators was reflected in the

43. "Letters on the Organization of Liberal Clubs," *ibid.*, *2*, Appendix xxv, cxlv–clxxi.

44. Thomas Wyse, *The Political Catechism Explanatory of the Constitutional Rights and Civil Disabilities of the Catholics of Ireland* (London, 1829). The catechism contained over 1,400 questions and answers under four general headings: What Is a British Freeman? Is an Irish Catholic a British Freeman? Why Is Not an Irish Catholic a British Freeman? Ought Not a Catholic Be a British Freeman?

gradually increasing concern for Irish affairs shown by Parliament. As early as June 1823 notice was taken of the renewal of Irish agitation in a brief debate on the Catholic question in the Commons. But Plunket's motion of that year for a committee to consider the question was defeated by a majority of 202, the largest since 1805. During 1824, although the question did not come to a vote, much of the session was taken up with Irish matters: in May an inconclusive debate in the Commons turned on the issue of the legality of the new organization in Ireland, and select committees were set up by both houses to inquire into the disturbed state of the sister island. Where formerly, as Peel remarked, not forty members would be present for an Irish debate, now four and five times that number attended.[45]

The session of 1825 was devoted almost entirely to Irish legislation: Goulburn's act suppressing the association and Burdett's emancipation bill, with its freehold and clerical wings, which was passed by the Commons 248 to 227 but thrown out by the Lords 178 to 130 after a spirited denunciation by the Duke of York. Some of the Lords tempered the rebuff with a conciliatory gesture. A group of Protestant peers owning property in Ireland, English Whigs of the prominence of the Dukes of Devonshire and Buckingham and Lords Lansdowne and Fitzwilliam, as well as Irish noblemen led by the Duke of Leinster and Lords Donoughmore and Charlemont, met at Buckingham House in Pall Mall, June 27, 1825, to draw up a series of resolutions advocating civil equality for Catholics. They warned that it was expedient "to confer with advantage what cannot be refused with safety and to adopt in peace a measure which may be forced upon us in war" and recommended their Catholic fellow subjects to be firm, temperate, and united.[46] The resolutions, signed by sixty-five noblemen, helped to soften the blow in 1825.

The passage of Burdett's bill by the Commons was the third instance in which the same house, which had sat since 1820,[47] had approved a relief measure. The event considerably worried Lord Liverpool and his ministers. After the defeat of Burdett's bill in the Lords, they thought of dissolving Parliament so that a new election might be held while public interest was still high and a no-popery cry could be raised at the polls. Wellington hinted to

45. Cited by O'Connell at a meeting, July 30, 1824, *DEP,* July 31, 1824.

46. "Resolutions of the Protestant Peers," in E. A. Kendall, *Letters to a Friend on the State of Ireland* (London, 1826), *3,* Appendix IV, xiv–xvi.

47. If not dissolved in 1825 the Parliament would be the first since the Septennial Act to run its full course.

Liverpool that he favored the step,[48] and in a letter to Lord Chancellor Eldon he was more explicit: the Roman Catholic question almost broke up the government in the last session, and if ministers did not dissolve now they would have the question all over again.[49] Liverpool himself was decidedly for an immediate dissolution if the question was to receive the support of those who were generally friendly to it in the government in the next session, but if they would discourage its being brought on, he would put off the dissolution until next year.[50]

Whigs in Parliament and Canningites in the cabinet, knowing that the Irish agitators, plagued by Goulburn's act and the wings quarrels, were in no position to be vociferous, did agree to bury the issue. They did not bring it forward in the session of 1826. But on the hustings the Catholic question was prominent. In Ireland the Catholics won seats in Waterford, Monaghan, Louth, and Westmeath, gains offset, nevertheless, in England, where the election was conducted under a mild no-popery slogan. The house that resulted seemed more decidedly Protestant. In 1827 the Commons negatived a motion of Burdett for a committee on the Catholic question 276 to 272. Yet it was notable that "the assemblage in the House of Commons was greater than it had been on any former division."[51] In 1828 renewed disturbance in Ireland once more focused attention on the emancipation issue. The same house which only a year before had defeated by four votes Burdett's motion now passed by a majority of six a resolution to consider the disqualifying laws. But in the upper house a motion introduced by Lord Lansdowne to concur in the resolution of the Commons was lost by a majority of forty-five, and there the matter rested for the remainder of the session.

In Ireland, meanwhile, one of the most vehement opponents of concession, George Dawson, M.P. for the Protestant stronghold of Derry, suddenly announced his conversion. He was convinced, he said in a speech on August 12, 1828, delivered, of all places, at a dinner to commemorate the siege of Derry, that the Catholic agitation was too menacing to warrant further resistance.[52] The furor created by Dawson's apostasy was heightened by his being secretary to the treasury and a brother-in-law of Peel, who, it was erroneously supposed, had foreknowledge of the speech. But Peel

48. Wellington to Liverpool, June 22, 1825, *Wellington Despatches, 2*, 463–465.
49. Wellington to Eldon, Sept. 7, 1825, *ibid.*, 482–483.
50. Liverpool to Peel, Sept. 15, 1825, BM, PP, 40305, foll. 86–87.
51. "The Catholic Question in Parliament," MS, *ibid.*, 40398, fol. 16.
52. *DEP*, Aug. 16, 1828.

was as startled as anyone [53] and condemned his kinsman's indiscretion as strongly as did the Duke of Wellington, who thought Dawson should be in a strait waistcoat. Dawson's defection from the hitherto solid ranks of the high Tories came as another blow to Wellington's government, already embarrassed by the repeal of the Test and Corporation acts and by the pro-Catholic vote in the House of Commons. It was doubly irritating in that Dawson compounded his offense by a frank avowal of motives at the very moment being weighed by Wellington and Peel as justification for action which was to earn for them also, within a few months, the epithet "apostates," spiced in many an ultra-Tory manor of England with an appropriate adjective.

Of all the tactics devised by the Irish leaders for bringing pressure to bear on legislators, the most persuasive was the upsetting of the traditional electoral pattern in Ireland. Petitions from the association in Dublin and from provincial, county, town, and parish meetings, while provoking debate in Parliament and attendant publicity in the press, persuaded few hostile M.P.'s to acknowledge the expediency of concession. The petty diplomacy of the London agent did little more than advertise Irish discontent in English newspapers and furnish friendly parliamentary leaders with useful material for their Irish debates. The deputation to London, along with the testimony of Irishmen before the select committees, only served to draw attention to the wretched state of the sister island and the underrated abilities of some of the Irish leaders. But the Waterford and Clare elections brought the pressure home. Irish members, especially those sitting for counties, began to realize their insecurity. Fear of losing personal importance attached to seats frequently won at ruinous expense brought men to think of concession who had never thought of it before.

Yet in the final analysis the chief impediment to emancipation was not to be found in Parliament. The Commons on six occasions since 1812 had voted in favor of concession and had passed emancipation bills three times, bills thrown out, to be sure, by the Lords,

53. William Peel wrote to his brother, Robert: "Good God! What can Dawson be about? I know no plea but insanity which can justify his conduct. . . . If the Catholic Association has such unbounded powers, why is he to proclaim its influence? . . . Why suffer the Agitators, the Emancipators, but above all the Canningites and the Converts to triumph over him? . . . as Secretary to the Treasury he had . . . no right to make the speech he did, unless he received the sanction of the Duke of Wellington. . . . He ought again and again to have guarded his hearers from supposing that his nearest connexions were parties to his apostacy." W. Peel to R. Peel, n.d., BM, PP, 40397, foll. 157–161.

but by peers relying on the Protestantism of their high Tory leaders, Liverpool, Wellington, and Peel, and the well-known hostility of the King. When once these supreme powers yielded, when they realized the necessity of making emancipation a cabinet measure, the House of Lords would perforce bow to the inevitable.

# 7. *The Most Difficult Problem That a Government Ever Had to Deal with*

THE Act of Union, although it did away with a separate legislature, left Ireland with its own executive government. In Dublin Castle there remained a viceroy, chief secretary, undersecretary, lord chancellor, attorney general and solicitor general, and a corps of subordinate officials to administer laws made no longer in College Green but in Westminster. While these authorities were, of course, still immediately subject to the Home Office, they exercised practically the same jurisdiction as had the pre-Union Irish Government. Thus, divided responsibility, shared by both Dublin Castle and Whitehall, besides highlighting a major weakness of English rule in Ireland, played into the hands of the Irish agitators and enabled them to bring pressure to bear on administrators in both islands.

The renewal of Catholic ferment in 1823 annoyingly increased the burden of the Irish Government, already hard pressed to keep peace and order in a land forever seething with religious factions, where the distinction of Whig and Tory was eclipsed by that of Catholic and Protestant, where the Union Jack attracted far less devotion than did orange ribbons and green cockades. After 1800 and previous to the 1820's there had been two great factions in Ireland. With the arrival in 1821 of a new lord lieutenant, the pro-Catholic Marquis Wellesley, a third party emerged, a small clique of liberal Protestants who sympathized with Wellesley and encouraged him in his attempts to steer a middle course between the extremes. But *virtus in medio* was an impossibility. While Protestant ultras, feeling themselves deserted by the government, denounced the viceroy for truckling to the demagogues,[1] the latter at first accused him of traditional viceregal partiality toward the Protestants

1. They accused him of preventing Orange processions while tolerating the association for the purpose of convincing the English Government that resistance to the Catholic claims was futile. Goulburn to Peel, July 25, 1826, BM, PP, 40332, foll. 65–70; Sir George Hill to Peel, Nov. 2, 1826, *ibid.*, 40389, foll. 221–226.

and then made an equally undesirable about-face by claiming him as an ally against the Orangemen. Naturally, the attentions of both parties were decidedly unwelcome.

Wellesley was the first Irishman to be named viceroy for centuries; he was a "Catholic" in politics and carried with him to Dublin express instructions to administer the existing laws "in a spirit of mildness and impartiality."[2] His official neutrality pointed, therefore, to a departure from the fixed habit of conducting the government by agency of the ascendancy, a sign which the majority of the faction bitterly resented. Self-interest explains their attitude. But their complaints were not wholly without justification. The Catholic Association was interfering in the administration of justice by prosecuting Orangemen and even the police;[3] it formed a special subcommittee "to watch over the police";[4] on at least one occasion it posted £500, "since no reward has been offered by the Government," for the apprehension and prosecution of an "Orange assassin";[5] and in 1828 it began to set up its own system of courts, two in every county with branches in the towns and villages, to settle disputes among the peasantry. The very existence of this popish parliament was a mockery of the legitimate government.

The difficulties of the lord lieutenant, beset by the clamor of both parties, were increased by division within his own camp. The chief secretary, Henry Goulburn, held political opinions, on the Catholic question at least, directly opposed to those of his superior and was reputed, moreover, to be a member of the Orange Society. In the post of undersecretary was an even more outspoken ascendancy man, William Gregory. Lord Chancellor Manners and the solicitor general, Henry Joy, were "Protestants," while William Plunket, the attorney general, was a "Catholic." Thus the most important offices in the Irish Government were filled by men who disagreed on the most pressing issue in Irish politics. Goulburn and Gregory, in their letters to Peel, accused Wellesley and Plunket of favoring the Catholics and not proceeding vigorously enough against the association.[6]

2. "A Sketch . . . of Lord Wellesley's Administration in Ireland," in Aspinall, *Letters of King George IV*, *3*, 297.

3. There were eight instances of such prosecutions before Goulburn's act made use of the association's funds for the purpose illegal.

4. Meeting of Aug. 4, 1828, Minute Book of the Association, AHD, CP.

5. *DEP*, Oct. 18, 1828.

6. O'Connell himself noted: "I never abused the Orangemen with half the violence they are now abused at the Castle." O'Connell to his wife, Jan. 11, 1823, O'Connell Letters to His Wife.

The liberal policies of Wellesley and of his successor, Lord Anglesey, aroused sympathy, nevertheless, in one quarter, among a small group of Irish Protestants who had a sort of headquarters in the Dublin salon of the witty Lady Morgan. While Lady Morgan's famous journals contain little about politics, her drawing room in Kildare Street was actually the foyer of Dublin liberalism, where she and her husband, Sir Charles, received other prominent leaders of the government party, Protestants acting frequently under the title of Friends of Civil and Religious Liberty and sympathizing with the aims, if not always with the vulgar methods, of O'Connell and Sheil.[7]

The contrast to Lady Morgan's salon was to be found in the Dublin Beefsteak Club, the resort of the extreme ascendancy faction. In 1828 the new and inexperienced viceroy, Anglesey, almost got himself in hot water with his own party by entertaining an invitation to dine with the club, where he might very well have heard such fantastic toasts as "The Pope in the pillory of Hell and the Devil pelting priests at him." Before he accepted, Lady Morgan intervened: "A rumour prevails at present in Dublin, that Lord Anglesea means to accept the invitation to be given to him by the *Beef Steak Club*. . . . should Lord Anglesea take his place in a Society which has so long offended the nation, and so utterly insulted the King in the person of his representative, the Marquis of Wellesley, not all the efforts of the Catholic leaders now disposed to support and uphold the popularity of Lord Anglesea's government, would suffice to keep quiet that nest of hornets, the Catholic Association." [8] Lady Morgan's warning was effective: the lord lieutenant did not dine with the beefsteakers. The incident disclosed not only the sort of petty diplomacy carried on by the liberal Protestants but also the fine line which Anglesey, as well as his predecessor, had to tread in a country where the slightest official gesture had political significance, in a city where "a community of information and gossip . . . makes it impossible to communicate anything without its becoming a topic of general conversation." [9]

7. W. Hepworth Dixon, ed., *Lady Morgan's Memoirs: Autobiography, Diaries, and Correspondence* (London, 1863), *2*, 266 and 271.

8. Lady Morgan to Lord Aylmer, April 18, 1828, *ibid.*, *2*, 256–257.

9. Gregory to Peel, Feb. 3, 1828, BM, PP, 40334, foll. 199–200. Even official correspondence was not safe from party prying. William Lamb, chief secretary in 1827, was informed by the Home Office that the seals of his letters were frequently tampered with. Thomas Spring-Rice to Lamb, Oct. 2 and Oct. 29, 1827, in W. M. Torrens, *Memoirs of Viscount Melbourne* (London, 1878), I, 255–256.

Playing upon this friction both within and outside the Castle, the Catholic leaders shrewdly and mercilessly exploited the known sympathies of the viceroys. At the outset of Wellesley's tenure O'Connell frequently heckled him with impudent public letters demanding prohibition of the annual Orange processions and the dressing of King William's statue. Since Wellesley had already decided to take such a step, O'Connell's importunity only served to embarrass him. But the letter was merely the beginning of an insidious strategy of committing the government against the Orangemen. The association protested loudly its eminent loyalty to the throne and its representative in Ireland, displayed prominently in its meeting room a portrait of George IV, and had the effrontery to print some of its popular anti-Protestant ballads under a crude cut of the royal features.[10] In 1824, when O'Connell sent to Plunket a long letter informing him of the spread of illegal secret societies among the peasantry of Tipperary, Goulburn instantly reported the maneuver to Peel, commenting shrewdly that O'Connell was laying in a stock of loyalty should the association ever be prosecuted.[11] Two years later O'Connell informed Plunket that in the country districts the Orangemen and the lower orders of the Catholics were secretly arming themselves with daggers in expectation of a clash. He must scarcely have suppressed a smile when he concluded the letter: "I have no remedy to suggest save the increase of the King's troops in Ireland. I have done my duty in communicating these facts to you." [12] Again Goulburn remarked caustically that the Irish leader was "playing his hand so as to be able to prove his loyalty." [13]

Yet the aim of O'Connell and his cohorts was not so much to prove their loyalty as to harass the Irish Government. And they succeeded. Anglesey, especially, was exasperated by their needling tactics, complaining to Peel in July 1828: "I am put into rather an awkward predicament by an application on the part of Mr. O'Connell for an audience. . . . I give you this information in advance, as I am aware that this occurrence may and probably will be in-

10. An irate Dublin Protestant noted: "The printing of and singing such songs under the effigy of His Majesty is calculated . . . to have two dangerous effects, namely, that of encouraging one Party in the idea that His Majesty is favorable to their views, and of creating a doubt in the minds of the other Party that the Royal House of Hanover is unfavorable to them." G. G. Gordon to Peel, Dec. 1, 1824, BM, PP, 40370, fol. 261.

11. Goulburn to Peel, Nov. 10, 1824, *ibid.*, 40330, fol. 175.

12. O'Connell to Plunket, March 7, 1826, Parker, *Peel, 1,* 409.

13. Goulburn to Wellesley, March 11, 1826, BM, WP, 37304.

sidiously commented upon." [14] The lord lieutenant's expectation was not disappointed: a few days later Gregory wrote to Peel: "The conference which O'Connell had with Lord Anglesea has created some jealousy. It is whispered that he was speaking of certain arrangements with regard to the Question." [15]

The purpose of the agitators was to keep the whispering alive, to make it appear that the government was in communication, if not in league, with them. Publicly in their meetings they lauded Anglesey and his chief secretary, Lord Francis Leveson Gower, both supporters of emancipation; O'Connell in August sent to Gower a letter "full of compliments and offering me information and assistance"; [16] and in the following month the association published an address proclaiming their determination to protect the lord lieutenant from the violence of the Orangemen. The result, as Gower admitted to Peel, was that "The High Protestant party believes that there is communication underhand between the Lord Lieutenant and the Agitators." While he pledged himself for "the entire falsity of this supposition, both with regard to the Lord Lieutenant and myself," [17] the chief secretary was afraid O'Connell would eventually "praise me out of office." [18] In November, when O'Connell again requested an interview, Gower quite lost his much-tried patience:

> I am harassed to death with the whole business, and particularly annoyed at this request on the part of Mr. O'Connell which for many reasons I think it mischievous to comply with, but at the same time there is I think no ground to refuse it. . . . One eternal prayer is dinned into my ears from morning till night, viz., for troops and magistrates and I have worn threadbare all the received forms of refusal. This ill-timed request of O'Connell's annoys me as much as all the rest, as I am convinced the mere circumstance of his obtaining an interview will have a bad public effect, but it is one of his means of annoyance.[19]

Gower expressed his vexation in many such letters to Peel and usually ended them with either repetition of his denial that he and his superior were taking sides with the Catholics or an assertion

14. Anglesey to Peel, July 26, 1828, BM, PP, 40325, foll. 146–147.
15. Gregory to Peel, Aug. 12, 1828, *ibid.,* 40334, fol. 237.
16. Gower to Peel, Aug. 20, 1828, *ibid.,* 40335, fol. 47.
17. Gower to Peel, Sept. 27, 1828, *ibid.,* foll. 172–173.
18. Gower to Peel, Oct. 7, 1828, *ibid.,* 40336, fol. 35.
19. Gower to Peel, Nov. 17, 1828, *ibid.,* foll. 127–128.

that it was one of O'Connell's purposes "to excite distrust of the Lord Lieutenant on your parts." [20] The chief secretary's assurances inspired little confidence; the tactics of the agitators were making the Irish Government suspect to the high Tory ministers of England as well as to the ultra-Protestants of Ireland.

The basic cause of the friction between the two governments was the existence of the Catholic Association. To most Englishmen, to all high Tories, and to the ultra-Protestants of Ireland, the association was symbolic of rebellion and of destruction of the Protestant constitution of "church and throne"; to supporters of the Catholic claims, Whigs, Canningites, Grenvillites, and liberal Protestants in Ireland, it was dramatic evidence of the necessity of granting emancipation before it was extorted by democrats and priests. Both sides were agreed on one point only: the body must be put down. The problem facing the pro-Catholic lords lieutenant was how to suppress it without inflicting a major setback to the Catholic cause; for Peel and the high Tories if suppressing the association meant a deathblow to that cause, so much the better.

There were three possible ways of proceeding against the Irish leaders: prosecute them collectively as an illegal organization, charge them individually with sedition, or enact new laws aimed specifically against them. The state of the law in 1823 was such that in order to prosecute the association the government had to prove that by performing an illegal act or a lawful act in an illegal way it was an unlawful assembly under the common law or that it contravened the Act of 1793 against representative societies. But in its constitution the association expressly disclaimed any representative or delegated character, and in all its proceedings its lawyer members were careful to forestall the slightest imputation of illegality. The government reporter who attended its meetings noted: "Many of the members are suspicious of each other and are constantly cautioned by Mr. O'Connell, whose eye is ever on the alert and whose apprehensions keep him perpetually at the task of restraining the members within limits. . . . They take every opportunity of saying that the Association is not a representative body." [21]

The Irish Government exercised a constant vigilance. It had in its employ a corps of informers as omnipresent and as active in the

20. Gower to Peel, Sept. 8, 1828, *ibid.*, 40335, fol. 8.

21. Report to the Head Office of Police, Dublin, Dec. 7, 1824, copy, ISPO, SCP, carton 47.

1820's as they had been in the 1790's.[22] The main field of their operations was secret societies and conspiracies among the peasantry, and although a few of them did recount in detail the parts taken by some members of the association in the rebellions of 1798 and 1803,[23] and although Gregory had one agent on a half-yearly pension who was an active member of the body,[24] they could furnish little information that was not already well known. The agitators boasted that all their proceedings were public and quickly challenged the slightest accusation of secrecy. It was fortunate that they did so, for from the beginning a reporter under orders of the police regularly attended their meetings.[25] Later Wellesley directed that a special agent be employed to make complete transcripts of the proceedings of each meeting and be prepared to verify them on oath.

Stephen Nolan Elrington, a reporter for *Saunder's News Letter*, was the first to hold the post, and for a little over a year his function was kept a strict secret. He generally spent four hours in attendance at each Catholic meeting, where he was known only as one of the newspapermen, and often six hours afterward in transcribing his reports for the government. In December 1825 Elrington's usefulness came to an end when Plunket had to produce him as a witness against O'Connell in the latter's indictment for sedition; thereafter he was branded "a wretched informer," lost his job on *Saunder's* through the influence of O'Connell and his friends, and was dropped by the Castle.[26] His place was taken by W. B. Gurney, a shorthand writer who, with the aid of two assistants, reported the remaining meetings of the association.[27] The government agents

22. ISPO, SCP, carton 47, 1823–32, contains many copies of informers' reports to James Tandy, chief magistrate of police in Dublin. They are signed only with various identifying symbols, such as ⊙, P, W, ≠, and ✕. The importance of these informers, as well as the efficiency of the system, is revealed in one of many letters from Gregory to Peel on the subject: "I am very sorry Q's name has been divulged; it was quite unnecessary; but it is the consequence of inferior agents wishing to make themselves of importance, and I suppose the Doctor has thought my absence a good opportunity of bringing himself into the notice of Lord Francis. Pray when you write to him, say how necessary it is that this man's name should be concealed; it has hitherto been unknown to all the Police of every description, and even to some of our Crown Lawyers." Gregory to Peel, Oct. 16, 1828, BM, PP, 40334, foll. 255–257.

23. Goulburn to Peel, Jan. 5 and July 22, 1825, *ibid.,* 40331.

24. Gregory to Peel, Feb. 4, 1825, *ibid.,* 40334, foll. 112–113. Gregory does not name him in the letter but was probably referring to F. W. Conway, editor of the Dublin *Evening Post.*

25. Wellesley to Peel, Nov. 2, 1823, copy, BM, WP, 37301, foll. 302–303.

26. Memorial of Elrington to Peel, Feb. 26, 1827, ISPO, CSORP, 1176/Whitehall 17.

27. Gurney was paid 23 shillings for each meeting he attended and 1 shilling per

forwarded their transcripts immediately to the Castle where they were read without delay by the lord lieutenant,[28] referred weekly to the law officers of the Crown in Ireland, and copies of the more important sent to Peel. Thus the proceedings received a thorough screening for the slightest evidence of illegality.

When the association was barely a month old, the solicitor general, Henry Joy, in answer to a request from Wellesley, delivered his opinion that the constitution of the new organization did not afford sufficient proof that it was to be a representative body.[29] Plunket, the attorney general, in England at the time, when consulted by Peel agreed with his colleague. Peel in conveying the information to Wellesley commented: "At present the duty of Government must be limited to keeping a strict watch on this association. . . . An interference without a strong assurance of a successful appeal to the law would evidently be impolitic, because the failure . . . must be injurious to the strength and character of the Executive Government." [30] Later Peel was to forget his own cautionary advice and to blame the Irish Government for making too much of the risk involved in prosecuting. In 1823 the association seemed far from formidable, and the Irish law officers, when asked a second time for their verdict, had to repeat that it violated no statute law.[31] The seriousness of the situation became apparent in the following year, with the launching of the Rent program. The crown lawyers were asked to write out another opinion and again declared that the association did not afford sufficient evidence of illegality: it was not representative so as to come under the terms of 33 Geo. III c. 29; it was not an unlawful debating society according to 60 Geo. III c. 6; and it did not so endanger the public peace as to be against the common law. When the matter was submitted also to the English law officers Copley and Wetherell, they concurred.[32]

The demagogues were guarding themselves too well against prosecution under the existing laws; it seemed that only a special act of Parliament would be able to get rid of them. Wellesley, close

folio page for his transcripts, an average of about £1,350 yearly. His transcripts from Sept. 1826 to Sept. 1827 totaled 51,746 pages. "W. B. Gurney's Account for Attending the Catholic Association," ISPO, OP II, 588/672/10.

28. That Wellesley performed this tedious task faithfully and scrupulously is evident from the many underscorings and comments with which he annotated suspect passages in the speeches of the agitators.

29. Joy to Wellesley, May 12, 1823, copy, BM, WP, 37301, foll. 57–58.

30. Peel to Wellesley, May 16, 1823, copy, BM, PP, 40324, foll. 156–159.

31. Wellesley to Peel, July 12, 1823, *ibid.*, 40611, foll. 54–67.

32. Wellesley to Peel, Nov. 30, 1824, BM, WP, 37303, foll. 9–15; Opinion of Copley and Wetherell, Dec. 20, 1824, *ibid.*, foll. 81–82.

to the scene, earlier anticipated this necessity than did Peel. In June 1823 he recommended legislation to put down the infant organization and early in 1824 sent over to the cabinet an outline of a bill for the purpose. Peel, arguing reasonably enough that it would be difficult, in the precarious state of the Catholic question, to get Parliament to act against such an insignificant body, advised the lord lieutenant that the existing laws were "sufficient to enable you to contend with any probable evil which may arise out of the proceedings of the association now sitting in Dublin." [33] Peel's error of judgment was short lived. A few months later he suggested to Goulburn that it might be prudent after all to amend and strengthen the law,[34] and within the year he wrote to Wellesley: "We cannot, however, reconcile it to our sense of duty to remain passive any longer, and to permit the functions of the Executive and Legislative Authorities of the State to be usurped by a body whose proceedings are at variance with every principle of the Constitution." [35] So belated an admission brought little satisfaction to Wellesley, piqued by Peel's disregarding his suggestions earlier in the year when, he noted ironically, he had "submitted to the judgment of superior wisdom and authority." [36] Peel, in his turn, resented a statement attributed to the lord lieutenant, "that *he* had not shrunk from vigorous measures, that the responsibility did not rest with him, that others had a different view of the danger." [37]

Regardless of personal recrimination, it was apparent by the close of 1824 that drastic steps were needed to rid Ireland of this incubus. To do nothing would increase the prestige of the thing; merely to abuse it in Parliament would invite retaliation, and "the association would beat us at the scolding match"; [38] the laws against political societies could not be brought to bear. Consequently on February 10, 1825, Goulburn in the House of Commons introduced his bill, curiously entitled indeed, "against unlawful societies in Ireland," whose main clause prohibited political bodies of longer duration than fourteen days. Goulburn's bill had a smooth passage. In the Commons only Brougham, Burdett, and

33. Peel to Wellesley, June 29, 1823, *ibid.*, 37301, foll. 154–156, in answer to Wellesley to Peel, June 22, 1823, copy, NL, WP, MSS 322.

34. Peel to Goulburn, April 14, 1824, copy, BM, PP, 40330, foll. 35–37.

35. Peel to Wellesley, Dec. 18, 1824, copy, NL, WP, MSS 322.

36. Wellesley to Peel, Nov. 20, 1824, BM, PP, 40330, foll. 205–206.

37. Peel to Goulburn, Nov. 2, 1824, copy, *ibid.*, foll. 161–162. Goulburn, in another example of faction play within Dublin Castle, consoled Peel with the remark that Wellesley "is always the first to impute the difficulty to others." Goulburn to Peel, Nov. 8, 1824, *ibid.*, fol. 173.

38. Peel to Goulburn, Nov. 6, 1824, copy, *ibid.*, foll. 163–167.

Mackintosh spoke forcefully against it; the rest of the opposition gave it every facility in order to make way for Burdett's emancipation bill; and the most prominent advocates of the Catholics, Canning and Plunket, actually spoke in favor of suppression.

Goulburn's act soon proved ineffective. O'Connell redeemed his promise of driving a coach-and-six through the "Algerine Act" by reconstituting the association nominally as a nonpolitical society. In 1828 when Goulburn's act was due to expire and the agitation was more virulent than ever, Anglesey predicted that even if the law were renewed, improved, and rendered perfect, he would back O'Connell's and Sheil's evasions against the ingenuity of the crown lawyers.[39] Peel glumly summed up the situation: "We cannot deny that the law has been on the Statute Book three years, and that the Catholic Association exists apparently in defiance of it, without any abatement of violence, . . ." [40] The law was not renewed, and its lapse terminated the sole experiment of the government with special legislation.

The effort was itself a source of increased friction between the English and Irish administrations. In a memorandum for the cabinet in March 1828 Peel remarked: "It certainly does appear to me that the position of the Government in abandoning the Law without having made a trial of it is a very embarrassing one. . . . I think the worst part of the case of the Executive Government is that it has remained a quiet spectator of the increasing evil, and that it has been too much afraid of the possible failure of an attempt to enforce the law." [41] Peel implied that the fault lay mainly with the Irish Government, and he had some justification for the charge. Wellesley and Plunket in 1826 and 1827 hesitated to commit themselves. The latter, in a private letter to Canning in December 1825, while admitting there were grounds for prosecuting the new association, asserted that such action would only reinvigorate it.[42]

Expediency was the excuse now used by the pro-Catholic members of the Irish Government: when the agitation was at a low ebb they argued that interference would revive it; when it was strong they feared there was little chance of a favorable verdict against it. They were, indeed, not solely responsible for such a dilatory

39. Anglesey to William Lamb, March 20, 1828, *Peel Memoirs, 1,* 23–24.

40. Peel to Lamb, March 31, 1828, *ibid., 1,* 30.

41. Memorandum of Peel for the cabinet on the Catholic question, March 31, 1828, copy, BM, PP, 40430, foll. 4–9.

42. Plunket to Canning, Dec. 18, 1825, in David Plunket, ed., *The Life, Letters, and Speeches of Lord Plunket* (London, 1867), *2,* 224–226.

policy. In England the law officers sometimes proved even more reluctant than their Irish colleagues to recommend prosecution. In January 1826 Plunket and Joy delivered a judgment that a Catholic meeting advertised for the following week would contravene Goulburn's act; they cautioned, nevertheless, that their opinion was exposed to doubt and that a jury conviction was uncertain.[43] In England when Copley and Wetherell hesitated to pronounce the intended assembly illegal,[44] Lord Liverpool summoned a special cabinet meeting. Peel sent to Wellesley the cabinet's decision: "We are disposed to think that, on account of its declining authority, it would not be advisable at the present moment to interfere with it [the association], either by direct proceedings or by the solemn admonition of a proclamation." [45] The recommendation of the cabinet, coupled with the reluctance of the English crown lawyers even to judge the intended meeting illegal as the Irish law officers had done, was ample excuse for caution. In the opinion of the lord lieutenant Peel had no reason for complaint if his own advisers favored winking at the association. But the body soon did grow in importance.

The election successes of 1826 brought Plunket face to face with the old dilemma: the new association appeared to be identifying itself completely with the old one and daily violating Goulburn's act, but to proceed against the members would be "to prosecute the Roman Catholic people, who from head to foot make common cause with them." [46] In November when Wellesley again requested a formal opinion, his law officers, replying that the association was an illegal assembly, advised that the difficulty of obtaining a verdict made a prosecution imprudent. This time the English lawyers agreed that the organization was unlawful, although they gave no opinion regarding the expediency of acting against it. Even Goulburn, hastily consulted by Peel, feared that a prosecution would only strengthen the association.[47] The coincidence of his opinion, as Canning remarked after seeing the whole correspondence on the matter, with that of the "Catholic" members of the Irish Government appeared to set the matter at rest.[48]

When Wellesley quit Ireland at the end of 1827, he had some reason to feel that responsibility for toleration did not lie solely

43. Copy of opinion of Plunket and Joy, Jan. 8, 1826, NL, WP, MSS 322.
44. Peel to Eldon, Jan. 6, 1826, BM, PP, 40315, fol. 234.
45. Peel to Wellesley, Jan. 3, 1826, BM, WP, 37304, foll. 1–6.
46. Plunket to Canning, Oct. 10, 1826, *Life of Plunket, 2,* 235.
47. Goulburn to Peel, Dec. 17, 1826, Parker, *Peel, 1,* 429–431.
48. Canning to Peel, Dec. 28, 1826, BM, PP, 40311, fol. 215.

or even mainly with himself. His early draft of a bill against the association was rejected, and later, when English ministers finally recognized the necessity of special legislation, his suggestions were considerably softened down to make the bill palatable to Parliament. When Plunket was attacked in the House of Commons for his ill-fated prosecution of O'Connell, not a voice was raised in his defense, an experience that taught him caution for the future. Finally, English ministers and law officers had concurred with their Irish colleagues in the instances when a proposed prosecution was abandoned. In fact Peel, a few days before leaving office in 1827, declared in the House of Commons that the cabinet had entirely approved the conduct of the Irish Government toward the Catholic Association; for their forebearance he took his full share of responsibility.[49] In private, while still at the Home Office, he had been more specific. Constantly badgered by Lord Eldon's insistence that in his day things would have been different, Peel summarized the difficulties of the situation:

> If the Roman Catholic Association has not been prosecuted, I consider if any blame attaches for the forbearance, that the Government of Ireland and the Government of England, and certainly the Secretary of State for the Home Department, are quite as subject to that blame as any other persons. But I am by no means prepared to admit that blame does attach. The degree of influence which such a body as the Roman Catholic Association possesses, the chance of increasing it by prosecution, the consequences of failure in such prosecution, the effect of a judicial declaration that the Society prosecuted does not offend against the law, are all matters to be maturely weighed before the Government commits itself to legal proceedings.[50]

Lord Anglesey inherited the problem that had plagued Lord Wellesley. When, soon after his arrival in Dublin, the association announced its new program of appointing churchwardens, the series of legal consultations began all over again, this time at the instigation of Peel and Wellington. The Irish law officers could find no legal objection to the churchwarden scheme,[51] and once again the matter was dropped, much to the relief of the new lord lieu-

49. Memorandum of Wellesley, n.d., 1827, prepared in consequence of his being desired to show why he did not put down the Catholic Association, BM, WP, 37305.
50. Peel to Eldon, March 10, 1827, copy, BM, PP, 40315, foll. 295–296.
51. Joy to William Lamb, May 8, 1828, PRO, HO, 100/224.

tenant, whose growing sympathy for the Catholic cause made him increasingly reluctant to act against an organization which was the strongest argument for concession. For his part he saw only three alternatives open to the government: to try to ignore the whole thing, to grant emancipation, or to crush the association and the power of the priests. The first was impossible, the third impractical unless habeas corpus was suspended, the country put under martial law, and all liberty of speech and of public meeting suppressed, a course to which the House of Commons would never consent unless there was actual rebellion in Ireland. The second was the only prudent policy.[52]

From a viceroy with such convictions, Wellington and Peel could expect little cooperation. In October the Duke, while admitting privately the hopelessness of putting down the association,[53] urged that one last attempt be made. "If the effort succeeds," he wrote to Peel, "we shall be masters of the game. If it should fail, Parliament and the country will see what it is they have to deal with."[54] Peel immediately relayed the Duke's advice to the viceroy, and the legal machinery was set in motion. After reading the transcripts of the association's meetings for the past six months, the Irish law officers gave their formal opinion that the assembly had violated the Convention Act of 1793 by exercising an authority to represent the Catholics of Ireland. Still they advised against a prosecution: the case would have to come before a jury and, in addition, the branch of the act prohibiting organizations from assuming a representative character had never undergone any judicial determination.[55] Once again Peel consulted the English crown lawyers. They were even more hesitant: "Although it might be justified in law we conceive it would be too hazardous for the Executive Government to take such a step . . ."[56] There ended the matter, except for the unpleasant duty of telling the King that it was inexpedient "in the present state of the Law to commit the Government in a contest with the Association."[57]

Prosecution of the organization itself was not the only resource considered by the authorities. In December 1824 Peel counseled Wellesley that since the association could not be prosecuted or dis-

52. Anglesey to Gower, July 3, 1828, BM, PP, 40335, foll. 18–20.

53. Wellington to Dean Phillpotts, Oct. 18, 1828, *Wellington Despatches, 5,* 145–146.

54. Wellington to Peel, Oct. 21, 1828, *ibid., 5,* 152.

55. Opinion of the law officers of Ireland, Nov. 17, 1828, *Peel Memoirs, 1,* 247–252.

56. Opinion of the law officers of England, Dec. 10, 1828, *ibid., 1,* 255.

57. Peel to George IV, Dec. 14, 1828, copy, BM, PP, 40300, foll. 267–268.

persed, "it appears to be of great importance that if a proper opportunity should occur of prosecuting an individual, either for delivering or for publishing a speech . . . such an opportunity should not be lost." [58] A few days before Peel's letter reached Dublin, O'Connell, expressing publicly his confidence that Ireland would soon be restored to her rights, warned that if she were eventually driven mad by persecution he hoped, "a new Bolívar . . . may arise and that the spirit of the Greeks and of the South Americans may animate the people of Ireland." [59] The Irish Government instantly seized on the words as seditious libel, arrested O'Connell, and indicted him, only to have its case dismissed by a Protestant grand jury eager thereby to embarrass Wellesley and Plunket.

When the next opportunity presented itself, the viceroy and his attorney general showed that they had learned a lesson from the incident. In October 1826 Sheil publicly attacked the Duke of York, with bitter condemnation of his personal life as well as his fanatical opposition to the Catholic claims. The vilification of his brother incensed the King, who sent off to Peel an angry letter complaining of the silence of the Irish Government and directing an immediate prosecution of Sheil.[60] Only with difficulty could Peel persuade his impetuous sovereign, on the advice of the lord lieutenant and the law officers of both islands, that although the speech was, indeed, libelous, a public prosecution might well embarrass the ailing Duke and his friends. Once again the norm was expediency and an opportunity for vigorous action was abandoned, mainly on the responsibility, as Peel admitted to Eldon, of the English Government.[61]

Within a few months Sheil again became a target. Using the occasion of a speech on the Memoirs of Wolfe Tone to remind the government of the horrors of civil war, he made his words more a threat than a warning. Wellesley desired an immediate prosecution. Plunket, more wary, refused to comply until he had the opinion of the English law officers, a condition which Goulburn, as usual, denounced to Peel as merely another maneuver of the attorney general to appease his Catholic friends, to whom he could plead, if the prosecution was successful, the compulsion of the British Government.[62] The English lawyers did concur. The cabinet, with the notable exception of Canning, who held that the seditious nature

58. Peel to Wellesley, Dec. 18, 1824, copy, NL, WP, MSS 322.
59. Meeting of Dec. 16, 1824, ISPO, CAP.
60. George IV to Peel, Oct. 16, 1826, BM, PP, 40300, foll. 161–162.
61. Peel to Eldon, March 10, 1827, copy, *ibid.*, 40315, foll. 295–296.
62. Goulburn to Peel, Jan. 24, 1827, *ibid.*, 40332, foll. 264–265.

of the speech would be hard to prove, likewise were for vigorous action. But once more the play of politics on the Catholic question intervened. Within a few weeks Canning was prime minister, Plunket promoted to the peerage, and Sheil's prosecution quietly dropped.

The Irish leaders soon resumed their violent language with greater confidence from the failure of past attempts to silence them and from a knowledge of the definite pro-Catholic sympathies of the new lord lieutenant, Anglesey. In July 1828 when Peel suggested that renewed attention be paid to Sheil and his inflammatory speeches, Anglesey coolly replied that his law officers agreed with him in considering the speeches, remarkably mischievous though they were, artfully guarded against prosecution, "and there I conceive ends the question." [63] Anglesey was more blunt than his predecessor, and more intractable. When Peel suggested the arrest of John Lawless, the firebrand of the Corn Exchange, for his rabid speeches in the North of Ireland, Anglesey replied that he doubted whether "in the present inflammable state of the country it will be advisable to prosecute." [64] But Peel insisted, and he was supported by Wellington and the King. The former, exasperated by the inertia of the lord lieutenant, declared himself "for the prosecution of everybody that can be prosecuted." [65] Lawless was arrested, held for a short time, released, and never brought to trial.

By the end of 1828 the efforts to suppress the organization in Ireland had succeeded only in increasing the friction between the governments of the two islands. One final, dramatic incident was to bring into the open the rift between the two. On December 4, 1828, the Catholic primate, Archbishop Curtis, resumed his correspondence with his old friend, the Duke of Wellington. He was prompted, he wrote, to break his three years' silence by the rumor that the Duke meant to have the Catholic question finally settled.[66] Wellington's reply a week later contained the remarkable sentence, "I am sincerely anxious to witness a settlement of the Roman Catholic question." [67] Curtis, amazed and elated at receiving such a frank answer "from a Prime Minister said to be so closely buttoned up and reserved," professed a desire to keep the contents of the letter as secret as possible. But he showed it to a few friends who had

63. Anglesey to Peel, July 20, 1828, *Peel Memoirs, 1,* 157.
64. Anglesey to Peel, Sept. 30, 1828, BM, PP, 40326, foll. 131–132.
65. Wellington to Peel, Oct. 14, 1828, *ibid.,* 40308, fol. 11.
66. Curtis to Wellington, Dec. 4, 1828, *Wellington Despatches, 5,* 308–309.
67. Wellington to Curtis, Dec. 11, 1828, *ibid., 5,* 326.

in the first place urged his writing to the Duke [68] and permitted transcripts to be sent to O'Connell and Sheil, on condition that they should not be published. Even Lord Anglesey learned of the letter and asked for a copy.[69]

Someone along the ever-lengthening line of confidants [70] now decided to make capital of the Duke's indiscretion. The letter appeared in the Dublin *Evening Post* on December 23. The cat was out of the bag and squalling through Dublin when it was suddenly forgotten amid a greater commotion. On December 25 Anglesey wrote privately to Curtis to express his surprise and satisfaction on learning, at long last, Wellington's real intentions and to urge that the Catholics be united and firm in their demands. The business of letter writing to the rather sheepish Dr. Curtis was now becoming almost a comedy, working up to a melodramatic denouement. On the very day that the lord lieutenant wrote his letter, Wellington, out of all patience with what he considered the maladministration of Ireland, proposed to the King his recall. The rumor sped across to Dublin. Anglesey, fuming at the disgrace, agreed to have his letter to Curtis made public. It appeared in the newspapers on the first day of the new year; the open break between viceroy and prime minister was on everyone's lips, in Dublin, in Ireland, and soon in England; and Peel, when he formally communicated the order for his recall, advanced as the reason Anglesey's letter to the Primate.[71] It was really a pretext. The move had been under consideration for months and only delayed for fear of the disturbance it would create in Ireland.

The indiscretion of both Wellington and Anglesey and the removal of the latter were merely the culmination of long standing disagreement. In one final, revealing letter, to his friend Huskisson, the ex-viceroy summed up his version of the affair: "You are the older politician, but I am the older soldier. You was caught in a trap. But I would *not* be *driven* to resign. Indeed I have too much identified myself with this people to abandon them in a difficulty. I bore much and would have borne more for their sakes, but I have

68. Curtis to Archbishop Murray, Dec. 15, 1828, AHD, Murray Papers.

69. Curtis to Murray, Dec. 24, 1828, *ibid.*

70. Curtis suspected it was O'Connell. Curtis to Murray, Jan. 6, 1829, *ibid.*

71. Peel to Anglesey, Jan. 10, 1829, copy, BM, PP, 40326, fol. 181. In a letter to the chief secretary, Peel, the statesman caught between two irascible soldiers, remarked: "I was surprised I confess by Lord Anglesey's letter to Dr. Curtis, . . . I was almost as much surprised when I read for the first time in its printed form the Duke's letter to the same Reverend Divine. I say this to you of course in strict confidence." Peel to Gower, Jan. 6, 1829, copy, *ibid.*, 40336, foll. 199–200.

been relieved from a distracting dilemma." [72] Yet the dilemma remained. George IV in 1827 had querulously demanded of the Duke of Newcastle, "Why do you suffer the damned Association in Dublin?" [73] The answer was not easy. Even Lord Eldon would have found it difficult to convince the King that Irish clamor could not be hushed by suppressing one organization; another, as actually happened, would rise immediately in its place, so long as liberty of public meeting remained in Ireland.

In the home island, also, administrators felt the pressure of the Catholic Association. Emancipation had long been an acute issue in British politics.[74] Differences of opinion on the question among ministers in the same cabinet were characteristic of every administration since the Union, and so evenly balanced were the numbers and talents of "Protestants" and "Catholics" that it had been found impossible to maintain an exclusive government, one whose members were united on the basis of either resistance or concession. The high Tories, clinging tenaciously to the penal code and the old commercial and representative systems, resisted all change, while liberal Tories, Canningites, and Grenvillites, advocating administrative and legal reform, emancipation, and free trade, maintained a resolute opposition only to parliamentary reform.

In 1812 both factions were united under Lord Liverpool in a restoration of the old "church and king" party of Pitt. Liverpool, belonging to neither wing, held important tenets of both. He was able to keep the precarious allegiance of such ultras as Eldon, Wellington, Bathurst, Westmorland, and the heir to the throne, the Duke of York, by sharing with them the conviction that English rule in Ireland was founded on Protestantism, that however useful for propaganda purposes the ancient bugbear of Catholic dual loyalty and the Pope's political power, what Catholic Emancipation really implied was a first step toward separation of the two

72. Anglesey to Huskisson, Jan. 3, 1829, BM, Huskisson Papers, 38757, foll. 177–178.

73. Entry of March 27, 1827, *Diary and Correspondence of Lord Colchester, 3*, 473.

74. The Catholic question played a prominent part in six of the eight cabinet changes from 1800 to 1829: in 1801 Pitt resigned because of the King's opposition to emancipation; in 1804 Addington resigned because his government was too weak without Pitt; in 1807 the Grenville ministry refused to pledge itself to resist emancipation and resigned; in 1809 the Whigs and Grenvillites rejected an invitation of Perceval to join the government on account of the same pledge; and in 1827 and 1828 the Catholic question presented the major difficulty in the forming of Canning's ministry and the main reason for the collapse of Goderich's.

islands and an Ireland ruled by priests, in which English power would be broken forever and from which a horde of demagogues would descend yearly on Westminster. On the other hand, Liverpool sheltered under his benign mantle liberal Tories like Canning and Huskisson, whose foreign and commercial policies he championed against the ultras.

For fifteen years Liverpool held together the Tory party by offering a compromise on the Catholic question, leaving it to its fate in a House of Commons where the anti-Catholics could command a slight majority and permitting all government supporters to speak and vote upon it as they chose. Thus were the Canningites and Grenvillites wooed from flirtation with the Whigs, the men who would have surrendered to Napoleon, who would now let in popery, who identified themselves with the unseemly democracy of the Radicals. It was an uneasy alliance to be sure. The appointment of Wellesley as Irish viceroy in 1821, intended as a gesture of appeasement toward the Grenvillites, who for the past two years had been hovering between Tory and Whig, raised qualms in high Tory hearts, as did another scent of a "Catholic" plot two years later when Canning visited Wellesley in Dublin, a trip the ever suspect foreign minister was permitted to undertake only after a promise of good behavior. Wellesley was succeeded in 1828 by Anglesey, "a true Protestant" as the King mistakenly thought. When Anglesey was recalled the emancipation problem had assumed such proportions that Wellington confided to Peel: "The whole question of Anglesey's successor turns upon the Roman Catholic Question. If we are to concede we may find one qualified." [75]

It was the Catholic Association that brought things to such a pass. Even Canning admitted that the association was "the most difficult problem that a Government ever had to deal with." [76] As early as 1824 George IV, viewing the proceedings of this hornets' nest as little short of rebellion, threatened that if they continued he would no longer consent to emancipation being left an open question. "This indulgence," he wrote to Peel, "was originally granted on the ground of political expediency, but that expediency dissolves when threatened rebellion calls upon the King for that which the King never will grant." [77] George, blustering as usual, allowed himself to be mollified by the suppression of the association in 1825. He knew that even the astute Lord Liverpool could

75. Wellington to Peel, Dec. 30, 1828, BM, PP, 40308, fol. 122.
76. Canning to Peel, Nov. 6, 1824, Parker, *Peel, 1,* 345.
77. George IV to Peel, Nov. 19, 1824, BM, PP, 40300, foll. 17–18.

not, if he would, form a stable government exclusively of the ultras.[78]

In February 1827 a stroke of paralysis incapacitated the prime minister and brought a sudden end to the fifteen years' truce. Canning, after much jockeying, was summoned to form a government. When Peel and Wellington, followed by five other high Tory former ministers,[79] refused to serve under him, he was forced into a shaky coalition with the Whigs. But in August Canning was dead. Goderich barely succeeded in holding together the fast disintegrating coalition for a few more months, until in January 1828 it collapsed. Into the breach stepped the Iron Duke, with a ministry containing at first the remnant of the Canningite "Catholics" [80] and later almost all "Protestants." [81] It seemed at long last that the King had an exclusive government. Yet, paradoxically, it was this "Protestant" ministry that was to carry emancipation, a phenomenon of which Peel, describing in a "most private" letter to his old friend in Dublin Castle, Gregory, the depressing state of affairs, gave a melancholy prediction:

> You and I have seen bad times in Ireland, but I quite agree with you, we never saw anything like the present. The radical evil is, and has long been, a divided Government, but what are you to do, when the House of Commons votes 276 to 272 on the Catholic Question? The House of Commons is in as unsatisfactory a state as the Government. Neither party is strong enough to carry anything. The consequence is inaction and passiveness on the part of the Protestants and growing strength and triumph on the part of the Catholics. It is quite clear that this cannot long last.[82]

78. The Catholic question threatened even the stability of Liverpool's compromise government. After the elections of 1826, although the ministry came back with an increased majority, the division between high and liberal Tory was more pronounced than ever. The great Tory peers grumbled at the administration, and Liverpool expected the Catholic issue to lead to the government's dissolution in the next session.

79. Eldon, Westmorland, Bathurst, Melville, and Bexley.

80. Huskisson, Dudley, Palmerston, Grant, and Lamb.

81. Huskisson, the leader of the Canningites, considered himself "very uncourteously turned out" by Wellington: "Our majority (an unexpected blow) on the Catholic question and other proceedings had created great soreness; and there were not wanting those who were constantly at work to foster the irritation. The Duke and Peel felt they were, by their moderation, losing all hold over the Ultras, and I must suppose that, on their parts, I was the victim of which the sacrifice would appease their wrath." Huskisson to Anglesey, May 26, 1828, copy, BM, Huskisson Papers, 38756, foll. 175–177.

82. Peel to Gregory, Aug. 26, 1828, BM, PP, 40334, foll. 238–241.

Peel, more than the other ministers, felt the weight of the Irish problem. From 1812 to 1818 as chief secretary for Ireland he had studied at first hand the mazes of the eternal Irish question.[83] From 1823 to 1829, with the exception of ten months, he received as home secretary weekly reports of the proceedings of the association and carried on a voluminous correspondence with Irish officials, of a formal nature with the lords lieutenant and confidentially with the chief and undersecretaries.[84] The responsibility was exhausting. Habitually cool, precise, methodical, with a genius for administration and a proud self-consciousness of the reputation he had earned as "the manly Peel," he sometimes, in more irritating moments, showed the strain: Sheil, on one occasion having accused Peel of intolerance, was guilty of "a damned lie"; O'Connell was a "cowardly scoundrel," and for his true character Peel had "very unfeigned contempt." [85] Such confessions of exasperation, had they been known to the Irish leaders, would have been as gratifying as were the public indications that they were a sore trial to the government. It was their aim to irritate, to confuse, to embarrass, to exasperate, in short, to make their very existence unbearable.

One of the first grievances taken up by the association was the legislation prohibiting priests from officiating at the burial of their parishioners in what had once been Catholic but were now Protestant cemeteries. In February 1824 when Sir John Newport presented one of the many petitions against the laws and moved for an inquiry into the subject, he caused a hurried exchange of letters among Peel, Goulburn, Wellesley, and Plunket. Peel, as home secretary and leader of the House of Commons, taken by surprise by Newport's motion, wrote immediately to John Leslie Foster for information on "this embarrassing question . . . with the agitation of which we are now threatened." [86] One of the laws, that of William III preventing Catholics from burying in the yards of suppressed monasteries, was repealed, but only, as Canning remarked to Peel two years later when the same question returned

83. As chief secretary Peel, while attempting to reform the abuses of the Castle system, sufficiently conformed to the idea that Ireland could not be governed without bribery and jobs to practice corruption, as the only means of maintaining the indispensable Protestant ascendancy. But he did so in a thoroughly disinterested spirit, for the benefit solely of the government and his party.

84. Almost daily letters passed between Peel and Lord Gower, the chief secretary, in 1828.

85. Peel to Gregory, Dec. 8, 1824; to Colonel Brown, Dec., n.d., 1825; to Vesey Fitzgerald, Oct. 16, 1828, copies, BM, PP, 40334, 40383, and 40322.

86. Peel to Foster, Feb. 10, 1824, RIA, Peel Letters to J. L. Foster.

to annoy Parliament, after causing "us so much trouble and difficulty." [87]

The burial question was only a phase of the running attack on the Irish church establishment. In 1825 when Joseph Hume was fulminating against that institution in the Commons, Sir Henry Parnell managed to persuade the Irish hornets to be silent on the issue, but in 1828 they again stung the government by flooding Parliament with petitions in favor of the dissenters. The repeal of the Test and Corporation acts was in effect a sort of minor victory for the Catholics; the measure was a liberal one; and Wellington's ministry, after opposing it in the lower house and being defeated there by a majority of forty-four, did not resign.

In the foreign as well as in the home department Irish clamor created difficulties. Strategically Ireland has always been England's Achilles' heel, and the frequent appeals of the association to foreign sympathy, the interest and financial aid aroused by it in Europe and in America, and the articles in the foreign press describing the woeful state of the Irish and likening their struggle to that of the Greeks and the South Americans, could not but disturb English ministers.[88] Moreover, attempts to silence the disaffected Irish had unpleasant repercussions. The selection of O'Connell's Bolívar speech for prosecution was a particularly unhappy choice since it occurred at a time when Canning, as foreign secretary, was trying to convert the King and the high Tories to his policy of recognizing the result of Bolívar's rebellion, the new republic of Colombia.[89] George IV, while extremely eager to punish O'Connell, did not see much consistency in the prosecution considering the line the government was about to take respecting the South American colonies.[90] Liverpool, Wellington, and Peel all admitted that the words selected for prosecution were most unfortunate, but they could not refuse to back up the Irish Government.[91] Peel, nevertheless, noted that Canning had written to the

87. Canning to Peel, May 26, 1826, BM, PP, 40311, foll. 178–181.

88. Canning complained that the appeals of the association to foreign sympathy would injure the prospects of pro-Catholic candidates in the English elections of 1826. Canning to Plunket, Dec. 13, 1825, *Life of Plunket, 2,* 221–223.

89. Only a few months previously Wellington had warned Canning against encouraging insurrection in the Spanish colonies as a bad example to Ireland. Wellington to Canning, June 12, 1824, *Wellington Despatches, 2,* 277–278.

90. Wellington to Peel, Dec. 26, 1824, BM, PP, 40306, foll. 99–101; Peel to Liverpool, Dec. 30, 1824, *ibid.,* 40304, foll. 328–329.

91. Liverpool resolved the difficulty in a typical but curious manner: "I am sure we must prosecute O'Connell, and the reasons for acknowledging Bolívar are much stronger than before the prosecution was thought of, for giving up the recognition

lord lieutenant to tell him that if Bolívar's expedition to Peru was successful, the British Government meant to recognize Colombia; with this knowledge counsel at O'Connell's trial might avoid in their speeches matter which would be indiscreet.[92] The trial never came off, and thus what might have developed into a highly distasteful incident was accidentally averted.[93]

Still the Bolívar affair taught a lesson in caution. Two years later when the question arose of prosecuting Sheil for a speech in which he indirectly threatened the government with rebellion and foreign invasion, Wellesley hesitated to act on his own authority and submitted the matter to the home secretary with the comment: "For however atrocious the libel certainly is in every view, it may perhaps appear to those in His Majesty's Councils, who are best qualified to form a correct judgment on the matter, that such a prosecution might not be advisable in the present state of our foreign relations." [94] Canning was the minister best qualified, and he advised against a prosecution because, even though the general effect of Sheil's speech was "to suggest to France the facility of an invasion of Ireland," it would be hard to prove that such was his intention. In addition, there was the dangerous construction that was apt to be made in France if Sheil was acquitted.[95] So delicate was the bearing of the Irish problem on British foreign relations that ministers thought twice before taking even such a seemingly minor step as a prosecution. Their hesitancy gave the law officers of Ireland a welcome excuse for not proceeding more vigorously against the association: "Individual members in speeches have afforded just grounds for prosecution. Yet because this thing has ceased to be of local importance only but is of imperial concern we have often not acted where our action might have embarrassed the Government or been against its policy." [96]

The burial question, the petitions in favor of the dissenters, and the relation of the Irish struggle to foreign policy were sources of petty aggravation. More disturbing was the threat that the

. . . would be to consider Bolívar as great a traitor as O'Connell and to avow this was our opinion." Liverpool to Peel, Dec. 31, 1824, BM, PP, 40304, foll. 330–331.

92. Peel to Goulburn, Dec. 27, 1824, copy, *ibid.*, foll. 342–346.

93. Plunket was quite content. He had feared that the prosecution "may force on the notice of other countries the unsettled state of Ireland." Plunket to the Duke of Buckingham, Jan. 9, 1825, in Duke of Buckingham and Chandos, *Memoirs of the Court of George IV, 1820–1830* (London, 1859), *2*, 194.

94. Wellesley to Peel, Jan. 25, 1827, BM, PP, 40324, fol. 283.

95. Canning to Peel, Jan. 29, 1827, *ibid.*, 40311, foll. 226–227.

96. Opinion of Joy and Doherty, sent to Anglesey Nov. 17, 1828, *ibid.*, 40326, foll. 154–158.

Irish leaders might extend their program to include two objectives more serious even than emancipation: parliamentary reform and repeal of the Union.

During the 1820's the movement for parliamentary reform was practically stagnant in England. There were no county associations, no corresponding societies, no Hampden clubs to register organized protest against an allegedly corrupt electoral system and an unrepresentative House of Commons. Across the Irish Sea the voice of the radical reformer was not quite so feeble, and there were signs that there the movement might once more be reinvigorated. Indeed, emancipation and reform had been linked once before, by the United Irishmen from whom O'Connell and his middle-class confrères inherited their tradition of political radicalism. In 1817 reform meetings had been held in Cork, Castlebar, and Belfast, while in Dublin O'Connell had helped found a short-lived society of Friends of Reform in Parliament, at a meeting of which he declared that every man should have the vote. Two years later an appeal from Henry Hunt to O'Connell and the Irish Catholics to join forces with the English Radicals went unanswered, but early in 1821 O'Connell stated in a public letter that it was "the extreme of folly and absurdity to imagine that an unreformed Parliament would or could consent to give us relief." [97] He urged his readers to petition no longer for emancipation but for reform.

With the founding of the association there were indications that the body might include reform in its demands. Some of the early petitions requested disfranchisement of Irish rotten borough corporations, and O'Connell more than once recommended that the Irish Catholics be brought to act with the reformers of England, a proposal to which the aristocracy and gentry, some of the wealthier merchants, and Sheil objected. It soon became evident that rather than risk the danger of breaking up the new organization over the issue, the members were prepared to use reform merely as a threat. Some of them, especially John Lawless, frequently argued the futility of seeking emancipation from an unreformed legislature, but in November 1824 when the London *Courier* was condemning the association as a hotbed of radicalism, O'Connell went out of his way to protest that there was no danger of the Irish people being driven "into the ranks of the real Radicals." [98] Even when Bentham subscribed to the Rent and sent a letter urging the necessity of reform, O'Connell disregarded the advice and in a

97. *Catholic Advocate,* Jan. 14, 1821.
98. *DEP,* Nov. 25, 1824.

speech praising the master alluded only to his great project for codification of the law.[99] Two weeks later, with his eye on the approaching discussion of the Catholic question in Parliament, O'Connell so far retraced his steps as to declare: "It was a rank falsehood that reform was any part of their object." [100] His mercurial statements on the subject were, perhaps, only additional proof of his confirmed Benthamism. The great objective was emancipation. If and when the threat of reform aided the cause, he declared himself a reformer.

In 1825 O'Connell's willingness to compromise led him into a trap. By agreeing to disfranchisement of the Irish forty-shilling freeholders he brought down upon himself the denunciation of English and Irish reformers. Cobbett, previously an ally, turned on him savagely; [101] in Ireland the radical members of the association, led by Lawless and George Ensor, an Irish Protestant, kept up a running newspaper and pamphlet attack on him for his apostasy. In a feeble effort to undo the damage O'Connell hastily reasserted that he was "a Parliamentary Reformer of that class called Radicals," [102] but he did not read his final recantation until after the Waterford election. Even then he was cautious, or wily. During the whole of 1827 the association coyly avoided the reform question out of deference to Canning and Goderich, until, with Wellington and Peel once more in office, the motive for restraint vanished. Early in 1828 when O'Connell proposed that the association go on record as advocating parliamentary reform, the conservatives, led by Lord Killeen, succeeded in shelving his motion, but only after a long, heated debate in which Killeen caustically observed: "It was not two months ago when a resolution somewhat similar had been brought forward by Mr. Lawless and it was with difficulty he could find a seconder. Now this motion was numerously and he confessed ably supported. Then, he was aware, there was an administration friendly, there was now one inimical to the Catholics." [103]

Within a few months the Clare election provoked additional and more emphatic declarations in favor of reform. On the hustings O'Connell promised that if returned he would support "every meas-

99. *Ibid.,* Dec. 24, 1824.

100. Meeting of Jan. 8, 1825, ISPO, CAP.

101. *Cobbett's Extraordinary Address to the People of Ireland* (pamphlet, London, 1825).

102. O'Connell at a meeting of the English Catholic Association in London, May 21, 1825. Henry Hunt also addressed the meeting but was halted by the chairman, the Duke of Norfolk, when he advocated reform. London *Morning Chronicle,* May 23, 1825.

103. Meeting of Feb. 13, 1828, ISPO, CAP.

ure favourable to radical Reform in the representative system, so that the House of Commons may truly . . . represent all the People." [104] He was fast burning bridges. Alarmed, some of the "Catholics" in Parliament induced Lord Rossmore to send to the new member for Clare "a hint which all your friends here agree in. They do not think the time is arrived for its being necessary that a man should declare himself a reformer. He may do so hereafter, but they think it injures the cause greatly here at present and prevents them from being of the use they otherwise could." [105]

The association ignored the hint. In the pledges which it drew up for submission to all future Irish parliamentary candidates it included one to support constitutional reform. The word *constitutional* had been substituted for *radical* as a last minute concession to the conservatives, but in an exchange of letters between Henry Hunt and O'Connell to which it gave rise the Irishman avowed that he looked to universal suffrage, biennial parliaments, and the ballot.[106] The change of words also elicited a mild lecture from Bentham who, although he realized the phrase *constitutional reform* was intended merely for public consumption, warned O'Connell that any reform that was not *radical* was moderate, and a moderate reform was a Whig reform.[107] This time O'Connell heeded Bentham. In a speech at the annual dinner of the East London Catholic Institute, February 25, 1829, he repeated his demands for manhood suffrage, frequent parliaments, and the ballot. The speech immediately reconciled Cobbett, who declared renewed devotion to the Irish leader in a public letter to the *Morning Herald*.[108]

Radical or constitutional, the terms were of less significance than the fact that the agitators had at last emphatically committed themselves to reform. The implications of their decision, heightened by the Clare election and the promised election pledges, dismayed even the supporters of emancipation in England, and in the House of Commons Lord John Russell was persuaded to withdraw notice of a motion he had given for consideration of the Catholic claims: "Never was such a clamour as was made in the London world against my motion; ministers, opposition, Huskissons, and all were frightened at the threats of a few stupid Ultras." [109] The stupid

104. *DEP,* June 24, 1828.

105. Rossmore to O'Connell, July 11, 1828, UCD, O'C P.

106. *Morning Register,* Aug. 5, Sept. 17, and Sept. 29, 1828; *Morning Herald,* Aug. 9, 1828; *DEP,* Sept. 18, 1828.

107. Bentham to O'Connell, Aug. 31, 1828, *Works of Bentham, 10,* 598.

108. *Morning Herald,* Feb. 28, 1829.

109. Russell to Thomas Moore, July 29, 1828, BM, Correspondence of Lord John Russell, 1819–1860, 38080, foll. 37–38.

ultras were quite reasonably alarmed. Two months after the Clare election Wellington's ministry had to decide whether or not to risk another contest in Ireland by fulfilling a promise of a peerage for one of the members for Galway. The resultant by-election would be a test case of the association's pledges. While Peel, at first, was all for taking the chance of a successful struggle with the demagogues,[110] the Duke was more pessimistic: in his reply to Peel he dolefully described the impasse to which the association had brought his government:

> I doubt the expediency of the contest in Galway. . . . By beating the Association in Galway do we not cut the ground from under our own feet on which we are to stand in order to prevail upon Parliament to legislate upon the franchise of forty-shilling freeholders, and for the purpose of establishing the influence of the Crown over the Roman Catholic clergy? I confess that what has moved me has been the Monaghan, the Louth, the Waterford, and the Clare elections. I see clearly that we have to suffer here all the consequences of a practical democratic reform in Parliament, if we do not do something to remedy the evils.[111]

A democratic reform in Parliament! Few threats evoked such ministerial nightmares. O'Connell and his band, long toying with the idea, had now pledged themselves to include reform in their demands. If they were not appeased, their clamor might prove just the stimulus needed to arouse once again a strong radical movement in England.

The hornets' nest also gave signs of extending their protest in another direction. In 1800 Pitt had persuaded the Irish Catholics not to oppose the Act of Union on the understanding that it would be followed by full emancipation. To the disillusioned Catholics, as well as to a small group of liberal Protestants cherishing the tradition of Grattan and Flood, the Union soon appeared a blight on Ireland's prosperity, the basic cause of the majority of her woes. In 1832 one of the veterans of the Corn Exchange noted: "There was scarcely an Agitator, who, like myself, can remember times prior to the Association era, but knows that it [repeal] was ever the ultimate object of all who co-operated in the work of political contention, save the Catholic nobility and some of the patrician gentry. I have often heard O'Connell declare, in the days when the

110. Peel to Wellington, Sept. 11, 1828, Parker, *Peel, 2,* 63.
111. Wellington to Peel, Sept. 12, 1828, *ibid., 2,* 63–64.

prospect of emancipation appeared most distant, that he would consent to forgo the accomplishment of that measure for the restoration of our national independence." [112]

Yet repeal, even more than reform, was a delicate question. O'Connell on this issue also moderated his tone when the mention of repeal was thought to hinder the emancipation cause. In November 1823 when a member of the association, a Mr. Flanagan, gave notice of a motion for the repeal of the Union, he was stopped short and told that he could not proceed since he was not yet a week enrolled as a member.[113] The body was not yet prepared to commit itself on such a dangerous issue; the most it would resolve was: "Had the Union not taken place, we are convinced the Protestants of Ireland in parliament would have long since conceded equalization of civil rights." [114] Later the agitators grew more confident. At a public dinner in Cork in September 1824 O'Connell stated that he was devoted first to parliamentary reform and then to repeal of the Union. Two months later Lord Cloncurry, recalling that repeal was the last wish he had heard from the venerable Grattan, urged the association to avow it: the ills of Ireland, Catholic grievances, the unmodified tithe system, absenteeism, the drain of wealth from the country, and a partial magistracy were all due in great part, Cloncurry asserted, to the Union.[115] Lawless and the more radical members seconded Cloncurry's proposal, but once again the matter was hushed, as was the question of reform, for fear of antagonizing the "Catholics" in Parliament on the eve of the 1825 debate on the Catholic claims.

Still the discussion did not go unnoticed, as Sir Henry Parnell attested in a letter to the Duke of Buckingham: "The evil now to be apprehended is, that the proper season for carrying emancipation is gone by; and that this measure will not take the people out of the hands of those of the Catholic leaders who seek only the separation of the two countries." [116] Another of Buckingham's correspondents noted that the association was giving "very great and serious uneasiness to Ministers, who fear a new Volunteer crisis, though there is no Charlemont, Grattan, or Flood." [117] Did they forget O'Connell and behind him a more complete and fore-

112. Thomas Kennedy, "Reminiscences of a Silent Agitator," *Irish Monthly Magazine, 1* (May 1832–April 1833), 511.

113. Meeting of Nov. 15, 1823, ISPO, CAP.

114. Meeting of Feb. 24, 1824, *ibid.*

115. Letter of Cloncurry to the association, *DEP,* Nov. 11, 1824.

116. Parnell to Buckingham, Nov. 25, 1824, Buckingham, *Memoirs, 2,* 160.

117. R. Plumer Ward to Buckingham, Nov. 27, 1824, *ibid., 2,* 163.

boding mass movement than Charlemont, Grattan, Flood, or even Wolfe Tone and Robert Emmet had ever been able to muster? And O'Connell, after the disappointment of 1825, seemed teetering on the brink: "The Union has been the great curse of this country . . . I will not stop my exertions . . . till I see a Domestic Legislature in this country . . . The subject has not been before discussed at Catholic Meetings. . . . From this day forth we shall seek a higher flight." [118] O'Connell suddenly suspended the higher flight lest it annoy Canning. For a moment, in March 1827, immediately after the defeat of the Catholic question in the Commons, he broke his silence to urge instant preparation of a petition for repeal. But petitioning was scarcely a forceful weapon.

In 1828, as was to be expected, repeal again raised its head. Violent speeches issued from the Corn Exchange, and there loomed the possibility that emancipation long delayed would drive the Catholic leaders to merge their grievances in a wider, full-scale struggle for national rights. O'Connell, for onc, made no secret of his impatience: "My object is to make one step at least in the amelioration of mankind by carrying Emancipation. This measure would reconcile Ireland to England. If it is not carried soon these countries will certainly separate. I see the growing materials of separation. Emancipation may blight them for centuries. Without it there is a moral impossibility to continue the connexion although the disastrous struggle be delayed by us who *now* profess influence. But come it will." [119] Come it did. Repeal of the Union was left as the goal of O'Connell's second great agitation, which ended, disastrously indeed, in his capitulation at Clontarf in 1843 and his own death four years later in the shadow of failure and of the great famine that withered his "lovely green land."

118. *DEP,* Jan. 20, 1827.

119. O'Connell to Richard Bennett, Sept. 26, 1827, NL, Autograph Letters of O'Connell to Counselor Bennett, 1815–31, Add. MS R1.

# 8. *Fierce, Fearless, and Desperate Peasantry*

NEVER far from the surface of any popular movement in Ireland lay the ugly possibility of violence. Rebellion and terror seemed endemic to Irish history. Whether confronted with the organized resistance of the Fitzgeralds and the O'Neills, Sarsfield, Wolfe Tone, and Robert Emmet, or the sporadic midnight raids of Limerick peasants, English governors seldom had respite from armed protest against their domination of the island. True, the country had been singularly quiet during the Jacobite risings of '15 and '45. Yet the century had culminated in the horrors of 1798 and 1803, and during the latter part of it there had grown up a formidable system of secret societies.

In 1761 the Whiteboys arose among the peasantry of Tipperary, providing an example soon imitated in other counties by the Rightboys, Oakboys, Hearts of Steel, Levelers, Shanavests, and Corkboys. Mainly agrarian in nature, these organizations had their religious counterparts in the Catholic Defenders and the Protestant Peep-of-Day Boys.[1] For a time the rebellions of 1798 and 1803 eclipsed the secret societies, but they reappeared around 1806 in the Threshers and from 1803 to 1835 in the Ribbonmen, to pass on to later generations of Young Irelanders, Fenians, and the Irish Republican Army their tradition of violence.

In the 1820's the most widespread form of secret organization was that of the anti-Protestant and antilandlord Ribbonmen, who flourished as a result of the postwar agricultural depression and the famine conditions of 1817 and 1818. Waging a bloody campaign of reprisal against high rents, tithes, and evictions, the Ribbonmen brought the southwestern counties to the verge of civil war. There was a lull in 1819, but in the following year agrarian outrage reappeared with increased viciousness. Masked, white-shirted, poteen-inflamed bands of Whiteboys, Ribbonmen, and

1. In 1795 the Peep-of-Day Boys became the Orange Society.

Rockites terrorized the countryside with their nightly marauding, rick burning, cattle houghing, and murders. The Irish Government retaliated with applications of the Insurrection Act and the Habeas Corpus Suspension Act to the disaffected areas, so frequently, indeed, that only ten of the years from 1800 to 1824 did not see one or both of the acts in force in some part of the country.[2]

With 1824 the incidence of agrarian crime declined. Under the terms of the Insurrection Act nine of the thirty-two counties of Ireland were proclaimed to be in a state of total or partial disturbance in 1823; two years later the last of them was declared free of disorder, and the Insurrection Act, repeatedly renewed by Parliament since 1796, was allowed to lapse. Why the sudden change? Dublin Castle and the Catholic Association both took credit for it. While Peel, in congratulating Wellesley on the improved state of the country, advanced as the reason the laws and the firm administration of the government,[3] O'Connell boasted, to greater effect, that the association, by organizing the peasantry and offering them a constitutional outlet for their protests, had succeeded where the Castle, with its coercion, had failed for centuries. And on his side lay the weight of evidence. Indeed, the underground agrarian organizations help to account for the sudden, country-wide success of the Catholic Association. A network of local societies was ready to hand. Normally the Ribbonmen had no political representation and, except on the level of laborers, no connection with the urban Catholics. Neither did they have much trust or interest in such public leadership as there was. But when they found O'Connell, whose reputation through rural Ireland had been growing long before 1823, appealing to them in terms of immediate realities, they decided to work with him.

Reluctantly, even O'Connell's opponents acknowledged his and the association's control over the peasantry. Major Warburton, inspector general of police for Connaught, testified that the Catholic leaders, lay and clerical, had pacified the country,[4] and the Earl of Clancarty, spokesman for the Orangemen, angrily complained to

2. From 1815 to 1824, when the Insurrection Act was in application for six of the ten years, 1,767 persons were tried under it in Tipperary alone. ISPO, SCP, carton 48. During the same period 6,442 convicts were transported from Ireland to New South Wales. Statistical report sent by Goulburn to Peel, July 20, 1825, BM, PP, 40311, fol. 106.

3. Peel to Wellesley, Feb. 3, 1826, NL, WP, MSS 322.

4. Testimony of Warburton before the select committee on the state of Ireland, June 21, 1825, *Parl. Papers* (1825), *8*, 840.

Goulburn that O'Connell and his ilk were responsible for quieting a people "who had so long withstood all the efforts of His Majesty's Irish Government." [5] Clancarty was protesting against the insolence of the popish parliament, but he scarcely overestimated its influence. The association, to be sure, counseled prudential conformity to the laws. Yet there remained the prospect that a traditionally lawless peasantry, whose secret organizations might now be under the central command of the association, would welcome less pacific instructions. As early as the spring of 1824 the association was assailed in the House of Commons as a formidable instrument of insurrection, and two years later Goulburn, in a report on the state of the country, warned that O'Connell controlled the Catholic clergy who, in turn, were complete masters of the people, "and upon him and them it depends whether the country shall or shall not be quiet during the winter." [6]

Although the country was quiet in 1826, the spirit of resistance to the law was still much in evidence. The number of persons convicted of criminal offenses, unlike the incidence of organized agrarian outrage, kept rising even after 1824.[7] The increase, while in proportion to the rapid growth of population, was, nevertheless, convincing proof that felonious tendencies on the part of individuals were undiminished. Moreover, the lull in the activities of the secret societies was not so promising as it seemed at first glance. From County Cork, for instance, the inspector of police reported that the Ribbonmen had come to regard their previous outbreaks as premature and rash, indeed, but preparatory to the general organization developed by the association; [8] in Limerick they were taking a new oath "to be faithful to the Catholic Asso-

5. Clancarty to Goulburn, Dec. 5, 1824, ISPO, SCP, 445/2624/30.

6. Goulburn to Peel, July 25, 1826, Parker, *Peel, 1,* 417.

7. Summary of persons charged with criminal offenses in Ireland, 1820–26. PRO, HO, 100/221:

| | *Charged* | *Convicted* | *Sentenced to Death* | *Executed* |
|---|---|---|---|---|
| 1820 | 11,645 | 5,667 | 239 | 71 |
| 1821 | 12,005 | 5,921 | 173 | 52 |
| 1822 | 15,251 | 7,572 | 341 | 101 |
| 1823 | 15,363 | 8,016 | 241 | 61 |
| 1824 | 16,078 | 8,562 | 295 | 60 |
| 1825 | 16,273 | 9,329 | 181 | 18 |
| 1826 | 17,159 | 9,557 | 281 | 34 |
| | 103,774 | 54,624 | 1,751 | 397 |

During the same period 5,095 were transported.

8. Maj. S. Carter to Goulburn, Dec. 21, 1824, ISPO, SCP, 444/2617/49.

ciation"; [9] and in various parts of the South and the Southwest blacksmiths were continuing their furtive manufacture of pikes against the day when O'Connell would call them out.

At one of the meetings in the Corn Exchange the secretary read a letter from several Dublin ladies warning that their subscription to the Rent must not be spent for powder and shot. While it provided amusement at the time, the letter was not ridiculous. Memories of '98 and '03 were still fresh. Informers attending the underground meetings of the Ribbonmen constantly reported that the irreconcilables had "every hope that O'Connell will stand their friend at the last push." [10] In Limerick an officer of the yeomanry noted that the people boldly spoke of strong measures if their rights were denied; their numbers were great; they could command arms; they were fast collecting money in the form of the Rent.[11] From the traditional centers of unrest, the southwestern counties, magistrates, circuit judges, police officers, and informers observed that the priests, in urging collection of the Rent, were telling the people it was for their own good to pay it and significantly withholding any further explanation: "This undefined and mysterious mode of acting leaves the people to their own construction. Therefore, a rumour . . . prevails among them universally that we are to have a rebellion." [12] Another informant, in County Cork, noted that both farmers and laborers believed the avowed purposes of the Rent were fictitious and that it was really to be used to buy arms and to engage foreign officers and emigrant Irish from America; when the time was ripe a word from either the demagogues or the priests could "set the mass in motion in less than forty-eight hours." [13]

Setting the mass in motion was something the Catholic leaders professed to dread as keenly as their opponents. Yet the very speeches in which they affected concern were often but thinly veiled warnings to the government not to drive the people to rebellion. O'Connell, for one, had a sincere abhorrence of bloodshed. But his was the equivocal method of carefully avoiding any insurrectionary activity while employing a revolutionary organization. While he did not, indeed, adopt a tactic suggested by Thomas Moore of beginning Irish petitions with the words, "We the fighting men of

9. Francis Blackburne to Goulburn, Jan. 14, 1825, *ibid.*, 447/2731/2.
10. Report of "W" to James Tandy, June 10, 1824, *ibid.*, carton 47.
11. Maj. Henry Croker to Gregory, May 31, 1824, *ibid.*, 445/2627/8.
12. J. Lloyd to Francis Blackburne, Dec. 14, 1824, *ibid.*, 445/2619/56.
13. Maj. S. Carter to Goulburn, Dec. 21, 1824, *ibid.*, 444/2617/49.

Ireland," he did frequently exploit the threat of physical force. A favorite remark of his was that in 1822 the secret societies had brought the country to the brink of civil war: "The contest was approaching. I assert fearlessly that civil war would shortly have raged, and the next thing I assert is that the Orangemen would not have been successful. There is a steadiness, coolness, and firmness among the Irish people." [14] In crediting the association with having averted the calamity, O'Connell obviously implied that what it had prevented it could, if driven to desperation, as readily promote. Such was the underlying theme of his warning to the Duke of Wellington in 1827: "We are stronger than may be imagined. Why even in London if Pat took it into his head, he would go near to beat the guards; but for efficient strength at home it is but folly not to appreciate us justly." [15] Emboldened by the Clare election O'Connell boasted: "Allow me now, Duke of Wellington, to send one whisper to your ear. Three hundred soldiers threw up their caps for me since I left Ennis." [16]

Other voices took up the refrain. Sheil, commanding as large an audience, was even less restrained than O'Connell:

> There are six millions of Roman Catholics in Ireland—a vast proportion of that immense body is alienated by the law. It is impossible discontent should not exist; it does exist —and what lines of difference should be drawn between discontent and disaffection, I leave the nice appreciators of phrase to determine. . . . This vast body of fierce, of fearless, and desperate peasantry, would be easily allured into a junction with an invader, . . . if, after a mature and deliberate preparation of the public sentiment, the united fleets of France and of America were to appear, with 20,000 men, and 100,000 stand of arms off our coast, gracious God! What would be the result? [17]

Such a prospect was equally repellent to Dr. Doyle. In his public letters the bishop asserted frequently that his chief anxiety for emancipation arose from an expectation of civil war if it was longer denied; [18] he, too, described the Catholics as "a mighty living mass, restless and agitated, . . . liable to be precipitated into some gulf,

14. Aggregate meeting of July 5, 1827, NL, CA MSS.
15. O'Connell to Richard Bennett, Jan. 15, 1827, NL, O'Connell Letters to Bennett, Add. MS R1, 18.
16. *DEP,* July 12, 1828.
17. *DEM,* Jan. 14, 1825.
18. J.K.L., *Letters on the State of Ireland* (Dublin, 1825), p. 291.

carrying with them in their fall the whole edifice of society"; [19] and he made bold to predict: "If a rebellion were raging from Carrigfergus to Cape Clear, no sentence of excommunication would ever be fulminated by a Catholic Prelate." [20] Such language from the foremost bishop in Ireland quite naturally led extremists, Ribbonmen, Whiteboys, and Rockites to expect eventually more than mere threatening words from their leaders. So far popular feeling was venting itself in declamation. The government should have been grateful for so many orators.

A rebellion scare in the winter of 1824–25 showed, nevertheless, how narrow was the gap between oratory and action.[21] During 1824 a pamphlet, *Pastorini's Prophecies*, was in circulation among the Catholics. Although the bishops condemned it and O'Connell contended that it was actually distributed by the Orangemen in order to provoke the peasantry to an outbreak, the people took one prophecy in particular seriously: 1825 was to be the year of Catholic triumph over their enemies. Coupled with the inflammatory language issuing from the Corn Exchange and a papal designation of 1825 as a holy year, the prediction was evidence enough to ultra-Protestants that the Catholics were planning a massacre, probably for Christmas Day 1824. Weeks previous to that date letters from alarmed Protestants began arriving at Dublin Castle and the Home Office. The Earl of Clancarty, convinced that the state of disaffection was worse than on the eve of the Rebellion of 1798,[22] wrote to Wellington, master general of the ordnance, begging hand grenades and Congreve rockets with which to defend his estates.[23] The Protestant Bishop of Ossory reported that the nobility and gentry were unanimous in their anticipation of rebellion; the Catholics in Galway, eager for battle, had received new instructions from the association through three strangers, two dressed like farmers and the third like a common laborer, who had lately passed through the district; and he was in hopes of catching a smith in the act of making pikes.[24] Another letter, from King's County, stated that the "entire Catholic population are sworn,

19. *Ibid.*, p. 46.

20. Letter to Mr. Robertson, London *Morning Chronicle*, May 18, 1824.

21. A similar scare occurred in June 1823, when Wellesley reported to Peel, June 22, 1823, that there was serious fear of a clash between Orangemen and Catholics. BM, PP, 40324, foll. 171–180. The news that the guards in Dublin had been doubled on the occasion caused "considerable alarm" in England also. Peel to Wellesley, June 20, 1823, copy, *ibid.*, foll. 165–168.

22. Clancarty to Goulburn, Dec. 5, 1824, ISPO, SCP, 445/2624/30.

23. Peel to Goulburn, Dec. 7, 1824, copy, BM, PP, 40330, foll. 260–261.

24. Bishop of Ossory, no addressee, Dec. 6, 1824, ISPO, SCP, 443/2606/71.

organized, and in general armed with fire arms or pikes for the purpose of a simultaneous rising if possible, to annihilate the Protestants of this country." As evidence the writer adduced the fact that in one barony the Catholics were holding nightly meetings.[25] Even normally sober persons like Bishop Jebb were apprehensive. To Peel, through his friend Sir Robert Inglis, Jebb reported in December that in his usually troubled part of the country there was a cessation of all outrage "and a silence like that of the grave": a crisis was at hand. "This is not the panic of vulgar alarmists; it is the judgment of intrepid men, aloof from party, well-versed in Irish politics." The present calm, too general and too sudden to be quite natural, was proof of the association's power and more ominous than riots, house burnings, or assassinations.[26]

Bishop Jebb was sure that even the lord lieutenant was more disturbed than he admitted. The latter, indeed, although inclined to dismiss the outcry of the high Protestant party as an effort to offset the clamor of the popish parliament, observed that the Catholics "would be easily led by the Association into any course of measures however violent." [27] John Leslie Foster and Goulburn, also, while deprecating fear of a general insurrection, advised Peel that there was immediate danger of an outbreak of fanatical party spirit: a mob riot, an accidental fire, a poacher's shooting at night might set a match to the flax.[28] The four provincial inspectors of police likewise observed widespread alarm, and from Lord Combemere, commander of the forces in Ireland, came word that the peasantry were showing a sudden, marked disinclination to enlist in the army. Combemere also noted that the city of Galway had been "thrown into a state of great excitement a few days ago by a report . . . of the Roman Catholic Association having been put down by proclamation from the King, and the people have since been constantly assembling in small groups in the streets." [29] With information from such varied sources at his command, Peel believed Ireland to be in danger,[30] and he was joined by Wellington, who bluntly admitted: "We are in that happy state in Ireland

25. Thomas Pepper to Lord Norbury, Dec. 11, 1824, *ibid.*, 443/2607/10.

26. Jebb to Inglis, Nov. 19, 1824, BM, PP, 40370, foll. 187–189.

27. Colonel Shawe, Wellesley's private secretary, to Charles Arbuthnot, Dec. 6, 1824, *ibid.*, 40304, foll. 307–316.

28. Goulburn to Peel, Dec. 14, 1824, *ibid.*, 40330, foll. 269–274; Foster to Peel, Jan. 20, 1825, *ibid.*, 40372, foll. 152–155.

29. Combemere to Sir H. Taylor, Dec. 3, 1824, copy, *ibid.*, 40370, foll. 289–290.

30. Peel to Goulburn, Dec. 30, 1824, copy, *ibid.*, 40330, foll. 252–258.

that it depends upon the prudence and discretion of the leaders of the Roman Catholic Association whether we shall have a rebellion there or not within the next six months." [31]

The Catholic leaders were more prudent than the Duke expected. Nothing came of Pastorini's prophecies. Christmas Day, in preparation for which some Protestant squires had canceled their dinners, barricaded their manors, and sent their families to the security of county towns, passed without incident.[32] The following months were equally tranquil. Nevertheless, the rebellion scare was symptomatic of the general anxiety aroused by the Catholic Association. Unless the government could rid itself of this powder keg, Wellington warned Peel, it must look to civil war sooner or later.[33] Most of the information from Ireland seemed to bear out the Duke's judgment. His friend, Vesey Fitzgerald, reported that the mobilization of the people was complete and even moderate Catholics appeared sullen; those who had confided in him in 1820 now refused to communicate anything; the lower orders, he concluded, had discovered their strength, and it would be preferable that they break out now rather than wait for a maturer time and greater preparation.[34] In 1826 Goulburn confessed he never felt more anxiety over the state of the country,[35] to which Archbishop Magee of Dublin added: "Our Popish demagogues here are going completely mad. . . . The country is in a state of universal inflammation. . . . I can myself see no issue to the proceedings but in a rebellion." [36]

Concern over the possibility of rebellion was increased by another consideration. In the past insurrection in Ireland had almost invariably been the occasion for foreign intervention in aid of the rebels, and despite the fact that since the end of the Napoleonic Wars England had been at peace with the continental powers, her relations, particularly with France, were unpredictable. The attention aroused by the Irish struggle outside the British Isles was, therefore, a source of uneasiness.

Quite early in the agitation O'Connell hinted at the danger of a French alliance with "Captain Rock," and in the association's

31. Wellington to Peel, Dec. 30, 1824, *Wellington Despatches, 2,* 385.

32. Even in the environs of Dublin many families were afraid to attend church on Christmas. W. H. Ellis to J. W. Croker, Jan. 2, 1825, copy, BM, PP, 40319, foll. 136–141.

33. Wellington to Peel, Nov. 3, 1824, Parker, *Peel, 1,* 348.

34. Fitzgerald to Peel, Jan. 24, 1824, BM, PP, 40322, foll. 113–131.

35. Goulburn to Wellesley, July 2, 1826, BM, WP, 37304, foll. 154–155.

36. Magee to Lord Colchester, Oct. 2, 1826, *Diary and Correspondence of Lord Colchester, 3,* 449.

"Address to the People of England" in 1825 he was more explicit: "Those who are labouring under oppression . . . will be exposed to the strong temptation of receiving (if they can obtain it) assistance from any part of the world; . . . lead us not into temptation, . . . the possibility of seeing in foreign fleets or bands the deliverers of Ireland." [37] O'Connell's words, repeated in speeches at the Corn Exchange and the country meetings, were taken seriously by many actual and potential Ribbonmen among the peasantry. One informant found that at their secret gatherings the Ribbonmen hailed O'Connell as an instrument appointed by Providence to effect their wishes and were convinced that he had obtained foreign aid.[38] More than one of the ballads circulating through the country sang cryptically of "help from across the water" or lamented, "It would be better for us all brave Bonny was not dead." [39] And from County Clare in 1826 came reports of foreigners, supposedly Frenchmen, lately seen passing through the country and of Ribbonmen administering secret oaths to be ready at an hour's notice to help foreign allies.[40] There could be little doubt that extremists, at least, looked to aid from France and expected the association to acknowledge it when the hour came. Of this they were scarcely more hopeful than the government was suspicious.

Any unusual French interest in Irish affairs was disturbing. Shortly after the founding of the association Peel secretly instructed Goulburn to keep sharp watch on the French consul in Dublin: "He corresponds with Chateaubriand on all matters of Irish domestic policy, which I should apprehend are peculiarly interesting to the French Minister . . . He sends the population abstracts, with notes of admiration on the rapid increase of the Irish people. . . . There is nothing treasonable in his reports, but he does report, and in great detail, and *through the Post Office*." [41] The underscoring was not lost on the chief secretary, who suggested that the consul's letters might better be opened in London rather than in the Dublin post office, "where we have such bunglers . . . that our opening them would be immediately promulgated." [42]

37. London *Morning Chronicle,* Feb. 22, 1825.

38. Information of "H," Jan. 5, 1825, ISPO, SCP, 447/2731/1.

39. "The Poor Man's Complaint," a ballad sent by John Wallace to Peel, Feb. 14, 1825, BM, PP, 40373, foll. 130–131.

40. Reports from police and magistrates in Clare, Aug.–Sept. 1826, ISPO, SCP, 447/2768/16–19.

41. Peel to Goulburn, Oct. 27, 1823, copy. BM, PP, 40329, fol. 185.

42. Goulburn to Peel, Nov. 1, 1823, *ibid.,* fol. 189. Letters to O'Connell from a suspected Ribbonman in Cavan were also being opened, copied, and sent to the

Although nothing treasonable was discovered in the correspondence, Peel did not relax his vigilance. In December 1824 he suggested to Canning the advisability of keeping "a sharp look-out after Irish agents in Paris." [43] Two years later, after the election surprises of 1826, there appeared stronger reason for fear of what Wellington termed "eventual interference of the Roman Catholic party in France in this [Irish] question." [44] Plunket advised Canning that the French Government was looking more anxiously at Ireland than hitherto,[45] an opinion seemingly borne out by the appearance of an unusual number of French travelers in the country. The Duke of Montebello, in particular, participating in Catholic meetings and advising the Catholics that "a people determined to be free could soon make themselves so," [46] aroused the suspicions of the government. The *Courier* saw in his visit the first step of a foreign invasion; even the more moderate *Times* charged him with conspiring with Sheil for the overthrow of both the Protestant religion and the House of Hanover; and Goulburn observed that the French nobleman's appearance "has confirmed the opinion that the French are prepared to make common cause with the Roman Catholics." [47]

There was also a possibility, noted by Wellington,[48] of interference from another quarter, America. The United States, under the administrations of the Anglophobe Adams and the Irish-descended Jackson, stood in far from friendly relation to Britain as a result of disputes over the northeast and northwest boundaries and trade with the West Indies. From New Orleans to Quebec meetings and associations of Irish-Americans were publicizing the Irish struggle, and in 1825 a committee of agitators from Ireland actually toured the United States and was somewhat hysterically

---

Castle. R. Anderson, postmaster at Killesandra, to Sir E. L. Lees, Dec. 11, 1824, ISPO, SCP, 445/2622/20.

43. Peel to Canning, Dec. 18, 1824, copy, BM, PP, 40311, fol. 88.

44. Memorandum of Wellington, n.d., 1825, *Wellington Despatches, 2,* 593.

45. Plunket to Canning, Oct. 10, 1826, *Life of Plunket, 2,* 234–235. Lord Granville, English ambassador at Paris, also reported to Peel that the Jesuits, with the aid of the French Government, were trying to extend their influence in Ireland. Peel to Goulburn, Dec. 28, 1826, PRO, HO, 100/216.

46. Major Warburton to Goulburn, Oct. 15, 1826, ISPO, CAP, carton 1158.

47. Goulburn to Peel, Oct. 20, 1826, BM, PP, 40332, foll. 160–161. In 1827 an English agent in Paris informed Peel: "The French Government have within these few days directed a return to be made of the number of Irish officers in the service and of their capability to serve; several persons have been recently sent to Ireland to survey the coasts; and Irish officers who had solicited in vain for employment have been appointed to civil and military situations." William Stuart to Peel, March 12, 1827, BM, WP, 37305, foll. 51–52.

48. See note 44, above.

reported to be getting arms and talking of independence.[49] The prospect of American intervention, nevertheless, was more remote than that of French aid in the event of an Irish rebellion.

The difficulties of the British Government in Ireland, arising from the prevalence of disaffection and the organization perfected by the association, were demonstrated in one very concrete way, the necessity of maintaining an expensive army in the sister island. Agitation, as Wellington noted, meaning something just short of rebellion, placed the country in that state in which its government was utterly impractical except by means of an overwhelming military force.[50] The garrison in Ireland in 1823 was 28,000 men; during the next five years it was increased until at the end of 1828 it approached 35,000 and cost annually £5,000,000.[51] It was composed of the regular army, the constabulary, waterguards, revenue police, and militia,[52] and in addition there was the yeomanry numbering about 30,000 men,[53] who, while exercised only a few days a year and unfit for immediate use, could be embodied in an emergency. But mobilizing the Irish yeomanry was a risky business. Exclusively and pugnaciously Protestant, they perpetuated memories of the horrors of 1798 when, badly disciplined and shockingly out of hand, they had injected into the rebellion the savage spirit of religious bitterness. Using the opportunity to settle old scores with Catholic "croppies," they had resorted to flogging, burning, shooting, and hanging. The Irish Government had no desire to revive such cruelties and consequently showed itself extremely reluctant to encourage rabid Protestant squireens.[54]

49. S. C. Whiting to H. V. Addington, July 19, 1825, in Addington to Canning, Aug. 6, 1825, PRO, FO, 5/198. Canning relayed this information to Peel and to the King, in what was probably an attempt to influence them on the Catholic question, and it was possibly a reason for Wellington's fear of American intervention expressed in his memorandum of 1825.

50. Speech of Wellington in the House of Lords, May 4, 1829, *Parl. Debates*, 2d Ser., *21,* 1029.

51. Scotland, with a population one-third that of Ireland, required a military establishment only one-fifteenth as large.

52. In 1824 the approximate numbers were:

| | |
|---|---|
| regular army | 21,000 |
| constabulary | 4,000 |
| waterguards and revenue police | 1,500 |
| militia | 1,500 |

Goulburn to Peel, June 5 and Nov. 26, 1824, BM, PP, 40330, foll. 67–68 and 239–241.

53. The Irish Yeomanry in 1824 numbered 29,676, in contrast to the 28,631 yeomen for all of England, Scotland, and Wales. Memorandum of Lord Palmerston, March, n.d., 1824, BM, PP, 40363, fol. 216.

54. An indication of the gravity of the rebellion scare of 1824–25 was the fact that Peel, who from his personal experience as Irish chief secretary well knew the

The lord lieutenant preferred to rely on the regular forces and to increase them in face of the danger arising from the agitation.

From 1823 to 1829 the numbers of the forces rose by almost one-quarter. A notable growth was that of the Irish constabulary, established in 1822, which increased from 1,602 in that year to 5,871 in 1828.[55] Less public, for fear of rousing alarm, were the augmentation and deployment of the regular army. Despite the decline of Ribbon atrocities, Wellesley advised Peel in 1823 that the army could not safely be reduced.[56] Goulburn, indeed, recommended that it be strengthened.[57] In the Southwest it was still necessary to have the protection of the military for the collection of rents and tithes, and in all parts of the island the troops had to be dispersed to prevent local disturbances, a necessity which would expose them, in the event of general rebellion, to considerable jeopardy.[58] Once only during the period from 1823 to 1829 was the army reduced: in the winter of 1826–27 Canning's policy of assisting the constitutional party in Portugal to put down rebellion made it imperative to call suddenly for Irish troops. Although only about 1,500 were withdrawn, the move caused grave concern to the Irish Government.[59]

Another source of anxiety, in addition to the adequacy of the military forces, was suspicion of their loyalty. Ireland was a fertile recruiting ground for the British army. In the country itself a very large proportion of the troops was Catholic. Consequently, Lord Combemere in 1824 noted apprehensively that the priests, with customary insolence, were beginning to forbid their parishioners to enlist,[60] and a year later the association was making "a most mischievous and alarming trial of their powers" by including in their census returns a reckoning of the Catholic soldiers in various garrisons.[61] But it was not until 1828 that the problem of the

character of the yeomanry, suggested that they be mobilized. Peel to Goulburn, Dec. 6, 1824, copy, BM, PP, 40330, fol. 258.

55. Return of the armed constables in Ireland in 1822 and 1828, by Gregory, March, n.d., 1828, ISPO, OP II, 588bb/830c/5.

56. Wellesley to Peel, Nov. 15, 1823, BM, WP, 37301, foll. 319–321.

57. Goulburn to Peel, Nov. 15, 1823, *ibid.*, foll. 313–317.

58. Lieutenant Colonel Brown to Sir H. Taylor, Oct. 12, 1824, NL, MS 131; Sir John Elley to Lieutenant General Combemere, Dec. 9, 1824, ISPO, SCP, 445/2619/54. In 1816 the troops in Ireland were distributed among 441 stations from which were detached nearly 1,900 patrols. J. W. Fortescue, *A History of the British Army* (2d ed. London, Macmillan & Co., 1902–30), *11*, 55.

59. Goulburn to Peel, Dec. 15, 1826, copy, BM, PP, 40332, foll. 209–210.

60. Combemere to Sir H. Taylor, Dec. 16, 1824, *ibid.*, 40371, foll. 157–158.

61. "Mr. Martin's private opinion on the state of the country," Jan., n.d., 1826, ISPO, SCP, carton 49. The *DEP* of Jan. 17, 1826, listed some of the returns: of 350 soldiers in Clonmel 310 were Catholics, as were 323 of the 500 in Waterford City.

reliability of the forces became acute. Then Anglesey was afraid he could not depend on their loyalty; the Catholic troops were ill disposed and, like the majority of the population, entirely under the influence of the priests; at least one regiment of infantry was divided into bitter Orange and Green factions. Anglesey suggested, therefore, the gradual removal of Irish recruits, under the appearance of being required to join their regiments, and the substitution of troops from Scotland or "at all events, of men not recruited in the south of Ireland." [62] The concern of the viceroy was echoed by another famous veteran, the Iron Duke. Wellington admitted he was troubled by the high proportion of Catholics in almost every Irish regiment; there was none without them.[63] Whether or not he caught O'Connell's "whisper" about the soldiers in Ennis, he had reports enough from army officers in Ireland that their Catholic troops were being harangued by the priests at Sunday Mass, were subscribing to the Rent [64] and succumbing in large numbers to the contagion of O'Connellism. Perhaps the Duke was informed also of the comment of one Irish infantryman: "There are two ways of firing, *at* a man and *over;* and if we were called out against O'Connell and our country, I think we should know the difference." [65]

The questionable loyalty of the forces, accentuated in 1828 by the feverish state of the country, prompted extraordinary measures. In July Peel advised Anglesey to remove the militia and yeomanry arms stored in the several counties to the safer custody of the ordnance,[66] and two months later the lord lieutenant called in also all the small detachments of troops scattered up and down the country lest they be sacrificed in the very probable event of an outbreak.[67] In September all the disposable forces in England, seven battalions of infantry and three regiments of cavalry, were ordered to the west coast to hold themselves in readiness for embarkation; Anglesey was given authority, whenever he desired, to summon them instantly; and in the following month he did order two of them across the Irish Sea as a display of force to overawe the agitators. A futile experiment! One of the regiments, the Twenty-first Welsh Fusiliers, ordered from Bath at a moment's notice and marching into Waterford fully expecting to hear the

62. Anglesey to Peel, July 20 and 26, 1828, *Peel Memoirs, 1,* 158–159, 164.

63. Wellington to Peel, July 31, 1828, BM, PP, 40307, fol. 170.

64. There are numerous letters to this effect from Irish officers in PRO, HO, 100/222.

65. Requoted from O'Keefe, *Life and Times of O'Connell, 2,* 483.

66. Peel to Anglesey, July 24, 1828, BM, PP, 40325, fol. 141.

67. Entry of Oct. 1, 1828, Maxwell, *Creevey Papers, 2,* 174–175.

clash of civil war, were disappointed: during the night after their landing they heard only shouts for "O'Connell and the Association" from the straggling Irish soldiery in every part of the town.[68] The cries were, nevertheless, an omen of the perilous military state of the country. In the course of the autumn 25,000 out of a regular infantry force of 30,000 men in the United Kingdom were stationed either in Ireland or on the west coast of England in readiness for Ireland, a situation summarized by Wellington in quite discouraging terms: "In consequence of former arrangements every disposable soldier in England was put at the disposition of the Lord Lieutenant of Ireland in the end of the last month. . . . He may call for any or all of these on any day he pleases. But it must be observed they are the last we have disposable. When they go we must call out the militia, and of course call Parliament." [69]

The military precautions taken by Wellington, Anglesey, and Peel were a result of the extraordinary state of Ireland in 1828. The year began with the simultaneous meetings, a project employed previously on a small scale in 1798 and occasionally by the Ribbonmen but now for the first time made an impressive display of moral and physical force. Debaters at the Corn Exchange had discussed the idea as early as 1826 but dropped it because Wellesley, on the advice of the law officers of both islands, was prepared to proclaim such assemblies illegal.[70] Two years later the crown lawyers, more hesitant, decided it was inexpedient to interfere with simultaneous meetings summoned for the second week in January,[71] and accordingly on Sunday, January 13, 1828, about 1,600 of the 2,500 parishes in Ireland did convene. While the number of meetings and the attendance at some of them were not so large as the association had anticipated, they provided, as the attorney general noted, "a fatal precedent of a people gathered into a solid and perilous confederacy." [72]

During the summer, in addition to the now familiar provincial, county, and parish conventions, special local meetings were summoned by emissaries from Dublin for the purpose of settling disputes and feuds among the peasantry. But the latter soon began

68. O'Keefe, *Life and Times of O'Connell, 2,* 480–482.

69. Wellington to Peel, Oct. 20, 1828, BM, PP, 40308, foll. 24–26.

70. Peel to Wellesley, Feb. 3, 1826, BM, WP, 37304, foll. 95–96.

71. William Lamb to Wellesley, Jan. 2 and 6, Wellesley to Lamb, Jan. 10, Lansdowne to Wellesley, Jan. 14, 1828, *ibid.* 37305, foll. 236, 240–241, 246–247, 254–256.

72. "Mr. Joy's Opinion," April 12, 1828, *Peel Memoirs, 1,* 50. The simultaneous meetings were followed by renewed violence from the Ribbonmen. The January and February police reports for 23 out of the 32 counties listed 17 murders and 206 outrages. Anglesey to Peel, March 31, 1828, *ibid., 1,* 33–35.

to take the initiative themselves and to assemble without waiting for instructions. In various parts of the Southwest large crowds were observed marching in the fields and on the hills, many of them in green uniforms or with green cockades in their hats. In a town in Tipperary when the constables confiscated the fife of one such marcher the enraged mob demolished the police barrack; on the same day, Sunday, October 28, hundreds of farmers and laborers, again with green flags, sashes, feathers, and ribbons, paraded through Castleconnell in Limerick, insulted Protestants, and finally provoked a riot.[73] At Templemore, late in September, between 2,000 and 3,000 of the peasantry, attended by about 10,000 spectators, marched in military array; at Killenaule there was a crowd of 8,000; at Cahir 700 cavalry, 300 infantry, and 12,000 attendants.[74] So great was public tension that in Limerick the mere sight of one of the regiments, with several artillery pieces, leaving the town on maneuvers started a panic among the citizenry, alarmed by rumors that the army had been called out to put down a rebellion.[75]

The North was only slightly less disturbed. In Ulster "Radical Jack" Lawless was invading the citadel of Irish Protestantism, gathering mobs of ten thousand Catholics who rallied wildly to his call, "Are the Ardee Boys here? Are the Sea Side Boys here? Are the Kells Boys here?" threatening to exterminate the "Orange reptiles" and whip the Brunswickers into the walls of Derry, advocating parliamentary reform, repeal of the Union, and total overthrow of "that robbing Church Establishment." He was met by almost equally fanatical crowds of Protestants who at one place, Ballybay, refused him entry to the town. There a pitched battle was averted only by the presence of the military and a strategic retreat on the part of Lawless.

73. Entries of Sept. 19 and Oct. 1, 1828, Journal of G. Ross-Lewin.

74. Anglesey to Peel, Sept. 20, 1828, *Peel Memoirs, 1,* 219.

75. Anonymous letter to Wellington, Aug. 3, 1828, BM, PP, 40307, fol. 195. A foreign traveler in the South of Ireland received a first-hand account of the enthusiasm of the peasantry: "I made inquiries of my guide as to the present state of his country. 'Yes,' said he, 'it's quiet enough here at present, but in Tipperary . . . they know how to stand against the Orangemen. O'Connell and the Association have organized us there, like regular troops; I belong to them, and I have a uniform at home; if you saw me in it, you'd hardly know me. Three weeks ago we all met there, above 40,000 men, to be reviewed. We had all green jackets . . . We have chosen our own officers; they drill us, and we can march and wheel like the redcoats. We had no arms to be sure, but they could be had too if O'Connell chose. We had flags, and whoever deserted them or got drunk we threw into the water till he was sober again; but that seldom happened. They call us O'Connell's Militia.' " Pückler-Muskau, *Tour, 2,* 27–28.

By autumn the situation throughout Ireland was formidable. Many liberal Protestants who had originally encouraged O'Connell, dismayed in 1828 by the pledges to be demanded of parliamentary candidates as well as by the threat of nonpayment of rent and tithes,[76] began to absent themselves from the Corn Exchange. The ultra-Protestants reacted more strenuously by forming Brunswick clubs, with subscriptions as low as a shilling in imitation of the association's Rent, to rally the opposition with the old Derry cry of "No surrender." The Brunswick clubs spread rapidly. Their stronghold, naturally, was in the North, but by the end of 1828 they numbered 148 in the towns and 26 in the counties of Ireland and about 40 in England.[77] Mainly Irish Orangemen and English high Tories, the Brunswickers displayed a fanaticism quite as violent as that of their opponents. In November, when Earl Talbot, lord lieutenant of Staffordshire, asked the advice of Peel in regard to forming a Brunswick Club in his county, the latter, while discouraging the project, added the significant comment, "I do not say what I would do if I were a gentleman resident in Ireland, menaced by such scoundrels as those who direct the Roman Catholic Association."[78] Peel well knew the flaming state of party passion in the sister island, and he sympathized with the exasperated Brunswickers who were taking matters into their own hands.

He knew also that the Protestants were alarmed at the prospect of the association's adopting a program of exclusive dealing, a foreshadowing of the latterly famous boycott. It came near to doing so in 1828 when it debated a motion recommending the Catholics to deal only with "friends of civil and religious freedom." While many members supported the motion, the Catholic aristocracy and even O'Connell, deeming it too radical, succeeded after a six-hours' debate in relegating it to a committee.[79] Any general system of exclusive dealing was bound to play havoc in Ireland. Yet there remained the grim possibility that the agitators might eventually, in exasperation, be driven to it. Moreover, the proposer of the project, a solicitor named Forde, had intended to follow up his motion with another urging owners of Bank of Ireland stock, nine-tenths of whom were Catholics, to sell out and convert into gold. Forde's tactic was timely. Just a few weeks previously

76. Entry of Oct. 5, 1828, Journal of G. Ross-Lewin.
77. Entry of Dec. 8, 1828, *ibid.*
78. Peel to Earl Talbot, Nov. 27, 1828, copy, BM, PP, 40308, foll. 88–90.
79. Meeting of Dec. 4, 1828, DEP, Dec. 6, 1828.

the Rent collectors of Wexford had organized and carried through a run on the provincial bank there, and the example had been imitated in Clonmel and Kilkenny. To avert panic gold was rushed from London, and happily the runs were limited to the three towns. The portent was ominous.[80] In many places during 1828 the peasantry were showing a "spirit of resistance to the collection of tithe, rent, or any such legal process whatever," and Lord Francis Gower, the chief secretary, expressed to Peel fear that the association might soon forbid the payment of rent and tithes.[81] In his reply Peel observed that "nothing, not even the murders you allude to, can be more formidable," [82] and Wellington used the incident as an argument to convince the King of the dire state of Ireland. It was possible, he wrote to George IV, that the Irish peasantry might soon refuse to pay tithes and rent. How could the law be enforced? "How can they [clergy and landlords] distrain for rent or tithes millions of tenants?" [83]

In Ireland the Catholic bishops and clergy were quite genuinely alarmed.[84] Dr. Doyle, less likely than his fellow prelates to succumb to panic, confided to Sir Henry Parnell that he was filled with apprehensions.[85] In some instances the parish priests, trying to prevent the unauthorized meetings and processions, had been repulsed angrily by their congregations. Anglesey informed Peel that the priests who had hitherto maintained their influence by supporting the agitation now seemed to be losing all control "over these infuriated people." [86] Even the popish demagogues professed to be doubtful of their authority. Sheil, an occasional guest at Anglesey's little dinner parties, in response to a discreet hint from his host that any outbreak would inevitably delay emancipation, undertook to halt the processions of the peasantry.[87] The associa-

80. F. L. Gower to Peel, Nov. 4, 1828, BM, PP, 40336, foll. 91–92. Three years later Francis Place used the same device in his famous exhortation, "To stop the Duke, go for gold."

81. Gower to Peel, Oct. 23 and Nov. 9, 1828, *ibid.*, foll. 79 and 103.

82. Peel to Gower, Oct. 27, 1828, copy, *ibid.*, foll. 85–87.

83. Wellington to the King, Oct. 14, 1828, *Wellington Despatches, 5,* 135.

84. Anglesey to Peel, Sept. 24 and 26, 1828, *ibid.*, 81–85.

85. Doyle to Parnell, Aug. 31, 1828, Fitzpatrick, *Doyle, 2,* 84–85.

86. Anglesey to Peel, Sept. 20, 1828, *Peel Memoirs, 1,* 220. In February 1829 when the question of dissolving the association was being debated by the members, the decisive argument for the move was the threat of the bishops to withdraw their support if the body was not immediately disbanded. Edward Dwyer, secretary of the association, to O'Connell, Feb. 11, 1829, UCD, O'C P.

87. W. Torrens McCullagh, *Memoirs of Richard Lalor Sheil* (London, 1855), *2,* 24.

tion sent down to the country several thousand copies, poster size, of an "Address to the Catholics of Tipperary" imploring them to be quiet; [88] O'Connell composed a public letter commanding the Irish of the Southwest, by their devotion to "our lovely land, green Erin, of the rivers and streams," to discontinue their meetings; [89] and two "Pacificators" were dispatched to the South. The orders of the association and the exhortations of its two emissaries proved effective. The progress of the latter, indeed, became a sort of triumphal procession through Tipperary, Clare, and Limerick, with the people drawing their carriages through the streets, illuminating the towns, and escorting them in huge crowds, with torches and lanterns, along the road by the side of Lough Derg to a midnight meeting in the chapel at Newport.[90]

Such commotion was not readily forgotten. To be sure, the peasantry of the South discontinued their independent proceedings —but only in expectation of greater things. They seemed, the chief secretary noted, to be looking forward to a rising whenever O'Connell should be prevented from taking his seat in Parliament as member for Clare, and O'Connell himself, finding it difficult to keep up his authority, was "obliged to swim with the stream of violence." [91] Both he and Sheil appeared to be extremely alarmed by increasing discontent in the country, especially in Tipperary and Mayo.[92] They realized that the slightest incident, a clash of Orangemen and Catholics in the North, for example, might well touch off retaliation in the South. On the other hand, they were reasonably certain, despite their fearful pretensions, of their control over the masses; only a few months previously they had given proof of it in putting down the processions of the peasantry. Still the game they were playing was decidedly hazardous. While rebellion was no part of their program, they had to keep popular passions at a fever pitch in order to intimidate and to extort.

The Catholic leaders were aided in their strategy by numerous reports and warnings reaching English ministers. Five days after his famous Derry speech, George Dawson wrote to his brother-in-law, Peel: "The system of espionage and organization is complete.

88. A copy of the placard was enclosed in F. W. Conway to F. L. Gower, Sept. 27, 1828, PRO, HO, 100/223.

89. Wyse, *Historical Sketch, 2,* appendix XXVII, clxxvi–cxciv.

90. London *Morning Chronicle,* Oct. 6, 1828.

91. Gower to Peel, Nov. 9 and 25, 1828, BM, PP, 40336, foll. 103, 147–148.

92. Gower to Peel, Dec. 2, 1828, *Peel Memoirs, 1,* 253; Gregory to Peel, Dec. 6, 1828, BM, PP, 40334, foll. 262–263.

. . . the Catholic Association can call upon every man by name, whenever it shall suit their purpose to summon them into action." [93] The Earl of Mount Cashel, in a letter circulated among the cabinet, stated that he lived in constant expectation of a rising; if matters grew worse he planned to send his family out of the country.[94] From a Protestant dean in a town near Ennis, whom he termed "a very respectable clergyman," Peel learned that the townspeople had planted the Tree of Liberty in the market square, were threatening the Protestants with massacre, and had frightened many of them into leaving for America. The peace-loving dean himself was driven to "sleep every night with a blunderbuss and a case of pistols double loaded." [95] An accumulation of such letters, patently alarmist though some of them were, could not but trouble the home secretary.

Official reports sent by the lord lieutenant were equally discouraging. In a letter read to the cabinet and shown to the king, Anglesey, early in July, remarked of the Catholic leaders: "I am quite certain they could lead on the people to open rebellion at a moment's notice; . . . There may be rebellion, you may put to death thousands, you may suppress it, but it will only be to put off the day of compromise; and in the mean time the country is still more impoverished, and the minds of the people are, if possible, still more alienated, and ruinous expense is entailed upon the empire." [96] Wellington and Peel were well aware that Anglesey's pro-Catholic sympathies colored his view of the situation, but when he spoke of rebellion, however ambiguously, they could not discount his opinion. In one letter he stated that he did not calculate upon immediate danger, only to warn a few lines later: "But I will not answer for it if an extraordinary occurrence should produce collision. Tomorrow for instance being the twelfth of July." [97] Another letter two weeks later contained the startling sentence: "I cannot persuade myself that immediate danger is to be apprehended; at the same time I cannot say that it would surprise me if insurrection were to break forth at once." [98]

The viceroy's actions were even more exasperating than his cor-

93. Dawson to Peel, Aug. 17, 1828, BM, PP, 40397, foll. 244–245.

94. Mount Cashel to Peel, July 18, 1828, *ibid.,* foll. 171–172.

95. Richard Hood to Peel, July 10, 1828, *ibid.,* fol. 146.

96. Anglesey to Gower, July 2, 1828, *Peel Memoirs, 1,* 147.

97. Anglesey to Peel, July 11, 1828, BM, PP, 40325, foll. 87–90. July 12 was the day when Orangemen annually commemorated the defeat of the Irish army at Aughrim in 1691.

98. Anglesey to Peel, July 26, 1828, *ibid.,* foll. 146–150.

respondence. Although he continually alluded to "frightful reports from the South," he delayed, in disregard of Peel's urgent advice to use force if necessary, proclaiming the meetings and processions of the peasantry until the association itself discouraged them and thus snatched from the Irish Government the credit and prestige for preserving the peace. Such a display of power by the demagogues and of weakness by the King's representative infuriated Peel. Anglesey was impossible; his lack of a forthright and vigorous policy added to a danger which, in a "most private" letter to his father, Peel admitted had brought Ireland to "the brink of civil commotion." [99]

To the Duke of Wellington the Irish crisis appeared even more threatening. At least he acknowledged his anxiety more bluntly. During the summer and autumn of 1828 he received, in addition to the official reports, many letters warning him that the Catholics were "pledged body and soul to risk and even lose all in the struggle." [100] His pro-Catholic friend, the Knight of Kerry, stated that every Irish parish was a regiment; the military force in the country was inadequate and its loyalty questionable; Protestant gentlemen wanted ships with marines and soldiers anchored along the coast, especially in the South and West, to protect and give refuge to their isolated families; the peasantry expected their foreign friends to land arms from France or America; in fine, "Dan literally has the peace, or otherwise, of the country in his hands." [101] Another correspondent, a retired Catholic soldier living on his pension in Clare, reported that the Catholics of that county were so well organized and watched the Protestant gentry so closely that on a few hours' notice the whole of the latter could be seized and massacred. The writer, afraid to give his name, assured the Duke he had served under him in Spain.[102]

Perhaps it was the affection of an old commander for his troops. In any event Wellington judged the soldier's information "but too true." To Peel he observed that the state of society in Ireland could not be worse than it was, civil war not existing,[103] and to a Tory friend who kept urging him to recall Anglesey he explained that the only motive preventing his doing so was dread of "even a

99. Peel to Sir Robert Peel, Feb. 7, 1829, copy, *ibid.*, 40398, foll. 181–183.

100. Anonymous letter from Limerick to Wellington, Aug. 3, 1828, *ibid.*, 40307, fol. 175.

101. Knight of Kerry to Wellington, Aug. 9 and Sept. 29, 1828, *Wellington Despatches*, *4*, 584–588; *5*, 96–97.

102. Wellington to Peel, Oct. 25, 1828, *ibid.*, *5*, 172–173.

103. Wellington to Peel, Dec. 6, 1828, Parker, *Peel*, *2*, 74–75.

month of rebellion."[104] For the benefit of the King, Wellington summarized the situation in the following terms: Ireland was completely organized, more thoroughly and extensively, indeed, than in 1798; respectable men like retired army officers and officers on half pay were quitting the island as unsafe; the influence of the popish demagogues had paralyzed even the royal authority; they held the fate of the country in their hands; and, he concluded, "No one can answer for the consequences of delay."[105] The delay to which the prime minister referred was that of postponing emancipation.

What forces had finally compelled the leader of the high Tories to yield? On the surface was the probability of rebellion. Even more persuasive were the consequences inherent in a dramatic event of July 1828. In June, after the retirement of Huskisson and his fellow Canningites from the cabinet and in the subsequent reconstruction of his ministry, Wellington appointed Vesey Fitzgerald, M.P. for County Clare, to the presidency of the Board of Trade, a move undoubtedly considered as a gesture of appeasement to the Catholics since Fitzgerald was a consistent advocate of emancipation. In addition he was the son of an excellent and esteemed landlord of Clare, and himself personally popular among his constituents. Taking cabinet office automatically required his standing for re-election, but his chances of defeat, if his return was challenged, seemed remote. Even the association, bound by its resolution to unseat any Irish M.P. who supported Wellington's administration, began only a dispirited search for someone to oppose him. The only Protestant whom they could run against Fitzgerald with any hope of success, a Major McNamara, refused the nomination. Then, unexpectedly, almost in desperation, O'Connell announced himself a candidate. The news created a sensation.[106] A Catholic proposing himself a member of Parliament! Was it not just this right that the agitators were demanding? It was. But as Peel noted: "The Roman Catholic is not disabled as Roman Catholic, but by his own act subsequent to election, by his refusal to take certain oaths."[107] The oaths, of supremacy and abjuration, were administered not on the hustings but at the Bar of the House of

104. Wellington to Dean Phillpotts, Oct. 25, 1828, *Wellington Despatches, 5,* 174.

105. Memorandum of Wellington for the King, Aug. 1, 1828, and Wellington to the King, Nov. 16, 1828, *ibid., 4,* 565–570, *5,* 252–268.

106. "The accounts from Ireland that O'Connell means to stand for Clare make a great sensation." Entry of June 27, 1828, in Louis J. Jennings, ed., *The Croker Papers* (2d ed. London, J. Murray, 1885), *1,* 426.

107. Peel to J. L. Foster, July 2, 1828, RIA, Peel Letters to J. L. Foster.

Commons when the elected representative presented himself to take his seat. O'Connell, therefore, might stand.

Yet he could take little credit for the idea. Someone else suggested it, and O'Connell reacted, when he first heard it, with the same lack of enthusiasm he had shown in 1825 and 1826 when Wyse was promoting the Waterford contest. Sir David Roose, lately high sheriff of Dublin and, while a Tory in politics, a friend of O'Connell, met P. V. Fitzpatrick, a member of the association, in Dublin's Nassau Street on the morning of June 24. When he asked, half-jokingly, why O'Connell himself did not stand for Clare, the question roused in the mind of Fitzpatrick memories of a time in his youth when he had been taken to visit John Keogh, the patriarch of Catholic causes at the turn of the century. Keogh had remarked: "John Bull is very stolid and very bigoted. He looks upon Emancipation as meaning liberty to burn him in Smithfield, and hence is ignorantly opposed to the proposition. He is, however, particularly jealous of the constitutional privileges of the subject, and if a man, Catholic though he be, shall be returned in due form to Parliament, and then shall be refused the right to take his seat notwithstanding, John Bull will look very accurately to the nature of the impediment."[108] Fitzpatrick lost no time in passing on the suggestion. That same evening he accompanied a half-hearted O'Connell to the offices of the *Evening Post* where, amid the hubbub of the editor's room, the new candidate, gradually warming to the task, penned an electrifying address to the Clare freeholders. The *Post* published the letter that night, a wager of battle.

The events that followed in the next two weeks had all Ireland, and much of England, watching. On the hustings in Ennis, the county town, O'Connell was put in nomination as "The Man of the People." Between forty and fifty thousand frieze-coated peasants assembled, although less than one-tenth that number were entitled to vote. And despite the crowds, the excitement, the flutes, the skirling of pipes, and the fiddles, the bonfires on the hills, the clanging of the chapel bells, the dancing, and the heat of a sultry July, scarcely a drunken man among them—and not a blackthorn. When a parish priest remarked, in the course of a sermon in one of the local chapels, "I know that it is a great mortification to many of you to abstain from intoxicating liquors," a titter of laughter rippled through his congregation.[109] Yet they obeyed

108. Requoted from Fitzpatrick, *Correspondence of O'Connell, 1,* 160.
109. Clare *Sentinel,* Aug. 1, 1828.

him: more than forty thousand Irishmen renounced whiskey, poteen, and even ale for three days! [110] The marvel of disciplined fanaticism first displayed in Waterford was repeating itself, at an even higher pitch. The commander of the troops in Clare reported that the organization of the people and the rapidity with which masses of them were moved in and out of the town were phenomenal: they marched in regular columns under their own officers, whose orders, "keep in step" and "right shoulders forward," even the rudest among them obeyed smartly. Leading Catholics from almost every county were to be seen in Ennis, "where they will receive an admirable lesson . . . how effectually to reap the benefits of the telegraphic system established; the priests are telegraphs conveying intelligence with the rapidity of lightning and the silence of the grave." [111]

The striking scenes of the Clare election have been described many times, but their full impact is nowhere better conveyed than in a little-known record left by one of the chief actors in the drama. The letters of Vesey Fitzgerald to Peel show that the former, as early as June 5, having some misgivings that his return would not, as the Duke anticipated, be a mere matter of form, implored Peel to keep his appointment a secret until it was actually made in council, "as it would only give more time for organization against me in Clare." [112] The fears were justified. Two weeks later, passing through Dublin on his way to Ennis, the new cabinet minister reported that the association had taken the field in "this cursed affair." [113] It was small consolation to him when Peel replied that it was "quite unnecessary for a Gentleman and a Minister of the

110. "The enthusiasm of the people rose to such a height, that they themselves decreed and inflicted a punishment for drunkenness. The delinquent was thrown into a certain part of the river and held there for two hours, during which time he was made to undergo frequent submersions." Pückler-Muskau, *Tour, 1,* 333–334.

111. Sir Charles Doyle to Lieutenant Colonel Wedderburn, July 5, 1828, ISPO, SCP, 450/2883/3. The Clare election prompted Peel to write to Sir Walter Scott: "I wish you had been present at the Clare election, for no pen but yours could have done justice to that fearful exhibition of sobered and desperate enthusiasm. 'Be true' was the watchword which, uttered by a priest or an agitator, calmed in an instant 'the stormy wave of the multitude,' and seduced the freeholder from his allegiance to his Protestant landlord. We were watching the movements of tens of thousands of disciplined fanatics, abstaining from every excess and every indulgence, and concentrating every passion and feeling on one single object; with hundreds of police and soldiers, half of whom were Roman Catholics . . ." Peel to Scott, April 3, 1829, Parker, *Peel, 2,* 99–100.

112. Fitzgerald to Peel, June 5, 1828, BM, PP, 40322, fol. 262.

113. Fitzgerald to Peel, June 17, 1828, *ibid.,* foll. 263–264.

Crown to notice the low slang of a county election."[114] How could one not notice O'Connell on the hustings, pointing a scornful finger at his opponent and shouting: "This, too, is the friend of Peel—the bloody Perceval and the candid and manly Peel; and he is our friend! and he is everybody's friend! The friend of the Catholic *was* the friend of the bloody Perceval, and *is* the friend of the candid and manly Mr. Peel!"[115] In disgust Fitzgerald might murmur, "Is this fair? Is this fair?" To the unscrupulous Dublin lawyer it was fair enough for the mob jury that hung upon his words. From Ennis Fitzgerald wrote: "Nothing can equal the violence here. The proceedings of yesterday were those of madmen, but the country is mad . . . It will not, cannot end well!"[116] And it did not. The result of the poll was 2,057 for O'Connell, 982 for Fitzgerald.

Writing from Ennis on the noisy night of July 5, the defeated candidate acknowledged his humiliation: "The election, thank God, is over, and I do feel happy in its being terminated, . . . All the great interests broke down, and the desertion has been universal. Such a scene as we have had! Such a tremendous prospect as it opens to us! . . . no man can contemplate without alarm what is to follow in this wretched country."[117] The Catholic leaders, naturally, capitalized on the alarm. Sheil, with more than a suggestion that unchecked power could lead to tyranny, boasted:

> We are masters of the passions of the people, and we have employed our dominion with terrible effect. . . . Protestants, awake to a sense of your condition. Look around you. What have you seen during this election? Enough to make you feel this is not mere local excitation, but that seven millions of Irish people are completely arrayed and organised . . . Did you mark our discipline, our subordination, our good order, and that prophetic tranquillity, which is far more terrible than any ordinary storm? You have seen sixty thousand men under our command, and not a hand was raised, and not a forbidden word was uttered in that amazing multitude. You have beheld an example of our power in the almost miraculous sobriety of the people. . . . Is it meet and wise to leave us armed with such a dominion?

114. Peel to Fitzgerald, June 21, 1828, copy, *ibid.,* foll. 268–269.
115. Requoted from T. C. Luby, *The Life and Times of Daniel O'Connell* (Glasgow, 1871), p. 518.
116. Fitzgerald to Peel, n.d., BM, PP, 40322, foll. 265–267.
117. Fitzgerald to Peel, July 5, 1828, *Peel Memoirs, 1,* 113–115.

> Trust us not with it; strip us of this appalling despotism; annihilate us by concession; . . . if you do not, tremble for the result.[118]

Thus did the year 1828 bring the Catholic question to a dramatic climax. In a land where violence was traditional and insurrection periodic the gap between constitutional protest and physical force was slight. The association, founded at a time of renewed agrarian outrages, gave the first notable proof of its influence by succeeding, where Dublin Castle long had failed, in suppressing the midnight raids, arson, and murders of the Ribbonmen. But the danger was not thereby eliminated. In one respect, at least, it was increased. This island-wide organization presented a more formidable basis for revolution than had hitherto appeared in Irish history. What was lacking was the will to plunge the obedient and disciplined masses into civil war. It was a defect, so to speak, cleverly disguised. With the help of the rebellion scare of Christmas 1824, the ever-present likelihood of foreign intervention, and the precarious state of the military forces in Ireland, O'Connell, Sheil, and their fellow demagogues were able to play constantly upon the fears of the Irish Government. In 1828, especially, the simultaneous meetings, the unauthorized processions of the peasantry, the tour of Lawless in Ulster, and, to cap all, the Clare election emphasized the explosive nature of party passions. The Catholic clergy were sincerely alarmed. Even the lay leaders affected to be unsure of their control. Perhaps, if concession were longer denied, they would lose their influence, or, in desperation, abandon their pacifism. It was such considerations that outweighed, in the minds of English ministers, the probable reluctance of the agitators to resort to violence, and it was such considerations likewise that presented them with a suitable dilemma to lay before the King, concession or civil war.

118. Speech of Sheil at Ennis, July 5, 1828, *Sheil's Sketches, 2,* 149–156.

# 9. Victory and Aftermath

In 1829 only two men were strong enough to hold together a Tory government. Their capitulation, therefore, on the Catholic question virtually assured the passage of emancipation. While Wellington and Peel, in common with the King and their high Tory followers, persistently spoke of concession as incompatible with the Protestant constitution of church and state, both gave signs even before 1828 that they were prepared one day to abandon principle for expediency. In 1825, for instance, when Burdett's relief bill was before Parliament, Lord Liverpool and Peel were compelled to deny rumors that they were weakening in their opposition,[1] and in the following year political gossip to the same effect moved Peel once again to insist he knew "nothing of compromise." [2]

Yet the rumors did have some basis in fact. In 1825 Peel hinted, in a letter to his old friend Gregory, that if his opposition to Burdett's bill proved futile, he would make the best of the wings for the sake of Ireland.[3] More explicit in 1826, he actually foretold the course he later adopted: "When I see it [emancipation] inevitable I shall (taking due care to free my motives from all suspicion) try to make the best terms for the future security of the Protestant." [4] Wellington's wavering seemed even more pro-

1. The rumor, published in the London *Morning Chronicle,* March 10, 1825, probably arose from the mild, forbearing tone of the prime minister's speech of that year in favor of the suppression of the association. Liverpool inserted a contradictory statement in the *Courier,* an unusual course of action which, nevertheless, did not appease the ultras who considered the language of the denial not very emphatic. Liverpool to Peel, March 10, 1825, BM, PP, 40305, fol. 20; Peel to Dr. Lloyd, March 12, 1825, *ibid.,* 40342, fol. 216. Liverpool, in fact, was prepared eventually to concede emancipation. W. R. Brock, *Lord Liverpool and Liberal Toryism, 1820 to 1827* (Cambridge, England, The University Press, 1941), pp. 268–269; also Canning to Wellesley, May 22, 1827, BM, WP, 37297, foll. 272–280.

2. Peel to Sir George Hill, Nov. 9, 1826, copy, BM, PP, 40389, foll. 234–237.

3. Peel to Gregory, March 21, 1825, *ibid.,* 40334, foll. 118–127.

4. Peel to J. L. Foster, Nov. 3, 1826, Parker, *Peel, 1,* 422–423. A brother-in-law of Peel, William Cockburn, the dean of York, was responsible for some of the rumors in 1826. He let it be known he had heard Peel, at a dinner party, "express a doubt as to how long it might be expedient to endeavour to oppose in the House

nounced. In a private memorandum of 1825 he proposed that the English Government arrange with the Pope that the Catholic Church in Ireland "be missionary rather than national," its clergy paid by the state, and communication with Rome strictly regulated. In return the government would "repeal every law imposing any disability upon Roman Catholics." [5] One can well imagine the rage of high Tories had they seen the memorandum. It was not discussed in the cabinet. But its existence remained convincing proof that the Duke, also, was prepared to compromise.

Even in 1828 Wellington and Peel came to a decision much earlier than is generally realized. The canny Creevey noted in his journal on February 12: "My sincere opinion is, and I beg to record it thus early, the Beau *will* do something for the Catholics of Ireland." [6] Indefinite enough as to what that something was, Creevey did diagnose correctly the Duke's disposition. For obvious reasons Wellington and Peel kept their intention to themselves, and in secret during the whole summer, autumn, and winter of 1828 the former tried to prevail upon George IV.[7] On August 1 he sent a long memorandum to the King on the impossibility of withholding emancipation; to do so would imperil the royal authority in Ireland and the King's reputation in Europe; more practically, his ministers were helpless: they could not suggest a dissolution of Parliament for fear of rebellion in the sister island or, at least, the return of a still larger majority of "Catholics" to the House of Commons.[8] In reply to this memorandum the King, unable to gainsay his minister's description of Ireland, agreed to permit him to discuss the question with the lord chancellor, Lyndhurst, and with Peel, on the definite understanding that he was not pledging himself to any plan they might adopt.[9]

While the reply was, indeed, some slight concession, George IV was still hostile, and his resistance increased with the efforts of his chief minister to overcome it. Peel, more cautious than his colleague, adopted a less forthright course; even in letters to Wellington he continued to assert that his mind was unchanged on the Catholic question, although at the same time stating that he thought the

---

of Lords what might come frequently recommended by large majorities of the Commons." Cockburn to Peel, Jan. 30, 1827, BM, PP, 40391, foll. 175–176.

5. "Memorandum on the Case of the Roman Catholics of Ireland," n.d., 1825, *Wellington Despatches, 2,* 592–607.

6. Maxwell, *Creevey Papers, 2,* 152.

7. Wellington to Gower, Jan. 19, 1829, *Wellington Despatches, 5,* 456–457.

8. Memorandum for the King, Aug. 1, 1828, *ibid., 4,* 565–570.

9. George IV to Wellington, Aug. 3, 1828, *ibid.,* 573.

"open" cabinet principle must be given up, that it was "necessary to make your choice between different kinds and different degrees of evil, to compare the actual danger resulting from the union and organization of the Roman Catholic Body and the incessant agitation in Ireland with the prospective and apprehended dangers to the Constitution or Religion of the country." [10] Peel was hedging. While it appeared which course he recommended, he did not want to bear the onus of a decision for which, ironically, the King was later to condemn him anyway as "a rag of calico." Even Lord Eldon, although he tried to nerve George IV to further resistance, admitted glumly that he looked "on the Roman Catholic question as, bit by bit, here a little and there a little, to be ultimately, and at no distant day, carried." [11]

The day was closer than he thought. In January 1829 Wellington secured the royal permission for a discussion of the whole issue in the new session of Parliament. The King still refused to commit himself and in the course of February balked once again at the emancipation bill sponsored by the cabinet. Only on the threat of his ministers to resign did he finally capitulate: "As I find the country would be left without an administration, I have decided to yield my opinion to *that* which is considered by the Cabinet to be for the immediate interests of the country. . . . God knows what pain it costs me to write these words." [12]

The King was not the only one to feel pain. Tory ultras raged at the apostasy of their leaders.[13] Some rebelled,[14] but the majority had no alternative, other than immediately wrecking their party, to following the Duke and Peel and enabling them to carry the question assisted by "the main pillars of the monarchy" rather than by "the rump of the Whigs and Mr. Canning." The government's emancipation bill passed the Commons easily, the Lords with only a futile last-ditch stand by the irreconcilables; and on April 13, 1829, almost exactly six years after the first meeting of the Cath-

10. Peel to Wellington, Aug. 11, 1828, BM, PP, 40307, foll. 185–196.

11. Eldon to Lord Stowell, n.d. (probably Sept.), 1828, in Horace Twiss, *The Public and Private Life of Lord Chancellor Eldon* (Philadelphia, 1844), *2,* 208.

12. George IV to Wellington, March 4, 1829, *Wellington Despatches, 5,* 518.

13. Wellington had assured Rutland of his determination to "uphold the Protestant interest," while Lethbridge innocently volunteered to second the address. The Duchess of Richmond had the apostates' names tied to stuffed rats in her drawing room; Wetherell was dismissed for a violent speech against "contemptible apostasy"; and Lord Winchelsea had to fight a duel with Wellington for accusing him of deceiving the Protestant and High Church party. Keith Grahame Feiling, *The Second Tory Party, 1714–1832* (London, Macmillan & Co., 1938), pp. 370, 372.

14. 173 Tory members fought the second reading. Even when the King's surrender became known, 109 Tory peers opposed the government. *Ibid.,* p. 372.

olic Association, George IV, petulantly threatening to retire to Hanover, affixed his royal signature.

The act itself was simple and direct. For the old oaths of allegiance, abjuration, and supremacy, as qualification for Parliament and "any office, franchise, or civil right," it substituted a new one. Catholics were now obliged only to swear allegiance to the Crown in its Protestant succession, acceptance of the property settlement and the church establishment as provided by law, and disavowal of the deposing power of the Pope as well as his assumption of any temporal jurisdiction in Britain. The act, while framed primarily with a view to Ireland, was to apply also to England and to Scotland and thus to confer there a right which Irish Catholics had enjoyed since 1793, the elective franchise. In addition, throughout the United Kingdom Catholics might belong to any corporation and hold all civil and military offices, with the exception of regent, lord chancellor of either island, and lord lieutenant of Ireland. They could not, indeed, hold religious celebrations outside their churches or private houses; their bishops were forbidden to adopt the titles of sees belonging to the Established Church; and all members of religious orders who should in future enter the country were to be banished. But from the beginning these restrictions were almost a dead letter.

Emancipation was inevitable. But its enactment in 1829 rather than five or ten years later is attributable directly to the Irish situation and in particular to the association. In Ireland a handful of agitators created a mass movement extending from a central directory down to the remotest parish in the island and so mobilizing the Catholic population, through a pyramidal structure of provincial, county, town, and parish meetings and Rent committees, that they presented for the first time in the long struggle for emancipation, and, indeed, in the history of political agitation in the British Isles, the ominous spectacle of a formidable national solidarity. While the very existence of such a body constituted a challenge to the legitimate government, the pressure it was able to exert, through propaganda, harassment of legislators and administrators, and the threat of physical force, brought home to ministers the ultimate question, "Can we any longer delay to do something? Must not that *something* be either restraints in Ireland unknown in the ordinary practice of the constitution, or concession in some form or other?" [15]

The answer was concession, the only practical answer under cir-

15. Wellington to Peel, Sept. 12, 1828, *Wellington Despatches, 5,* 44–45.

cumstances that included the danger of civil commotion. At the least there was the prospect of exclusive dealing, run on the banks, and nonpayment of tithes and rent. Far more fearful was the possibility of insurrection and civil war. Even one of the coolest members of the association, Thomas Wyse, predicted: "Had things gone on in the state in which they were, it is quite certain the great mass of the Catholics, at no distant period, would scarcely have thought it worth their while to have continued asking any longer, for what had been so long and so punctiliously refused them." [16] The grim possibility of another rising was one of the most urgent arguments for concession, as Peel frankly admitted:

> In the course of the last six months, England being at peace with the whole world has had five-sixths of the infantry forces of the United Kingdom occupied in maintaining the peace and in police duties in Ireland. I consider the state of things which requires such an application of military force much worse than open rebellion. . . . If this be the state of things at present, let me implore you to consider what would be the [word indecipherable] of England in the event of war. Would an English Parliament tolerate for one moment a state of things in Ireland which would compel the [word indecipherable] of half her military force to protect or rather to controul that exposed part of the empire? Can we forget what happened in 1782, what happened in 1793? [17]

Dire as it was, the prospect of violence gave place in immediate concern to an even more pressing consideration: "The Roman Catholics have discovered their strength in respect to the elective franchise. Let us beware that we do not teach them how easy it will be to paralyze the Government and the law." [18] The return of O'Connell for Clare and the election pledges projected by the association proved that the Catholics were well on the way to learning the lesson. There could be no doubt that the contagion of Clare would have been irresistible in all but six or seven of the counties of Ireland, all the large towns, and all the boroughs with popular franchise. In 1828 Wellington could not appoint to cabinet office or raise to the peerage any representative of an Irish constituency. Much less could he dissolve Parliament and "permit the Roman

16. Wyse, *Historical Sketch, 1,* 323.
17. Rough draft of a letter of Peel, no addressee, Feb. 8, 1829, BM, PP, 40326, foll. 185–188.
18. *Ibid.*

Catholic Association to send fifty or sixty Radicals from Ireland." [19]

Had the prime minister had behind him the solid support of Parliament, he might, as Peel was able to do in 1843, have kept Ireland at bay through coercion. But as a result of the basically political and social, rather than religious, nature of the Irish problem and the consequent weakness of the Protestant argument that insisted on the suppression of the social and religious aspirations of the majority of Irishmen in order to perpetuate a political situation, the English hegemony, both Parliament and ministry were divided. For more than sixteen years the Lords and Commons had been at odds on the Catholic question. For over a quarter of a century it had been found impossible to exclude from the councils of the King such men as Pitt, Castlereagh, and Canning. Finally, as Peel sadly noted: "The opinions of the young men who are now entering into public life, and who are likely to distinguish themselves, are, *with scarcely an exception of even one*, in favour of an adjustment of the Question." [20]

On the other hand, the King, the church, and most of the English people were hostile to concession. For this reason Wellington and Peel were compelled to act secretly and swiftly in 1829, "without giving time for the excitement throughout England with which we are threatened." [21] But the animus of the people was a sporadic thing. While O'Connell and his friends did suffer some indignities from the London mob and saw "No Popery" chalked on walls, with placards and prints in the streets depicting the fires of Smithfield and Wellington and the King kissing the Pope's toe, there was little prospect of a Gordon riot. Lord Eldon commented glumly: "The country cares very little about the matter." [22]

Many of the Irish Protestants also showed themselves apathetic. They had come to share the view of Lord Hutchinson, who remarked to Creevey: "In this country the Catholics are fifty to one: in property we are twenty to their one. Let us start fair as to laws, and I have a *just cause* to embark in, and my mind is quite made up to fight them in defence of my property; but I don't like fighting in an unjust cause." [23] In March 1829 Peel remarked wearily to the new viceroy, the Duke of Northumberland: "I suppose the intelligent part of the Protestant Community is quiescent

19. Peel to Gregory, Feb. 1, 1829, *ibid.*, 40334, foll. 274–278.
20. See note 17, above.
21. Charles Arbuthnot to Peel, Feb. 10, 1829, BM, PP, 40340, foll. 211–212.
22. Eldon to Lady F. J. Bankes, n.d., 1829, H. Twiss, *Eldon, 2*, 215.
23. Entry of Oct. 1, 1828, Maxwell, *Creevey Papers, 2*, 174–175.

if not entirely contented."[24] Relief on the part of Tory leaders matched the satisfaction of liberal Protestants and the elation of Catholics. Emancipation in 1829 put an end at least to "the long litigated question that had for so many years precluded the cordial cooperation of public men, and had left Ireland the arena for fierce political conflicts."[25]

The sister island was to remain an arena. Had concession come in 1801 it might, as Lecky maintained, have conciliated Irish feeling. In 1829 it was too late.[26] The very manner of its granting confirmed Irishmen in their wildest impressions of their power. In 1824 Sydney Smith, with his usual incisiveness, had predicted that the business "will be done at last rather by fear than by any wit or reason."[27] The event justified his pessimism. The English Government made a great concession not from any sense of justice but avowedly in consequence of a powerful priestly and democratic agitation. Wellington publicly confessed that he was faced with the alternatives of surrender or civil war. How fateful such an admission for subsequent English-Irish relations! "I fear," said the Earl of Mansfield, "the Irish Roman Catholics will not be slow in perceiving, that as it is by combination that they have obtained concession to their present demands, they should remain combined, and thus they will obtain their ulterior objects."[28] Perhaps the Earl was thinking of repeal of the Union.

The Catholics did not remain combined. The association dissolved itself before Parliament tried once again to outlaw it, and the unprecedented alliance of the Catholic middle class with the peasantry waned. Thereafter the connection was unstable, until the "Mud Cabin Act" of 1884 gave the peasantry popular franchise and thus some means of controlling their representatives in Parliament. In the 1830's, when O'Connell was demanding peaceful support of his repeal agitation, the peasantry, inspired rather by the words of Bishop Doyle, waged a tithe war quite successfully by themselves. Not until O'Connell's union with the Young Irelanders in 1842–44 gave the peasantry the notion that he might be ready to lead them in the fight they wanted, did they give him

24. Peel to Northumberland, March 25, 1829, BM, PP, 40327, fol. 17.

25. *Peel Memoirs, 1,* 188–189.

26. As Lord Melbourne later remarked, on the Catholic question all the wise men proved to be wrong and all the damned fools right. Emancipation was only a prelude to the demand for repeal of the Union.

27. Smith to Thomas Moore, June 5, 1824, PRO, Papers of Lord John Russell, 30/22/1.

28. In the House of Lords, April 3, 1829, *Parl. Debates,* 2d Ser., *21,* 248.

mass support again. They had their own immediate, practical objectives. And simple repeal of the Union was not one of them. When emancipation was won and O'Connell began talking not about rents, tithes, evictions, duty labor, fines, and bribes, but about the restoration of Grattan's parliament, they lost most of their interest in him except as a personality. Yet they did not forget the lesson of organization or their desire to fight. Combination was to plague English rule in Ireland for the rest of the century,[29] indeed, until the establishment of Irish self-government in 1922. The Catholic question provided but another example of a fundamental and unhappy lack of understanding on the part of Englishmen of the distinctive problems of Ireland, of the vast differences in character and circumstance between the two peoples. Yet even though so long delayed, emancipation, had it been granted as a right and graciously instead of grudgingly and as a ransom extorted by threat of violence, might have helped to render less bitter subsequent relations between the two islands.

In Ireland itself the immediate effects of the measure seemed scarcely proportionate to the energy and enthusiasm that had gone into six years of turmoil. To be sure, the Catholic leaders achieved their main objective: they might now aspire to seats in Parliament and to all public offices under the Crown except those of lord chancellor and viceroy. But public and municipal posts were still controlled by a caste reluctant to share them, the ascendancy which had been in the saddle since 1660. For the middle-class Catholics, then, the actual rewards of emancipation were strictly limited; and for the masses, upon whom the leaders relied for their power and whose grievances they had so strenuously condemned, there was no direct benefit at all. In fact, emancipation was immediately followed by an act disfranchising the Irish forty-shilling freeholders.

The raising of the franchise from forty shillings to ten pounds reduced the Irish electorate from a little over 100,000 [30] to about 16,000,[31] and it destroyed the last safeguard of the small farmer

29. Of the 22 changes of cabinet between 1829 and 1900, 11 were due primarily to Irish questions.

30. Most historians have placed the number much higher, above 200,000. A statistical return of freeholders in the counties made by order of the House of Lords in 1829 totaled 212,594. But the list is cumulative; some of the returns dated from 1788; and by comparing them with the numbers entitled to vote in specific counties in 1826 and in Clare in 1828, one finds that over half the freeholds were unregistered or had become defunct. "Return of freeholders registered up to 1829," ISPO, OP II, 588zz/917.

31. The number of £10 freeholders registered from June 1829 to January 1830 was 15,800. "Return of freeholders in 1830," *ibid.*, 588zz/918.

against eviction by landlords to whom his vote was no longer a source of political power or an incentive for the multiplication of freeholds. O'Connell and his colleagues did protest in 1829 against the bill. They could not do less in view of their commitments during the wings controversy and the support the forty-shillingers had given them in Waterford and Clare. But it was a feeble effort compared with the resistance they might have made, with the resources of organization at their command, had the majority of them been sincerely dedicated to parliamentary reform. They never broke completely with the notion of accepting emancipation as a boon from an upper-class legislature rather than as a right won by the people. Indeed, they undermined their public protests with private communications reaching the eyes of ministers.

Letters from O'Connell, Sheil, Conway, and P. V. Fitzpatrick, addressed to a friend in London but obviously, on the basis of internal evidence, intended for the information of government, contained assurances that disfranchisement would provoke no dangerous reaction in Ireland. Fitzpatrick stated that the opponents of the measure in Dublin were neither many nor clamorous; [32] Sheil, testifying to the same conditions in the counties where he was on circuit, asserted that the franchise should not be weighed against the liberty and tranquillity of the country and promised, "We were formerly interested in awakening, we are now equally interested and bound to allay the popular ferment." [33] O'Connell wrote that he had "an insurmountable repugnance to give the Ministry any species of trouble," and was only too anxious to throw the people whom he had rescued from the toils of Captain Rock "into the hands of a just and paternal Government." [34] It was left for Conway to make the most candid avowal of the game the Irishmen were playing; their public remonstrance, he confided, was due merely to the necessity of saving appearances: "After all the resolutions of the Catholic Association, it cannot reasonably be expected that they could be suffered to go by the board without a protest. . . . But I implore you to be under no apprehension whatever." [35]

The letters do little credit to the reputation of the writers for sincerity, consistency, or foresightedness. So far as O'Connell was concerned, the loss of the forty-shilling freeholders in all probability prevented him from forming a solid bloc in the House of

32. Fitzpatrick to Pierce Mahony, March 8, 1829, BM, PP, 40399, fol. 97.

33. Sheil to Mahony, March 21 and 29, 1829, *ibid.*, foll. 98–99, 108–109.

34. O'Connell to Mahony, March 28 and 30, 1829, copies, *ibid.*, foll. 100–103. 113–114.

35. Conway to Mahony, March 29, 1829, *ibid.*, foll. 110–112.

Commons, an Irish party. On the other hand, the Irish leaders found themselves in a perplexing situation. Emancipation was an aim on which all could and did agree, but to reject it because accompanied by a raising of the franchise and to divert the agitation to parliamentary reform, as urged by Lawless at home and by Hunt and the Radicals in England,[36] was a course which, however much it might have hastened the revival of the reform movement in the United Kingdom, would have split the association. Some of its members, like Sheil, prepared only to threaten, were as reluctant as Wellington and Peel to face, much less to evoke, the specter of radical reform. Certainly the Catholic bishops would have dissociated themselves from such a purely political endeavor.

The opening of Parliament and government office and the reduction of the Irish electorate were the most immediate and spectacular results of the six-year struggle. Of far greater importance was the way the Emancipation Act had been forced on a reluctant ministry. In Ireland a national conspiracy of unprecedented proportions left a deep impress, for good and for ill, on the history of the country. For the first time all classes of the Catholic population were arrayed under leaders of their own race and religion in a tremendous mass movement. Such a lesson in effective political organization was not easily forgotten. O'Connell deliberately modeled his subsequent repeal associations on the pattern developed in the Corn Exchange. While less successful than their prototype, they passed on to later movements of the 19th century, notably those for land reform and home rule, the tradition that national benefits could be wrung from England only by the threat of tumult in Ireland.

The significance of any great movement lies not only in the aims and efforts of those who undertake it but also in its impact on their way of life. In this respect the lesson of the emancipation struggle had its weaknesses as well as its advantages. It bequeathed to Ireland a type of politician and a devotion to personalities rather than to political principles that remain to the present day. O'Connell, as one of his biographers has remarked,[37] was the father of the Irish Parliamentary party and of Tammany Hall, the epitome of the creative, witty, scurrilous, disingenuous Irish politician. The Catholic Association, by endowing him with an unchallenged primacy, earned for him the proud title "The Liberator," one which he never forgot and did not permit the Irish people to for-

36. Public letter of Henry Hunt to O'Connell, Leeds *Patriot,* March 14, 1829.
37. O'Faoláin, *King of the Beggars*, p. 220.

get. The knowledge that he, almost singlehanded, had been able to withhold 40,000 of his countrymen for three days from whiskey drinking and could with assurance dare any man, including the King, to repeat the experiment was itself a heady draught. It accounted for many of the demagogic blind spots he later suffered. From the necessity of circumstances he was more the politician than the statesman. At the Corn Exchange, where his unique authority led him to look rather to the management of underlings than to the inspiration of colleagues, more outspoken members frequently complained that he treated them like children, that he was prone to consider any opposition a personal affront. Such an attitude, while explaining much of his inconsistency, temporizing, and shortsightedness, leads one to speculate on the possibilities of the situation had a man of the caliber of Thomas Wyse, who first appreciated the importance of election strategy, had a larger share in the planning and direction of the movement. As it was, Wyse, with his intense concern for the long-range political education of the Irish people, and O'Connell, with his immediate absorption in doing battle with whatever weapon came to hand, were poles apart.

Even Wyse did not cope with many aspects of the complex Irish problem neglected by O'Connell and the other leaders. Concentrating on religious and political grievances, they failed to realize the crucial nature of the land question. O'Connell showed himself a bitter enemy of the Irish trade unions, which in Dublin in 1830 were the best organized in the islands; he opposed the introduction of poor laws into Ireland; and to many present-day Irish nationalists he is still anathema for his determined pacifism, his seeking only repeal of the Union and not complete separation from Britain, and his Benthamite attitude toward the Irish language. He considered the Gaelic way of life, as romanticized in the ballads of the people and later glamorized in the doctrinaire nationalism of the Young Irelanders, unrealistic and nostalgic. Irish, still the common tongue of over two millions of the people and a language he himself spoke fluently, he regarded as impractical, a barrier to the progress he envisioned for his country as part of the United Kingdom.[38]

The manner in which O'Connell addressed himself to the ques-

38. O'Connell made at least two speeches in Irish at local meetings. One of them, at Tralee, discouraged him from continuing the practice: the reporters from the London papers were ludicrously puzzled, sitting with pencils poised and not understanding a word.

tion of the Irish language was typical not only of the man but of the movement he led. The association was an opportunistic affair, and although it is easy in retrospect to consider how much it might have set itself to accomplish had its leaders only appreciated the more fundamental problems of their country and devoted themselves to wider, national aims, it did attain its principal objective, and much more besides. It brought about a revolution in Ireland by means of a colossus of democratic power which amazed and alarmed even its creators. They could not be expected, these men who had never tasted the responsibility of government office, to display the moderation, the statesmanship, the good form of a man like Robert Peel. The material was raw, the craftsmen uncouth. Emancipation, while not all they expected of it, was, to a dispirited people, a token of national rehabilitation, a measure more pressing and seemingly more attainable than parliamentary reform, repeal of the Union, disestablishment of the church, or settlement of the land problem. In setting this aim, one based on religious distinctions, before the Catholic masses and thus emphasizing religious cleavage in Ireland to the further embitterment of relations between the churches, the leaders contributed remotely to the antagonism which appears today most strikingly in Irish and English politics in the Border problem. It is difficult, nevertheless, to imagine how emancipation might have been won without antagonizing an already hostile minority, jealous of their ascendancy and for the most part insensitive to the legitimate protests of the majority of their countrymen.

The responsibility of the association for increasing religious tension was more than offset by its contribution to the general movement for political reform. It coordinated a mass movement throughout Ireland without contravening the laws against political organization, and it won its point without plunging the country, as so often in the past, into rebellion and civil war. It taught the peasant population of the island self-reliance, obedience to their chosen leaders, and the novel lesson that by union and discipline they could challenge and break the resistance even of a king. In the last decades of the 18th century a new patriotism had developed among the ascendancy minority, leaders of the popular struggle for an independent and representative parliament and for relaxation of the penal laws. The Rebellion of 1798 and the Union dealt a fatal blow to this Anglo-Irish Protestant liberal spirit. What survived was the republican tradition of Wolfe Tone, to fuse in the 1820's with the new Catholic democratic patriotism of

O'Connell and his association, and to continue later with the Fenians and still later with the IRA extremists.

The emancipation conflict had repercussions outside the narrow confines of Ireland. A direct and immediate result was the granting of civil equality to English, Scottish, and Welsh Catholics. Less perceptible, but scarcely less important, was the effect on political organization in England. Within four years another and even more spectacular reform was to be forced on the British Government in much the same way as Catholic Emancipation.

In 1829 Wellington and Peel found themselves on the horns of a dilemma: they had to choose between entering a constitutional struggle far more ominous than the Wilkes case and betraying their high Tory followers. They chose the latter course and, rather than resign and allow Whigs to carry the measure, remained in office to safeguard as best they could the Protestant establishment. By doing so they broke their party. Tory ultras were no longer capable of opposing a solid front to all reform. In addition, the association inspired the British reformers by providing an object lesson in the effectiveness of political organization and mass action from below. Since the great weakness of previous reform societies had been the lack of general organization and a central directing body, it is impossible to say how long a time might have elapsed before the defects were remedied by the English reformers had they been left to their own resources. As it was, Ireland presented a visible and impressive example of mass action, a lesson which Thomas Wyse hoped would guide the Englishman also "in the future struggles he may have to make for the restitution or improvement of national rights." [39]

Wyse's optimism was not immediately justified. The association, although it made a deep impression on English Radicals, did not suddenly arouse a powerful reform movement. Political agitation, dormant in England during the years that the Irish struggle absorbed public attention,[40] was to be revived on a wide scale only late in December 1829 with the founding of the Birmingham Political Union. Before that date there were, nevertheless, significant stirrings. A letter of Junius in 1827 recommended the formation of reform associations with a national rent based on the Irish model.[41] The suggestion was ineffectual, but in the following year

39. Wyse, *Historical Sketch, 1,* 7.

40. From 1824 to 1829 not a single English petition was presented in Parliament on the subject of parliamentary reform. Jephson, *The Platform, 2,* 31.

41. *A Letter from Junius to the People of Great Britain on Reform and Union of Sentiment* (pamphlet, London, 1827).

the London *Examiner* took up the theme, observing that the state of public feeling was favorable to renewed consideration of parliamentary reform, "and it is desirable that agitation and organization which have been working such wonders for Ireland should be made assistant to this great object for the Empire." [42] In 1829 recommendations to the same effect appeared in greater number; speakers at radical meetings pointed to the example set by Ireland; and during the latter half of the year attempts were made to found reform societies on the pattern of the association.[43] None of the efforts was successful, and it was not until Thomas Attwood launched his Birmingham Political Union on December 14, 1829, that an English equivalent of the Irish organization was realized.

Attwood plainly acknowledged, in a speech at Birmingham on May 8, 1829, the connection between the two agitations: "But Reform is not the work of a day. The Duke of Wellington has taught us how to command reform. By union, by organization, by general contribution, by patriotic exertion, and by discretion, keeping always within the law and the constitution. These are the elements of Reform. By the peaceful combination of means like these the Irish people have lately obtained a glorious and bloodless victory. . . . In this work I am willing to participate, and at a proper time I will cordially contribute my humble assistance to set it in operation." [44] The time came seven months later, and in the actual founding of his organization Attwood apparently consulted O'Connell. The Irishman replied in a letter stating the project to be lawful, summarizing the principles and constitution of the late Catholic Association, and requesting to be enrolled in the Birmingham Political Union.[45] In imitation of the Birmingham example political unions mushroomed throughout Britain to become the directors of the great struggle of 1830–32, fulfilling a prediction made by Lord Grey: ". . . you will probably see associations all over the country; and when once they have felt their power, the history of the Catholic question will show the consequences that may be expected." [46] The consequences were consti-

42. London *Examiner,* Aug. 31, 1828.

43. London *Examiner,* June 14, Aug. 26, Sept. 13, 14, Oct. 25, 1829; London *Morning Chronicle,* Aug. 11, Oct. 20, 1829.

44. Thomas Attwood, *Distressed State of the Country* (pamphlet, Birmingham, 1829), p. 80.

45. O'Connell to Attwood, Feb. 16, 1830, Fitzpatrick, *Correspondence of O'Connell, 1,* 199–200.

46. Grey to Sir H. Taylor, March 22, 1831, in Henry Earl Grey, ed., *The Reform Act, 1832* (London, 1867), 1, 186.

tutional crises and eventual concession extorted through the threat of physical force. The Reform Act of 1832, like its predecessor, Catholic Emancipation, was obtained under pressure from powerful, extraconstitutional, voluntary political associations.

Besides leading to a breakup of the Tory party and providing a stimulus to the English reformers, the Irish agitation made its impact felt in less obvious ways. The numerous Irish workers in England were everywhere active in the radical movement; the disfranchising of the Irish forty-shilling freeholders, seemingly a direct setback to reform, proved that the existing franchise was by no means sacrosanct; and, finally, emancipation opened the doors of Parliament to Catholic reformers. O'Connell, a radical, middle-class Irish Catholic, had pushed a middle-class measure through an aristocratic English Parliament in 1829; and he had done so with a warning: "How mistaken men are who suppose that the history of the world will be over as soon as we are emancipated! Oh, *that* will be the time to *commence* the struggle for popular rights." [47]

The struggle for popular rights in Ireland from 1823 to 1829 began not only a new epoch in the history of that island but also contributed indirectly to the social and political revolution that changed England in 1832. It was but a link in a chain. The lesson of the power of the organized masses was passed on by the reformers of 1832 to the Chartists, the Anti-Corn Law League, the second and third reform act agitations, the English trade-union movement.

In 1892 the historian Lecky, looking back over six decades, ventured the pessimistic judgment that "it was in the long popular agitation for Catholic emancipation that the foundation was laid for the political anarchy of our own day." [48] Lecky was referring to Ireland, with thoughts of Young Irelanders, the Fenians, the Irish party, the political influence of the Irish priesthood, and the decay of landlord sovereignty. But his comment could easily be expanded. Modern democratic government, in many of its aspects, would doubtlessly appear to him anarchical, for one thing because of the powerful pressure groups that operate within our political system. These organizations, catering to particular and often divisive interests, do seem at first sight anarchical. Yet in larger per-

47. O'Connell to James Sugrue, March 11, 1829, Fitzpatrick, *Correspondence of O'Connell, 1,* 176.

48. Lecky, *History of Ireland, 3,* 150.

spective they are seen to perform an essential, if not always well-ordered or altruistic, function of political representation. In the long history of their development the political agitation that convulsed Ireland and absorbed the attention of England from 1823 to 1829 played a major role.

# *Bibliographical Note*

THERE has been hitherto no adequate history of the Catholic Association of Ireland. Consequently, the following bibliography will be devoted mainly to source material and include only those secondary works which have been of immediate use to a study of the association and its agitation. The struggle for emancipation, both in Ireland and in England, began long before 1823, and for the fullest, but by no means complete, listing of the literature that has risen from the general movement one should consult H. W. C. Davis' bibliography for his essay on "Catholic Emancipation" in Lord Acton and others, eds., *The Cambridge Modern History, 10* (New York, 1911), 860–866.

## SOURCES

### I. MANUSCRIPTS

*A. The association's own records.* The papers of the Catholic Association have long been considered lost or destroyed, and not until 1942 were the secretary's minutes of four meetings, three in 1827 and one in 1828, discovered and deposited in the National Library of Ireland, where they are filed as Catholic Association MSS. They form only a fraction of what must have been an immense bulk of records of a society that held an average of 100 regular meetings a year for six years. In 1950, in the course of my researches in Ireland, I found a considerably larger store of the association's papers in the archdiocesan archives, Archbishop's House, Dublin, in seven large cartons labeled "Catholic Proceedings." While not complete, they are especially valuable for the light they throw on the latter phases of the movement in 1827 and 1828. They comprise minutes of meetings, Rent letters, census returns, lists of members, minute books of the finance and grievance committees, financial accounts, placards and handbills, reports of country meetings, and many letters of O'Connell, as well as one of his personal fee books. A smaller collection of similar material is preserved at O'Connell's family home, Darrynane Abbey, County Kerry, in a large file book of the association.

*B. Government reports.* The records of the association itself are supplemented by a valuable, and hitherto unused, collection of transcripts of its proceedings made by shorthand reporters employed by the Irish Government to attend all its meetings. With the exception of those for 1824 which were sent to Peel and are filed in the Public Record Office, London, Home Office, 100/213, these reports are in the State Paper Office, Record Tower, Dublin Castle. Since 1913 the majority of them had been listed as missing, but in February 1950 the deputy keeper of the records, in response to my inquiries, kindly undertook a search which resulted in recovery of the fugitives. They form a bulky (the average report of a meeting runs to fifty folio pages) and almost complete record of the association's Dublin proceedings. They are catalogued as the Catholic Association Papers.

*C. Documents of state.* Five other collections in the Irish State Paper Office contain material pertinent to the agitation and the general state of Ireland during the 1820's: the State of the Country Papers, Official Papers (2d Ser.), Chief Secretary's Office Registered Papers, Secret Service Accounts, and Private Official Letters. They are especially valuable for their hundreds of letters and reports from informers, magistrates, judges, police officials, and private persons throughout the country on the incidence of agrarian crime and disorder, the activities of the secret societies, the local organization of the association, military and constabulary statistics, and elections. Here also is to be found much of the official and private correspondence of the chief and undersecretaries on such matters as government patronage, charges on the secret service lists, payments to newspapers, and the friction existing within Dublin Castle as a result of the pro-Catholic sympathies of the viceroys.

One of the most important single collections of letters dealing with Irish affairs is to be found in the Peel Papers in the British Museum. Robert Peel was home secretary during most of the 1820's, and as a result, 79 of the 436 bound volumes of his correspondence consist for the most part of letters and memoranda to and from his fellow cabinet ministers, members of the Irish Government, and personal friends and minor officials in Ireland on the subject of the association. Next in usefulness in the British

Museum are the Wellesley Papers, comprising the formal reports and private letters of the Marquis Wellesley, lord lieutenant of Ireland from 1821 to 1828. Duplicates and additional letters are preserved in the Wellesley Papers in the National Library of Ireland. The Liverpool, Hardwicke, and Huskisson Papers, and the Correspondence of Lord John Russell, all in the British Museum, also contain occasional letters on the Irish agitation. The Public Record Office, London, in the Home Office Papers, 100 (Ireland), possesses, in addition to the government transcripts for 1824, official correspondence on the state of Ireland, and in the Russell Papers, 30/22, a few letters to and from Lord John Russell descriptive of the progress of the Catholic question in Parliament and ministry.

Information on the attitude of the Irish hierarchy toward the agitation is to be found in letters of Archbishops Curtis and Murray to their Roman agent, Dr. Michael Blake, and to Cardinal della Somaglia, prefect of the Congregation of the Propagation of the Faith, in the archives of that congregation in Rome (separate from the Vatican Library), Irlanda, Volumes *24–25*. The Cullen Correspondence in the library of the Irish College, Rome, also contains a few letters on Catholic affairs in Ireland for this period.

*D. Private documents.* The most fruitful source for a behind-the-scenes view of the struggle is the correspondence of O'Connell, which, unfortunately, has never been collected in one repository. Some of it, directly concerned with the management of the association, is in the archdiocesan archives, Archbishop's House, Dublin, and in Darrynane Abbey, as noted above. In the library of University College, Dublin, are twenty-four cartons of uncatalogued correspondence, much of which, between O'Connell and Sheil, Cobbett, Eneas MacDonnell, the Knight of Kerry, and Lord Rossmore, deals with political aspects of the Catholic question. The National Library of Ireland has a smaller collection of O'Connell MSS, notably his letters to Counselor Bennett, 1815–31. Another series of letters, from O'Connell to his wife, in the possession of a descendant, Col. Manners O'Connell FitzSimon, Newbliss, County Monaghan, presents a candid expression of O'Connell's attitude toward his fellow leaders and the problems he had to cope with at the Corn Exchange.

The Murray Papers in the archdiocesan archives, Dublin, include many letters between Archbishop Murray of Dublin and his brother prelates, particularly the primate, Dr. Curtis. Here are to be found the originals of some of the famous Curtis-Wellington and Curtis-Anglesey letters of 1828. Dr. Michael Blake, Roman agent of the Irish bishops during the period, later became Bishop of Dromore. His correspondence, preserved in that diocese in the Bishop's House, Newry, County Down, contains letters from other bishops, notably Murray, on the political state of the Catholic question.

Additional letters of Robert Peel, revealing his constant anxiety over the Irish situation, exist in the library of the Royal Irish Academy, Dublin. The same institution also possesses a MS Diary of Mr. Justice Day, 1828–31, which describes some of the popular excitement near the end of the movement. A similar and more detailed account is to be found in the Journal of G. H. Ross-Lewin, who was at Ross Hill, Kilkee, County Clare, in September and October 1828. I am indebted for use of this diary to its present owner, Professor John Wardell, Old Abbey, Shanagolden, County Limerick. Four other manuscript sources containing observations of first-hand witnesses are the eight volumes of Journals of Lady Morgan, a Collection of Songs and Addresses at the Monaghan Election (1826), Rambles Northward in Ireland in 1827 by Thomas Bell, and a Letter-book of Lieutenant Colonel Brown, all in the National Library.

### II. PRINTED MATERIALS

*A. Newspapers.* The gaps in the records of the association and the government transcripts of its proceedings are filled by the Dublin newspapers, citation of which has been made in the footnotes of this study whenever all three sources contain identical material. The Dublin press gave full coverage to the proceedings of the association. The *Evening Post*, in particular, frequently published the actual minutes of meetings and much of the association's correspondence, as well as the resolutions and synopses of the speeches at the country meetings. The reports in the *Morning Register*, *Freeman's Journal*, *Weekly Register*, and *Chronicle* are slightly more condensed, as are those of the *Evening Mail* and *Saunder's News Letter*, two ascendancy papers important because of their hostility to the movement. The London papers, notably the *Morning Chronicle*, *Examiner*, *Times*, and *Courier*, reprinted accounts from the Dublin journals, although at times they sent their own reporters to Ireland.

*B. Documents of state.* The increasing concern of the English Government for Irish affairs as a result of the agitation is reflected in the space devoted to them in parliamentary papers and debates. In addition to the usual volumes dealing with bills, committees, accounts, and reports relating to Ireland, 1824, Volume *8* of the *Parliamentary Papers* is devoted to reports from the select committee of the House of Commons on the districts in Ireland under the Insurrection Act; 1825, Volumes *7–9* to minutes of evidence and reports from select committees of both houses on the general state of Ireland; and 1825, Volume *12*, and 1827, Volumes *12–13* to reports from a special commission on education in Ireland. Hansard's *Parliamentary Debates* (2d Ser., 1820–30) is likewise an essential source for the increasingly frequent Irish debates in both houses, particularly in 1824, 1825, 1828, and 1829.

*C. Private documents.* The first, and hitherto only, history of the association was the work of one of the Irish leaders, Thomas Wyse, whose *Historical Sketch of the Late Catholic Association of Ireland* (2 vols., London, 1829), while for the most part cool and dispassionate in spite of the fact that it was written between 1826 and 1828, is on the whole a propaganda effort. Its chief value lies in appendices of documents and statistics which constitute almost the whole of the second volume.

The observations of travelers in Ireland in the 1820's form a significant body of source material. Duvergier de Hauranne, *Lettres sur les élections angluises et sur la situation d'Irlande* (Paris, 1827); a German Prince (H. von Pückler-Muskau), *A Tour in England, Ireland, and France in the Years 1828 and 1829* (English transl., 2 vols., London, 1832); and James Glassford, *Notes on Three Tours in Ireland in 1824 and 1826* (Bristol, 1832) are eyewitness accounts of many of the country meetings. Although primarily of importance for knowledge of Ireland in years prior to the 1820's, Edward Wakefield, *An Account of Ireland Statistical and Political* (2 vols., London, 1812) is indispensable for background material.

The major speeches and some of the correspondence of O'Connell have been published in three ill-edited and apologetic works: John O'Connell, ed., *The Select Speeches of Daniel O'Connell* (2 vols., Dublin, 1854); M. F. Cusack, ed., *The Speeches and Public Letters of the Liberator* (2 vols., Dublin, 1875); and W. J. Fitzpatrick, ed., *Correspondence of Daniel O'Connell* (2 vols.,

London, 1888). Of the three Fitzpatrick's is the most helpful if barely adequate. Important letters between O'Connell and Bentham are to be found in John Bowring, ed., *The Works of Jeremy Bentham* (11 vols., Edinburgh, 1843). Sheil has fared slightly better at the hands of his editors. Thomas MacNevin, ed., *The Speeches of Richard Lalor Sheil* (London, 1847) gives only a sampling of his oratory. More useful are M. W. Savage, ed., *Sketches, Legal and Political, by Richard Lalor Sheil* (2 vols., London, 1855); R. Shelton Mackenzie, ed., *Sketches of the Irish Bar by Richard Lalor Sheil* (2 vols., New York, 1854); and W. Torrens McCullagh, ed., *Memoirs of the Right Honourable Richard Lalor Sheil* (2 vols., London, 1855). W. J. Fitzpatrick also undertook the editing of *The Life and Correspondence of the Right Rev. Dr. Doyle* (2 vols., Dublin and London, 1861), and although his aim seems to have been to canonize his hero, the work does contain some of the famous public letters and a selection of the private correspondence of the prelate who was the episcopal mainstay of the association.

Much of the pertinent correspondence of Peel has not been published. Earl Stanhope and Edward Cardwell, eds., *Memoirs by Sir Robert Peel* (2 vols., London, 1857–58) admit that they suppress a great deal. Charles S. Parker, ed., *Sir Robert Peel from His Private Papers* (3 vols., London, 1891–99) includes some of the suppressed letters but only a fraction of those cited in this study. *Despatches, Correspondence, and Memoranda of Arthur Duke of Wellington*, edited by his son (8 vols., London, 1867–80), are more extensive and of particular usefulness for an appreciation of the Duke's gradual capitulation on the Catholic question. For the important papers of Wellington's brother, Lord Wellesley, one has to rely almost entirely on unpublished sources, since Robert R. Pearce, ed., *Memoirs and Correspondence of Richard Marquess Wellesley* (3 vols., London, 1846) and *The Wellesley Papers*, by the editor of the Windham Papers (2 vols., London, 1914), contain surprisingly little about Wellesley's difficulties with the association. Rollo Russell does better by his father in his edition of *Early Correspondence of Lord John Russell, 1805–1840* (2 vols., London, 1913). Lord John was, however, a youthful side-line observer. William Coyningham Plunket, on the other hand, was in the thick of things in Ireland, and David Plunket, ed., *The Life, Letters, and Speeches of Lord Plunket* (2 vols., London, 1867) published a good record of his grandfather's problems as Irish attorney general. William Lamb, later Lord Melbourne, was chief secretary in 1827. W. M. Torrens, *Memoirs of Viscount Melbourne* (2 vols., London, 1878) has a few of his letters which bear on the agitation. Lamb, Plunket, Russell, and Wellesley were prominent advocates of emancipation; excellent examples of the type of opposition they encountered are given in Arthur Aspinall, ed., *The Letters of King George IV, 1812–1830* (3 vols., Cambridge, England, 1938) and the Duke of Buckingham and Chandos, ed., *Memoirs of the Court of George IV, 1820–1830* (2 vols., London, 1859).

Useful commentaries on events in Ireland are also to be found in the memoirs of contemporary observers not immediately concerned with the administration of Ireland. Lord John Russell, ed., *Memoirs, Journal, and Correspondence of Thomas Moore* (2 vols., New York, 1857); Lytton Strachey and Roger Fulford, eds., *The Greville Memoirs, 1814–1860* (8 vols., London, 1938); *The Diary and Correspondence of Charles Abbot, Lord Colchester*, edited by his son, Lord Colchester (3 vols., London, 1861); Louis B. Jennings, ed., *The Croker Papers* (2d ed. 3 vols., London, 1885); Horace Twiss, *The Public and Private Life of Lord Chancellor Eldon* (2 vols., Philadelphia, 1844); and Sir Herbert Maxwell, ed., *The Creevey Papers* (2 vols., New York, 1904) all are of value for their frequent comments on the effect of Irish clamor on the political state of the Catholic question in England. W. Hepworth Dixon, ed., *Lady Morgan's Memoirs: Autobiography, Diaries, and Correspondence* (2d ed. 2 vols., London, 1863) and, to a lesser extent, Lady Gregory, ed., *Mr. Gregory's Letter-Box* (London, 1898) perform a similar function by retailing the gossip, intrigue, and political maneuvering provoked by the association in ascendancy and government circles in Dublin. Edward A. Kendall, *Letters to a Friend on the State of Ireland* (3 vols., London, 1826) is a useful, because hostile, commentary on the emancipation movement. John Wade, *The Black Book* (2 vols., London, 1820 and 1823), *New Parliament: An Appendix to the Black Book* (London, 1826), and *The Extraordinary Black Book* (London, 1831), although condensations of many of Wakefield's statistics, contain important revelations of the methods of ascendancy control in Ireland.

*D. Pamphlets and periodicals.* Since a proliferous pamphlet literature arose out of the Catholic question, it is impossible to do more than list the major collections that have been preserved. The most extensive of its kind, and a source on which Lecky relied heavily for his Irish history, is the Haliday Tracts and Pamphlets in the Royal Irish Academy, over two hundred volumes of which deal with the period from 1823 to 1829. The Haliday and Joly collections in the National Library, those in the library of Trinity College, and the Bradshaw Irish Collection in Cambridge University Library, although considerably smaller, have some pamphlets not found in the Royal Irish Academy. Controversial articles in the *Edinburgh*, *Quarterly*, and *Westminster* reviews, the *New Monthly Magazine*, and the *Irish Monthly Magazine of Politics and Literature* have also been of use in this study.

## Secondary Authorities

### I. Monographs

A valuable but, regrettably, unpublished survey of the relation between political agitations and radical movements in Ireland and in England from the Union to the first reform act exists in the form of a doctoral dissertation by Reinhard Cassirer, *The Irish Influence on the Liberal Movement in England, 1798–1832*, presented at the University of London in 1940 and on file in the university library. In two articles in the *English Historical Review*, Arthur Aspinall has provided pertinent information on subjects having an indirect but important bearing on the association: "The Coalition Ministries of 1827," *42* (1927), 201–226 and 533–559; and "The Irish Proclamation Fund, 1800–1846," *56* (1941), 265–280. Good appreciations of the roles of two of the Irish leaders are to be found in the Irish journal, *Studies:* Denis Gwynn, "Bishop Doyle and Catholic Emancipation," *17* (1928), 353–368; "O'Connell and His Lieutenants," *18* (1929), 255–270; and Michael Tierney, "Daniel O'Connell and the Gaelic Past," *27* (1938), 353–368. Other noteworthy articles descriptive of the state of Ireland and the emancipation movement have appeared in the *Dublin Review:* George O'Brien, "O'Connell and the Ireland in Which He Lived," *184* (1929), 182–193; J. W. Good, "O'Connell and Repeal," *ibid.*, 218–228; and Basil Whelan, "Behind the Scenes of Catholic Emancipation," *ibid.*, 295–328.

### II. General Works

Although Denis Gwynn's *The Struggle for Catholic Emancipation, 1750–1829* (New York, 1928) is an excellent survey of the whole emancipation movement, particularly in Ireland, there exists no thorough study of the Irish phase of the long struggle comparable to Bernard Ward's *The Dawn of the Catholic Revival in England, 1781–1803* (2 vols., New York, 1909) and *The Eve of Catholic Emancipation, 1803–1829* (3 vols., New York, 1911–12). Consequently, since emancipation was admittedly won in Ireland, one of the most significant aspects of the movement, the nature of the Catholic Association as a powerful political organization, has been neglected. Moisei Ostrogorskiĭ, *Democracy and the Organization of Political Parties* (2 vols., New York, 1902) and Henry Jephson, *The Platform, Its Rise and Progress* (2 vols., New York, 1892), while helpful in placing the association in perspective in the history of pressure groups, allude to it only cursorily. The emancipation movement in Ireland still awaits a careful, detailed study of the sort given the great measure that so closely followed it by George S. Veitch in his *The Genesis of Parliamentary Reform* (London, 1913), a work of special assistance for the correlation of the two movements in my introductory and concluding chapters. Four other authorities are essential to balanced appreciation of the reform movement and the state of the Catholic question in relation to English party politics: H. W. Carless Davis, *The Age of Grey and Peel* (Oxford, 1929); W. R. Brock, *Lord Liverpool and Liberal Toryism, 1820 to 1827* (Cambridge, England, 1941); Keith Grahame Feiling, *The Second Tory Party, 1714–1832* (London, 1938); and Michael Roberts, *The Whig Party, 1807–1812* (London, 1939).

The best single-volume general history of Ireland is Edmund Curtis, *A History of Ireland* (6th, revised ed. London, 1950). While there is nothing for the 19th century of the proportions and merit of W. E. H. Lecky's *A History of Ireland in the Eighteenth Century* (new ed. 5 vols., London, 1892), special studies do provide good background for the years 1823–29. The latest and most balanced appraisal of the political history of the period before the great famine is R. B. McDowell, *Public Opinion and Government Policy in Ireland, 1801–1846* (London, 1952). D. A. Chart, *Ireland from the Union to Catholic Emancipation* (London, 1910) is a short but well-measured survey of social and administrative conditions. As an economic study it is superseded by one of the better examples of modern Irish historiography, George O'Brien's *The Economic History of Ireland from the Union to the Famine* (London, 1921). O'Brien has been supplemented and at times corrected in two more recent social and economic histories by American scholars: John E. Pomfret, *The Struggle for Land in Ireland, 1800–*

*1923* (Princeton, 1930) and William Forbes Adams, *Ireland and Irish Emigration to the New World from 1815 to the Famine* (New Haven, 1932). R. Barry O'Brien's *Dublin Castle and the Irish People* (London, 1912) has proved a handy reference manual for information about the personnel and inner workings of the English Government in Ireland, and one aspect of that administration, government patronage of the press, has been exhaustively investigated in Arthur Aspinall, *Politics and the Press, c. 1780–1850* (London, 1949), a book especially valuable because of the important role played by the Irish press in the emancipation agitation.

Other authorities, who make only casual reference to the association but who supply useful background material, are Constantia Maxwell, *Dublin under the Georges, 1714–1830* (London, 1936) and *Country and Town in Ireland under the Georges* (London, 1940); John W. Fortescue, *A History of the British Army* (13 vols., New York, 1902–30), Volume *11* of which is devoted to the years from 1815 to 1838 and furnishes helpful information on the military situation in Ireland; William Carleton, *Traits and Stories of the Irish Peasantry* (6th ed. 2 vols., London, 1865); and Conrad Arensberg's anthropological study, *The Irish Countryman* (London, 1937).

### III. BIOGRAPHIES

Sketches of the leading agitators, particularly of those not listed in *The Dictionary of National Biography*, may be found in John S. Crone, *A Concise Dictionary of Irish Biography* (Dublin, 1928). There exists no full-scale life of O'Connell. Lecky's all-too-brief study in the second volume of his *Leaders of Public Opinion in Ireland* (authorized ed. 2 vols., New York, 1912) still remains the best-balanced, but by no means adequate, biography. It must be supplemented by two recent works, the one a fine psychological tour de force, Seán O'Faoláin, *King of the Beggars* (New York, 1938); the other a well-edited collection of analytical essays, Michael Tierney, ed., *Daniel O'Connell* (Dublin, 1949). Of the other ten lives of O'Connell a few are useful for factual data, but none meets the standards of serious and thorough scholarship. James J. Auchmuty's *Sir Thomas Wyse, 1791–1862* (London, 1939) is, on the other hand, a sound biography of the man who engineered the Waterford election and was the first historian of the association. L. A. G. Strong presents an excellent portrait of Thomas Moore in *The Minstrel Boy* (London, 1937); Lord Cloncurry's autobiography, *The Personal Recollections of the Life and Times of Valentine Lord Cloncurry* (Dublin, 1849) is useful as an exposition of the views of a prominent Irish Protestant patriot who sympathized with the Catholic leaders; Augustus G. Stapleton, *The Political Life of George Canning* (2d ed. 3 vols., London, 1831) and A. A. W. Ramsay, *Sir Robert Peel* (London, 1928) are helpful studies of the leading protagonist and opponent of the Catholic claims in Parliament and cabinet.

# Index

89717